Import Tariffs as Environmental Policy Instruments

Economy & Environment

VOLUME 19

The titles published in this series are listed at the end of this volume.

Import Tariffs as Environmental Policy Instruments

by

Christiane Kraus
The World Bank,
Washington DC, U.S.A.
and Hannover University,
Hannover, Germany

Springer-Science+Business Media, B.V.

A C.I.P. Catalogue record for this book is available from the Library of Congress.

ISBN 978-90-481-5461-6 ISBN 978-94-015-9614-5 (eBook)
DOI 10.1007/978-94-015-9614-5

Printed on acid-free paper

Originally published by Kluwer Academic Publishers in 2000.
Softcover reprint of the hardcover 1st edition 2000

Import Tariffs as Environmental Policy Instruments

ABSTRACT

This study presents an integrated theoretical and political approach to assess import tariffs to support environmental policy instruments.

To analyse rigorously the theoretical claim for such eco-tariffs, we provide a unified framework in form of an international trade model enriched by a domestic respectively global environmental externality. In the course of the investigation, we modify the model to analyse an array of contexts for which an environmental quality or welfare improving effect of eco-tariffs has been claimed. We characterise circumstances and conditions under which such tariffs can be shown to improve environmental quality and social welfare, taking into account general equilibrium effects.

Furthermore, we apply the theoretical results in a policy analysis of eco-tariffs and other trade instruments in the context of domestic and global environmental policy to assess the relevance of the theoretically analysed eco-tariffs.

Finally, we present the GATT/WTO rules and regulations which to date ban use of eco-tariffs for environmental objectives. Mapping those rules and regulations against our theoretical results, we attempt to isolate which rules ought to be changed.

ACKNOWLEDGEMENTS

This book is the result of more than three years of research that began in Brussels, continued in Kiel, was mainly undertaken in Hannover, and concluded in Washington, DC.

I first started thinking about the suitability of trade instruments to further environmental protection while working in 1995 for DG I at the European Commission where my Conseiller Ramiro Cibrian brought this question to my attention. Thereafter I began my doctoral studies at Kiel University where Prof. Dr. Michael Rauscher took an interest in my work. Prof. Rauscher subsequently agreed to co-supervise my doctoral thesis when I moved in 1996 to Hannover University to continue – and eventually finish – my doctoral studies in the department for Quantitative Economic Research under the supervision of Prof. Dr. Hans-Joachim Heinemann, chair for International Economics.

I am highly indebted to both Prof. Heinemann and Prof. Rauscher for their continued support over the course of this my doctoral studies. Prof. Heinemann provided excellent working conditions at Hannover University. He also sharpened my mind on issues of international monetary and trade economics, and challenged my views on various issues of this study.

Prof. Rauscher, chair for International Economics at Rostock university, encouraged and guided me in a truly marvellous fashion. Without his expert knowledge in the field and outstanding qualities as a supervisor I would not have mastered the challenge of a doctoral thesis.

Support by the Studienstiftung des deutschen Volkes is gratefully acknowledged.

My friends at Hannover University – Lars, Nelli, Boris, Karen, Adrian and Dirk formed a wonderful team. Special thanks go to Dirk for helping me with a lot of tricky analytical questions and reading the entire manuscript, and to Adrian for formatting the graphs.

I would also like to thank Martin for long discussions on GATT law issues, and Sophia and Stefan for their flexibility to turn a social visit into an intense last-minute proof-reading effort. Special thanks go to my mentoress Lilo who always had a supportive and watchful eye on me from Brussels. Finally, I would like to thank Jane for her invaluable editorial support.

I am deeply grateful to my friends Barbara, Ilse, Lilja, Marietta, Sophie and Philipp for providing the emotional backbone to live through the ups and downs of doctoral studies.

My greatest debt is to my parents who carried much of the burden and shared my joy in completing this book – I owe them so much more than my doctorate.

WER WEISS?

Ein Mensch schreibt feurig ein Gedicht:
So, wies ihm vorschwebt, wird es nicht.
Vielleicht hat Gott sich auch die Welt
Beim Schöpfen schöner vorgestellt.

(Roth [1983, 265])

TABLE OF CONTENTS

Page

LIST OF ABBREVIATIONS

BTU	British Thermal Unit
ch.	chapter
CFC	chlorofluorocarbon
CRS	constant returns to scale
CTE	Committee on Trade and Environment
ed./eds.	editor/editors
et al.	et alia/alii (and others)
ERTB	Environmental Race towards the Bottom
EU	European Union
EPA	Environmental Protection Agency
FOCs	first order conditions
GATT	General Agreement on Tariffs and Trade
GHG	greenhouse gas
ITO	International Trade Organization
NAFTA	North American Free Trade Agreement
NIMBY	not in my backyard
OECD	Organisation for Economic Cooperation and Development
PPM	production and process method
sg	sign
SPSS	Sanitary and Phytosanitary Standards
TBT	Technical Barriers to Trade
U.S.	United States (of America)
UV-B	ultraviolet-B
Vol.	Volume
w.r.t.	with respect to
WTO	World Trade Organisation

LIST OF SYMBOLS

Usually, lower case letters denote variables of the home country, upper-case letters denote variables of the rest of the world

c^i, C^i	consumption
f, F, h, H	production functions
g, G	environmental ('green') tax rate
k, K, $\tilde{k}$, ,$\tilde{K}$	capital stock
k^i, K^i, $\tilde{k}^i$, $\tilde{K}^i$	capital input
l, L, $\tilde{l}$, $\tilde{L}$	labour supply
l^i, L^i, $\tilde{l}^i$, $\tilde{L}^i$	labour input
p, p^i	product prices
r, R	reaction functions
s, S	polluting smoke
u, U,	utility functions
v, V	disutility functions
w, W	social welfare function
w_i	factor rates of return
x, X, $\tilde{x}$, $\tilde{X}$, y, Y, $\tilde{y}$, $\tilde{Y}$	supply of goods
β	parameter
κ	scale parameter
π, Π	profit functions
τ, T	tariff rate
φ, ξ	production function
l	political support function

LIST OF FIGURES

Page

LIST OF TABLES

Page

Chapter 1

Introductory Remarks

1. SUBJECT, MOTIVATION, OBJECTIVE, APPROACH AND STRUCTURE

SUBJECT AND MOTIVATION

Increasing economic integration of sovereign nations, reflected by the growth of trade flows in the past decades and associated with a rapid increase of economic activities and world-wide GDP, has also been accompanied by an alarming increase of local, national, international and global environmental problems. Economists tend to view this as a coincidence, treating the two developments as separate.

Free trade is generally considered a source of welfare improvement. The exchange of goods induces specialisation according to comparative advantages of the trading countries. By virtue of this improvement of the international division of labour, production becomes more efficient and world-wide output increases. Thereby, gains from trade accrue to all trading countries[1].

In economic terms, environmental problems occur when agents impose external costs upon society in the form of pollution, thereby reducing social welfare. These problems have been recognised and researched extensively; a set of implications has been advanced. The efficient solution of an

[1] See standard textbooks on international trade such as Gandolfo [1994] or Markusen et al. [1995].

environmental externality has pollution regulated at its source with appropriate policy instruments such as environmental taxes[2].

Still, some environmental problems have been associated with trade liberalisation and international trade flows; the claim has been made that free trade and the rules by which it is governed harms the environment[3]. Economic growth stimulated by international trade is feared to result in increased pollution if environmental externalities are not properly internalised, in particular in those countries specialising in environmentally disruptive production. Furthermore, the concern has been voiced that competitive pressure stemming from internationally integrated markets may tempt governments to neglect or reduce environmental regulation, thus engaging in eco-dumping which leads to an environmental race towards the bottom if eco-dumping becomes a world-wide phenomenon. Eco-dumping and environmental races towards the bottom have been investigated both empirically and theoretically and are increasingly an issue in the political debate over trade and environment.

A particularly pressing problem that has gained centre stage in the past decades is a degradation of the global environmental commons by spill-over pollution, i.e. pollution that results in world-wide harm regardless of its source. If such global environmental pollution is not internalised, trade-enhanced economic growth is feared to result in an intolerable deterioration of global environmental quality. To complicate matters for the protection of the global environment, internalisation of spill-over externalities by a subset of the trading community may remain ineffective, if competitiveness effects result in increased pollution in countries where no control measures are in place.

Since international trade relations are suspected to cause eco-dumping and reduce effectiveness of policies addressing global pollution, the potential of trade policy instruments to support environmental policies addressing these problems has been investigated. Both in the contexts of eco-dumping or environmental races towards the bottom and global environmental protection, results of theoretical and empirical studies imply that measures in the form of eco-tariffs addressing environmentally harmful production may serve to improve environmental quality and welfare.

As a consequence, trade restrictions addressing environmentally harmful products are deliberated by policy makers to complement domestic and global environmental protection efforts. However, so far such eco-tariffs have not become part of environmental or trade policy because among other

2 See for example Baumol & Oates [1989] for a comprehensive textbook of environmental economics.

3 See Esty [1994, 9pp] for a summary of environmentalists' critique of free trade.

reasons, they are not sanctioned by the multilateral trade regime[4]. The lack of environmental provisions in the GATT/WTO regulations and the fact that environmentally motivated trade restrictions may collide with current trade rules, have stirred much criticism of the GATT/WTO and prompted a plethora of reform proposals[5].

This study presents an integrated approach to assess import tariffs to support environmental policy instruments theoretically, as well as a policy analysis. To analyse rigorously the theoretical claims for eco-tariffs, we provide a unified framework in the form of an international trade model. Thereafter, we apply the theoretical results to a policy analysis of eco-tariffs and other trade instruments proposed in the context of domestic and global environmental protection.

OBJECTIVE AND APPROACH

The objective of this study is to determine both suitability and relevance of eco-tariffs supporting environmental policy instruments. **Suitability** refers to the question of whether such instruments have positive environmental and/or welfare effects; **relevance** addresses the policy issue, i.e. whether such eco-tariffs are demanded by policy makers, and whether they are sanctioned by the rules governing international trade relations.

To tackle the question theoretically, we set forth a general equilibrium international trade model enriched first by a domestic and then a global environmental externality. In the course of the investigation, we modify the model to analyse an array of contexts for which the suitability of eco-tariffs has been claimed. We characterise circumstances and conditions under which eco-tariffs may serve to improve environmental quality and social welfare, taking into account general equilibrium effects.

Furthermore, we analyse policy proposals for eco-tariffs and other trade instruments in the context of domestic and global environmental problems to assess the relevance of the theoretically analysed eco-tariffs.

Finally, we present the GATT/WTO rules and regulations which to date ban use of eco-tariffs for environmental objectives. Mapping those rules and regulations against our theoretical results we attempt to isolate an agenda for reforms.

4 It should be noted that GATT/WTO rules and regulations do not prevent trade measures taken pursuant to environmental objective in general. However, trade measures addressing production and process methods of imported goods are not sanctioned by the GATT/WTO.

5 For an extensive summary of the debate see Esty [1994].

STRUCTURE

This study consists of a theoretical investigation and a policy analysis. Chapters 2 – 11 contain the theoretical investigation of eco-tariffs in the context of domestic and global pollution. In chapters 12 and 13 we perform a policy analysis of eco-tariffs, again for domestic and global environmental problems.

The role of eco-tariffs as a corrective measure for eco-dumping and environmental races towards the bottom is subject of chapters 2 - 6. Chapter 2 gives a brief survey of empirical and theoretical evidence for eco-dumping, and environmental races towards the bottom and introduces the discussion of eco-tariffs to mitigate eco-dumping and environmental race towards the bottom. Chapter 3 presents a simple international trade model in which we incorporate an environmental externality. In chapters 4 - 6 this model is used to analyse different contexts in which tariffs have been proposed as corrective measures against eco-dumping and/or environmental races towards the bottom.

The role of eco-tariffs for an efficient control of global pollution and to achieve cooperation to address global environmental problems is the subject of chapters 7 - 10. Chapter 7 provides a survey of the role of tariffs for the protection of the global environmental commons. Chapter 8 shows effects of spill-over pollution in the model introduced in chapter 3. Chapter 9 analyses the role of tariffs as second best instrument for protection of spill-over externalities in the absence of cooperation. Chapter 10 investigates the incentive effects of eco-tariff to cooperate for protection of the global environment. Results of the theoretical investigation are briefly summarised in chapter 11.

The policy debate surrounding eco-tariffs is subject of chapters 12 and 13. Chapter 12 presents policy proposals for eco-tariffs in the context of domestic environmental problems. Furthermore, we describe clashes with current GATT/WTO rules regarding trade instruments and domestic pollution. Policy proposals and GATT/WTO regulations are discussed in the light of the theoretical evidence gathered in part chapters 4, 5 and 6.

In chapter 13, we summarise policy proposals of eco-tariffs for global environmental protection and clashes with current GATT/WTO rules. Policy initiatives and relevant multilateral trade regulations are discussed using results from chapters 8, 9 and 10.

In chapter 14 we evaluate suitability and relevance of eco-tariffs as environmental policy measures by summarising findings of the theoretical investigation and results of the policy analyses.

2. ISSUES, CONCEPTS AND DEFINITIONS

ENVIRONMENTAL EXTERNALITIES

Environmental externalities[6] can be categorised according to the spatial extension of the environmental harm they create. We briefly outline those environmental problems addressed in our study, namely domestically contained and global ones. Furthermore, we sketch how our model reflects effects of environmental externalities for society and the sources of environmental pollution. Finally, we provide a brief overview of linkages between international trade and environmental externalities.

Domestic environmental externalities are polluting emissions generated within a country causing environmental damage exclusively within this country's borders. This is the special case where boundaries of environmental systems coincide with policy frontiers[7].

Global environmental externalities are caused by pollution spilling across national borders and harming environmental resources shared by all countries, i.e. global environmental commons[8]. What distinguishes global from domestic externalities is therefore that the damage is independent of the geographic location of the source of pollution and may fall within different jurisdictions.

Global environmental commons are resources with value for the world community that are beyond the jurisdiction of individual states[9]. Most global

6 From a (neo-classical) point of view, environmental problems arising from human activities are subsumed under negative externalities or external effects; compare Rauscher [1997,19pp] for further elaboration on environmental problems as externalities.

7 Compare Baumol & Oates [1988, 258], Feess [1998, 207], and Siebert [1995a, 170]. Examples are pollution of inland water resources, or smoke generated by a production process which is not transported outside the vicinity of its source.

8 Some authors further distinguish regional environmental problems, i.e. spill-over externalities which affect a subset of the world community. Siebert [1995a, 187pp] and Feess [1998, 210pp] for example analytically differentiate regional and global externalities.

9 This reflects the legal definition. However, the definition used in non-legal literature for global environmental commons also encompasses resources whose value affects nations other than those having jurisdiction over them, i.e. portions of the globe located within the jurisdiction of sovereign states whose value accrues to all mankind (e.g. bio-diversity); compare Tschofen [1992, 1/2].

environmental commons are open access resources[10]. The 'tragedy of the commons'[11] therefore lies in the absence of well-defined property rights: the extent to which they are harvested, used or sustained is not determined by cooperation between all agents who derive utility from their existence, or whose welfare is reduced by their depletion.

Global environmental problems have gained political importance in recent decades, in particular with the discovery of the ozone hole and global warming[12]. Safeguarding the layer that protects the earth from harmful solar radiation and avoiding a destabilisation of climatic conditions are now recognised among the most serious challenges for international policymaking[13].

Regarding consequences of environmental externalities for economies, we distinguish two modelling approaches: externalities either affect welfare **directly** by causing disutility for society, or they affect welfare **indirectly** by harming productivity[14].

In the majority of economic models incorporating environmental externalities - including ours - the former approach has been chosen. In our formulation, social welfare is composed of two parts, namely consumption utility and disutility stemming from the environmental externality[15]. We furthermore assume that these two components are additively separable[16].

10 Global environmental commons comprise common pool resources such as minerals in deep sea beds, common sink resources such as the atmosphere and the oceans, and global public goods such as bio-diversity and the ozone layer. This tripartite nature of global environmental commons has been stressed by Siebert [1990, 1]. Yet other definitions only distinguish two aspects, i.e. common pool and sink resources (e.g. Eckhaus [1993, 3] and Vogler [1995, 3]), or subsume all global environmental commons under global public goods (e.g. Oberthür [1992, 11]).

11 The term 'tragedy of the commons' has been introduced by Hardin [1968] with respect to population growth. However, it is now commonly used with reference to global environmental resources.

12 The problems of ozone depletion and global warming are summarised in chapter 13.

13 See Blackhurst & Subramanian [1992, 248] and Sandler [1992].

14 E.g. Merrifield [1988] and Choi & Johnson [1992]. A combination of both, i.e. an externality which harms society directly and indirectly has also been considered (see Pethig [1992] and Rauscher [1997, ch.5]).

15 Similar formulations have been used by Hoel [1993] and Rauscher [1991a&b, 1994, 1995d & 1997 ch. 5].

16 This assumption is analytically convenient; it avoids environmental quality affecting the structure of demand. A further implication of additive separability is that both welfare components are superior. Hence, if consumption utility increases - e.g. as a consequence of trade liberalisation - society's desire for environmental quality grows as well. (For a detailed discussion of additively separable utility functions see Deaton & Muellbauer [1980, ch.5]. For the superiority feature in particular, see Deaton & Muellbauer [1980, 139]).The separability assumption is made in the majority of models similar to ours.

To analyse the questions raised in earlier, we set forth an international trade model of the Heckscher-Ohlin-Samuelson type, enriched by an environmental externality. We assume that the environmental externality is caused by the production process method (PPM)[17] in one of the sectors, more specifically in the sector where production is relatively capital-intensive. Apart from sector specificity, we also assume factor specificity of pollution, i.e. it is discharged as a by-product of the input factor capital[18].

In Heckscher-Ohlin-Samuelson models featuring environmental externalities, sector-specific PPM pollution is not an unusual assumption[19].

Sector **and** factor-specificity of PPM pollution, however, is somewhat rarer. Rauscher [1991b] provides an example: he develops a Ricardo-Viner model in which environmental pollution is sector and factor-specific. He considers environmental services ('clean air') as the sector-specific input factor; by virtue of the Ricardo-Viner approach, pollution is hence sector-specific as well[20].

To our knowledge, none of the existing Heckscher-Ohlin-Samuelson models set up to highlight aspects of the relationship between environmental and trade policy uses both sector and factor specificity of environmental

---

However, some authors choose a less restrictive approach (e.g. Copeland [1993 & 1994], v. Long & Siebert [1989], Ludema & Wooton [1994], Markusen [1975] Panagariya et al. [1993], Pethig [1976], and Siebert [1977]).

17 As regards the source of pollution, it is also possible to model externalities arising from consumption (e.g. Rauscher [1997, ch.5] and Beghin et al. [1994b & 1996]. However, for our purposes - i.e. addressing environmental policy and trade policy linkages - a PPM externality is more appropriate since multilateral trade rules ban trade instruments addressing PPM externalities, while trade instruments addressing consumption externalities are allowed. Chakarian [1994], Lee [1994], Tudini [1993], and Vaughan [1994] provide a survey of PPM pollution in the context of trade and environment.

18 Further specifications of environmental pollution, i.e. which environmental medium is affected and their dynamic features, i.e. whether the damaging effect arises from the stock or the flow of a pollutant, are neglected in our study. For a taxonomy of environmental pollution see Siebert [1995a, 21/22].

19 Choi & Johnson [1992], Markusen [1975], and McGuire [1982] for example use Heckscher-Ohlin-Samuelson type models with sector-specific environmental externalities. In Ricardo-Viner models Copeland [1993] and Rauscher [1991b] also use a sector-specific environmental externality arising as a by-product of production in one of two sectors. Heckscher-Ohlin-Samuelson models in which both sectors release environmentally harmful emissions are modelled by Pethig [1976] and Siebert [1977&1979]. n-sector international trade general equilibrium models where all sectors pollute the environment are considered by Copeland [1994] and Hœl [1993].

20 Yet, if this model was to be generalised to a Heckscher-Ohlin-Samuelson formulation, factor specificity would imply that both sectors pollute the environment as it does in Klepper [1994], Pethig [1976] and Siebert [1977&'79]. Panagariya et al. [1993] set our a similar model by augmenting an Heckscher-Ohlin-Samuelson model with a third, sector-specific input factor which causes an environmental externality.

externalities. However, we believe that our approach has a number of advantages: one of them is that the assumption of sector and factor specificity of environmental externalities, and particularly its linkage to capital input in the capital-intensive sector, highlights important aspects of environmental externalities[21].

The connection between **environmental externalities** and **international trade** can be highlighted by investigating how they mutually affect each other[22]. In our study, two aspects of the trade and trade liberalisation are relevant for environmental quality. These are the specialisation and growth effects of trade.

In a Heckscher-Ohlin-Samuelson model, trade liberalisation triggers **specialisation** as long as trading countries' endowments differ. Hence, trade liberalisation reduces pollution in countries which do not have a comparative advantage in producing the good whose PPM harms the environment. Domestic environmental externalities are aggravated in countries where production of the polluting good is stimulated.

World-wide division of labour leads to **growth** in the production of commodities. Therefore, aggregated pollution increases. If pollution affects the global environmental commons, the environmental externality for all countries thus increases[23]. Furthermore, owing to our assumption of additive separability of the two components of social welfare, trade liberalisation triggers a desire for enhanced environmental quality[24].

[21] Often environmental pollution arises in capital-intensive sectors (e.g. industrial sectors, energy generation) where they are largely determined by the production technology, which in turn reflects the particular capital stock available in the economy; compare Sohmen [1976, 228]. Furthermore, a number of pollutants (e.g. sulphur dioxide and carbon dioxide) are positively correlated with the capital stock of economies; see World Bank [1992, 11]. Further advantages of our modelling approach are that the model can be handled like a 'normal' Heckscher-Ohlin-Samuelson model; i.e. the environmental externality does not add analytical complexity. At the same time, we do not reduce the generality of the Heckscher-Ohlin-Samuelson approach.

[22] Focussing on the relation between the environment and trade as they appear in our model, we suppress many aspects feeding the 'awkwardness' (Rauscher [1997, 1]) of the connection. For example, we neglect environmental cost from transportation (see Helm [1995, 29pp]) and problems associated with cross-border waste disposal (see Rauscher [1997, ch.4]. A further dimension, namely the 'clash of cultures' (Esty [1994, ch.2]) between environmentalists and free-traders as protagonists in the debate is completely ignored in our study.

[23] Compare also Helm [1995, 34pp] and Rauscher [1997, 1].

[24] Hence, if an increase in environmental protection efforts stemming from the latter effect trigger environmentally less disruptive PPMs, the aggregate effect cannot be determined in advance. Furthermore, since the Heckscher-Ohlin-Samuelson model is static, empirical

Finally, environmental externalities change welfare implications of trade liberalisation: while in the absence of environmental externalities free trade has positive welfare effects, this is no longer necessarily true if environmental externalities are present[25].

ENVIRONMENTAL AND TRADE POLICY INSTRUMENTS AND POLICY FORMATION

For our theoretical investigation, we assume that government maximises its objective function using either environmental policy instruments alone, or in combination with trade policy instruments.

To internalise environmental externalities, government can introduce adequate policy measures. Efficient **environmental policy instruments** are[26]

- command & control measures[27],
- an environmental tax[28], and
- tradable permits[29].

In our model, we assume that government always has an emission tax to its disposal to maximise its objective function[30]. Since we also assume that

---

observations cannot be expected to reflect its predictions; see Helm [1995, 32pp] for a cursory empirical glance.

25 The validity of the gains of trade theorem (see Gandolfo [1994, 54pp] and Markusen et al. [1995, 61pp]) is based on a number of assumptions of which the absence of market failures such as (uninternalised) environmental externalities is just one.

26 This categorisation follows Rauscher [1997, 21]. Siebert [1995a, 125/126] lists in addition moral suasion, publicly financed pollution abatement and abatement subsidies. The three we have listed yield an identical allocation in a static competitive economy where welfare-maximising governments have perfect information.

27 Government allocates (optimal) pollution quotas or restricts technology choice of firms by setting PPM standards (if pollution is generated by PPMs).

28 To be an efficient instrument, this tax should be levied on emissions; its optimal level corresponds to the Pigouvian tax, i.e. is set equal to marginal social damage caused by the negative environmental externality.

29 Government determines the (optimal) emission level and distributes (or auctions) pollution permits accordingly. To yield an efficient solution, a perfect market for these permits is needed.

30 Rauscher [1991a,1995c&d] also uses taxes as regulatory instrument. We do not perform a comparison of alternative environmental policy instruments which has been frequently undertaken for closed (Bohm & Russel [1985] provide a survey) and also open (Verdier [1993], Rauscher [1992a]) economies.

pollution is a by-product of capital input, the internalisation of the sector and factor specific environmental externality by means of a tax makes the effect of the tax equivalent to a factor price differential. This observation allows us to rely to the literature on international trade and factor market distortions[31] for the derivation of our results.

The following **trade policy instruments** are available for governments wishing to affect trade flows:
- tariffs[32],
- quantity restrictions and
- the so-called grey area measures[33].

In our study, we shall consider tariffs as policy instruments for governments which can use trade policy measures in addition to the environmental tax to maximise their objective function[34]. Comparing one instrument with the situation when two are available allows us to investigate the theoretical implications of relaxing the ban on trade measures.

Throughout our model, governments are assumed to use the policy instruments at their disposal to maximise their objective function. Apart from the use of environmental policy instruments to achieve environmental goals and trade policy instruments to achieve trade policy goals, governments may also use *trade policy instruments to achieve environmental goals* and *environmental policy instruments to affect trade flows* if the direct instruments are not available.

Since we assume that governments always have environmental policy instruments at their disposal, only the latter case when they pursue trade policy goals using the environmental tax is considered[35]. We compare the

[31] E.g. Bhagwati & Srinivasan [1971], Hazari [1978], Herberg & Kemp [1971], Jones [1971], and Magee [1971,1973&1976].

[32] In general, tariffs can be positive or negative; negative tariffs correspond to an export subsidy. In our theoretical investigation, we shall restrict tariffs to positive tariffs.

[33] E.g. voluntary export restraints, local content requirements, administrative requirements and product standards (compare Krugman & Obstfeld [1997, 197] and Siebert [1994, 179]).

[34] Reasons for restricting our investigation to tariffs are twofold: tariffs and quantity restrictions are in the absence of uncertainty equivalent (see Vousden [1990, ch.2]). Furthermore, since we chose a tax rather than tradable permits as environmental policy instrument, we chose tariffs as environmental policy instrument as the corresponding (price) instrument in trade policy.

[35] It is also possible to analyse trade instruments as (sole) environmental policy instruments (as done by Brandner & Taylor [1998]). However, we confine ourselves to the case when environmental policy is used for trade policy objectives. In view of increasing

situation when government has both environmental and trade policy instruments at its disposal with the tax-only case. This offers insights regarding the effect of availability of the trade policy instrument on environmental quality and policy.

In neo-classical models, governments generally behave benevolently, i.e. maximise social welfare by setting their policy at the optimal level. However, this assumption may be violated if policy measures are used to achieve income distribution objectives. Since both environmental and trade policy measures have losers and gainers, those affected by environmental regulation or trade policy may spend considerable resources in seeking to influence the decisions of policy makers. The insights of the political economy approach indicate that these attempts of regulatory capture are often successful[36].

Thus, politicians may be modelled as tailoring their policies to the interests of voters in an effort to be re-elected, or lobbies who contribute resources to their political campaigns. The implication of either of these approaches is that certain groups within society acquire political importance, with the result that government gives greater weight to their interests in decision making[37].

While in most of our analysis we assume that government is in fact benevolent, we change this assumption in chapter 6 where we allow for regulatory capture by producers of the good whose PPM pollutes the environment. This is modelled by biasing government's objective function towards the welfare of producer of that good. In an Heckscher-Ohlin-Samuelson model, the reason why producers, i.e. owners of factors tied to a certain sector, would profit from political decision making is not obvious. There are no supernormal profits to be earned in either sector, nor do factor rewards differ between sectors. Hence, we assume that producers of the good whose PPM pollutes the environment enjoy either monetary or non-monetary benefits suppressed in our model[38].

---

environmental regulation and decreasing scope for trade policy, we think that this case is more realistic.

36 The term 'regulatory capture' is borrowed from Stigler; similarly adequate would be the term 'political capture'.

37 Compare Deardorff [1994].

38 While the assumption that producers of a particular good gain regulatory capture is rather ad hoc, the fact that producers (rather than consumers) are successful in manipulating government is not: since there are generally fewer producers than consumers, gains from rent seeking are larger for the former. Furthermore, members of a particular industry are often already organised which alleviates coordination for lobbying activities (compare Vousden [1990, ch.8].

ANALYTIC TOOLS

For the theoretical investigation we set forth a Heckscher-Ohlin-Samuelson model augmented by an environmental externality. We perform comparative static analysis with this model[39].

Furthermore, we consider interaction of **non-cooperating** governments. One of the features of the perfectly competitive market model is that cooperation is not required for an economy to reach a welfare optimum[40]. This result generalises to international economic relations: If perfectly competitive economies trade with each other, a Pareto optimum is reached in the absence of international policy coordination[41]. However, the optimality of uncoordinated actions is not robust against violations of underlying assumptions: Within economies, market imperfections lead to suboptimal allocation and welfare losses[42]. In this case, coordinated actions can overcome the respective market failures and restore a welfare optimum[43].

Between perfectly competitive economies, a welfare-maximising government can introduce distortions through trade policy, if the country is large, i.e. has market-power on its im- and export markets[44]. In this case, cooperation between the countries involved can also restore optimality[45]. However, if countries do not cooperate, their unilateral welfare-maximising behaviour leads to welfare losses.

In chapter 4, we analyse trading countries with market power who do not cooperate. In chapter 5 we address a case with imperfect goods markets and

39 For a detailed treatment of the comparative statics approach see Krauss & Johnson [1974].

40 I.e. a Pareto optimum, an idea originally developed by Pareto [1909]; compare Debreu [1983, ch.1] and Lockwood [1987] on the concept of Pareto optimality in economics.

41 See Gandolfo [1994, 57], and Markusen et al. [1995, 67p]. For this result, we also need the assumption that government intervention does not take place in these perfectly competitive economies.

42 Such is for example the case if an environmental externality is present, and prices resulting from decentralised, uncoordinated actions no longer accurately reflect environmental (and hence economic) scarcities. See Mas-Colell et al. [1995, ch.11] for externalities in general and Baumol & Oates [1988] for environmental ones in particular.

43 When for example an environmental externality is present, the Coase Theorem applies: if those suffering from the externality and those causing it can (costlessly) bargain, a welfare optimum is restored; see Coase [1960]. Alternative to the bargaining solution, a welfare-maximising government can also correct the market failure with the equivalent result if an efficient policy instrument is chosen, see above.

44 The parallel to market imperfections causing inefficient resources allocation within an economy is obvious: although none of the assumptions required for a competitive equilibrium in each individual economy is violated, the world market exhibits imperfections, i.e. market power by one of the market participants.

45 See Markusen et al. [1995, 258].

non-cooperating governments. In both cases, the outcome is not a global welfare optimum.

In chapters 8, 9 and 10 we consider the case of an environmental externality which spills across borders. In the presence of such a global environmental problem, non-cooperation between the countries involved also leads to a suboptimal outcome[46].

Investigating non-cooperatively interacting governments, we can distinguish two cases: a country with market power either faces many 'small' countries or one large trading partner. In the analysis of the latter, we use the Nash equilibrium approach[47].

Hence, each government determines its country's optimal environmental trade policy for a given policy in the other country. The optimal reaction to every possible choice by the other country can be traced as a country's reaction function (and vice-versa). At the point of intersection we find the Nash equilibrium, i.e. the locus where the two countries' policy choices are consistent in the sense that each one is the optimal reaction to the other one's choice.

Apart from determining and characterising the equilibrium outcome, we can also perform comparative statics of Nash equilibria by varying exogenous parameters or policy choices affecting countries' reaction curves.

DEFINITIONS

The terms we define - eco-dumping, environmental race towards the bottom, NIMBY policy, and eco-tariffs - are frequently used in our study. Furthermore, they stand for concepts which are either not frequently used in economic literature, or have never been coined the way we use them.

[46] Optimal domestic environmental policy does not restore global optimality since it does not internalise cross-border externalities. However, a supranational government - for whose establishment countries have to cooperate - can introduce global environmental policy measures to yield a Pareto optimum. Alternatively, governments can bargain to find a Coase solution.

[47] For an introduction to game theory see Rasmusen [1989]; for a sophisticated treatment of the issues see Fudenberg & Tirole [1991]. For the game theory used in our study a basic knowledge of the concepts as presented in Tirole [1988, ch.11] suffices. The Nash equilibrium concept was originally developed by Nash [1950&51] (compare Tirole [1988, 427]). If countries decide sequentially upon their policy measures, the relevant concept would be a Stackelberg equilibrium (originally developed by Stackelberg [1934]; compare Tirole [1988, 315]).

The term **eco-dumping** (or environmental dumping) has been employed in the public discussion with reference to internationally differing environmental standards for PPM externalities[48]. Governments engaging in eco-dumping curtail regulation of environmental externalities to improve competitiveness of domestic industries or to attract mobile factors of production[49]. Since internationally different standards can also reflect differences in endowments or preferences within societies, we use an alternative definition in our study. Eco-dumping in our definition refers to environmental policy whose level of environmental regulation (in form of taxes) is lower than the Pigouvian tax because of open economy reasons[50].

The term **environmental race towards the bottom** (henceforth ERTB) refers to the outcome of inter-jurisdictional competition when regulatory entities compete each other down to undesirably low levels of environmental regulation because some or all countries engage in eco-dumping[51].

[48] See for example Ranné [1996, 1]: "*In den Medien oder in der politischen Diskussion werden Handelspartner üblicherweise des Öko-dumpings bezeichnet, wenn ihre Umweltschutzvorschriften weniger streng sind als ein bestimmtes Referenzniveau. Dieses Referenzniveau kann sich .... an den in anderen Ländern üblichen Reglementierungen* [oder einem weltweiten Standard] *orientieren...Meist werden jedoch als Meßlatte die Umweltschutzvorschriften des eigenen Landes angelegt.*"

[49] The relation between eco-dumping and 'normal' dumping which refers to locally differentiated prices may not be immediately obvious. First of all, 'normal' dumping is undertaken by individual producers, while for eco-dumping governments are the relevant agents. Moreover, while 'normal' dumping refers to a situation when exported goods are sold at a price below the one prevailing at the domestic market, eco-dumping may be undertaken by import-competing countries as well. The parallel between them is the fact that 'normal' dumping may occur when governments grant subsidies to domestic firms; eco-dumping is thus seen as an 'implicit' subsidy (Ranné [1996, 3]; for a different view according to which eco-dumping has nothing to do with 'normal' dumping see Kuhn & Tivig [1996, 7]).

[50] This corresponds to a definition advanced by Revesz [1994, 376-9]. Similarly Rauscher's [1993a, 5] definition: "... *environmental dumping is pricing of environmental resources, that are used in the production of export goods, at less than marginal* <u>*domestic*</u> *social cost.*", which we augment by the fact that lax policies are introduced because of trade relations. Rauscher [1994, 825] advances and investigates a third definition of eco-dumping, namely the laxer treatment of an exportables sector with regard to environmental regulation.

[51] See Revesz [1994, 373] and Rauscher [1997, 279/280]. Often, the term used in this context is 'environmental race <u>to</u> the bottom', which might be interpreted to imply no regulation at all. This concept is not particularly useful, since strategic interaction resulting in too low levels everywhere does not depend on the level actually going all the way to zero (see Wilson [1996, 393, footnote 1]). Esty [1994] uses the term 'political drag' in similar circumstances.

NIMBY (not in my backyard)[52] **policy** is defined as the opposite of eco-dumping, i.e. regulatory choice of a higher tax than the optimal one which would prevail in the absence of trade relations.

Spill-over externalities which pollute the global environmental commons have not been an essential component in the discussion of eco-dumping and ERTB[53]. Still, when we come to discuss environmental spill-over effects in chapters 7 – 10, we shall keep the terms eco-dumping and NIMBY policy for simplicity if we refer to governments setting taxes below or above the level which would be optimal in the absence of trade relations.

Eco-tariff in our definition is an import tariff levied on the good whose PPM pollutes the environment. We mostly consider positive values for this tariff; i.e. when it is levied by countries importing the good whose PPM pollutes the environment. 'Eco' refers to the fact that the tariff is levied on the good whose PPM pollutes the environment. It does not necessarily imply that the tariff has positive effects for environmental quality[54].

Apart from tariffs levied on goods whose PPM pollutes the environment, we also consider **conditional eco-tariffs**, i.e. tariffs conditional upon environmental policy in the exporting nation.

52 See e.g. VanGrasstek [1992, 233]. The term is also used by Rauscher [1997] to describe situations when governments introduce too stringent environmental regulation.

53 See Wilson [1996, 395].

54 Whether it does is in fact one of the central questions addressed in this study.

Chapter 2

Eco-Tariffs to Avoid Eco-dumping and Environmental Races towards the Bottom (ERTB)

The aim of this chapter is to set out and discuss considerations that led to the suggestion of the use of trade instruments to combat eco-dumping and ERTB. We provide a survey of empirical and theoretical evidence for eco-dumping and ERTB when environmental problems are domestic in nature. In these contexts, it has been suggested that availability of eco-tariffs as additional policy instruments may be environmentally beneficial and/or welfare-enhancing. However, this issue has not been conclusively resolved. We raise some of the open issues regarding eco-tariffs to prevent eco-dumping and ERTB which shall be addressed in chapters 4, 5 and 6.

1. EMPIRICAL ASSESSMENT OF ECO-DUMPING AND ERTB

So far, no empirical evidence has been gathered to determine that countries engage in suboptimal environmental policies to promote exports[1]. Yet, there is anecdotal evidence such as aspects of the US legislative process and proposals for carbon and energy taxes[2].

[1] OECD [1995b, 20]: "*..the [OECD] has not identified evidence of countries* de*liberately resorting to low environmental standards to gain competitive advantages or to attract investment...*" See also OECD [1993] and Stevens [1995]. Similar results are found in Pearce [1993], Grossman & Krueger [1994], Jaffe et al. [1995] and OECD [1996] as reported by Ekins & Speck [1998, 46].

[2] GATT [1992, 29] cites the Wall Street Journal (8 July '91): "*The [US] Council on Competitiveness has taken on the task of helping polluters block [the] EPA's [Environmental Protection Agency] efforts to write clean-air regulation with the unabashed purpose of protecting industries from the cost of regulation.*" Furthermore,

As regards the actual effect of environmental regulation on competitiveness, they are negligible[3], although some evidence exists that countries with stringent regulation lose competitiveness in pollution-intensive industries[4].

The reason that environmental control expenditure does not seem to affect competitiveness is mainly due to the fact that costs imposed by environmental regulation are quite low, amounting for example in 1989 to only 2% of value added for most of the US industry and below 1% for most of Germany's industry[5]. Yet, environmental control costs are expected to rise considerably in the future, and thus competitiveness effects may become more apparent[6]. For example, simulation studies undertaken for the agricultural sector show that the introduction of more stringent, optimal environmental policies could lead to a considerable loss of international competitiveness[7].

As regards industry relocation owing to strict environmental regulation, a summary of existing empirical studies compiled by Levinson [1996] comes to the conclusion that inter-jurisdictional competition to attract mobile factors of production by means of low environmental standards has not occurred on a large scale[8]. Again, anecdotal evidence exists that some environmental laws have been softened to attract or retain industry[9]. As regards the actual effect of internationally diverging standards of environmental policy on industry relocation, the results of empirical

---

Esty [1994, 161] reports that President Clinton's energy tax proposal and the EU's carbon tax proposal were finally dropped or postponed for fear of negative competitiveness effects.

3 OECD[1995b, 20]: "*...no systematic competitive impacts from disparate environmental regulations nor loss of markets, domestically or abroad, due to 'eco-dumping' has been documented.*"

4 This is found by Robison [1988] for the United States. Similar findings are reported by Low & Yeats [1992] and Low [1992] investigating trade patterns from developing to developed countries (studies summarised in Levinson [1996, 435-438]). Gray & Shadbegian [1993] find evidence for competitiveness effects of environmental regulation; however, their results are disputed by Jaffe et al. [1995] as presented by Ekins & Speck [1998, 37].

5 See Esty [1994, 159] and Blazejcak et al. [1993], cited in Helm [1995, 59] and Sorsa [1994].

6 See Esty [1994, 161].

7 See Meinheit [1996, 60-62] citing simulation studies by Hartmann [1993&1994] and Gardner [1994].

8 Levinson [1996, 429].

9 Leonard [1988] finds for example that Ireland has attempted to attract polluting industry by low environmental standards (see Levinson [1996, 430]).

investigations point towards the conclusion that industry does not significantly respond to such differences[10].

The fact that neither trade nor investment patterns offer empirical support for the 'loss of competitiveness' or the 'industrial flight' hypothesis is explained by the low level of cost imposed on industry by environmental regulation[11]. However, it is a commonplace assessment that the level of environmental regulation implemented so far is well below the level recommended by optimality considerations[12]. Since the **fear** of loss of competitiveness and industrial flight have been used as arguments to postpone or cancel environmental regulation[13], the evidence does not rule out the possibility that countries engage in eco-dumping and ERTB[14].

2. THEORETICAL ASSESSMENT OF ECO-DUMPING AND ERTB

FIRST BEST WORLD AND SECOND BEST WORLD

In a first best world of open economies where

- governments choose policies to maximise welfare,
- countries are small,

[10] Such has been Leonard's [1988] result in a study that focused on pollution-intensive industries. He finds little to no evidence that industrial relocation has taken place (study summarised in Levinson [1996, 436/37]).

[11] See Cropper & Oates [1992].

[12] There is widespread agreement, that environmental policies implemented to date do not internalise all external environmental costs: Ursprung [1992, 7/8]: "*The reasons for the excessive pollution are well understood. Moreover, appropriate environmental policy instruments have been developed and are available. In spite of all that, one observes that environmental policies are introduced only very hesitantly.*" Klepper [1992, 248]: "*....one can confidently argue that most countries seem to pursue environmental policies which are less demanding than a special cost-benefit analysis would require.*" Also Klepper [1994, 3]: "*...environmental taxes are generally low - in most cases quite below their optimal level...*"; and Walter [1975, 37]: "*Historically, environmental damage has not greatly influenced international economic relations, simply because the associated costs were not internalised.*"

[13] See Cropper & Oates [1992, 695] and Pearson [1987] referred to in Levinson [1996, 450].

[14] It may even explain some of it: Klepper [1994, 3&19] for example argues that the fact that competitiveness effects of environmental taxes found so far are statistically insignificant may be attributable to the fact that taxes are set much lower than their optimal level.

– no cross-border externalities exist[15], and
– markets are competitive

international differences in the stringency of environmental regulation reflect differences in endowments or preferences with regard to environmental quality, hence comparative advantages[16]. In such a world, welfare - maximising governments have no trade-related reason to deviate from optimal environmental policies and thus, neither eco-dumping nor ERTB can occur[17]. Hence, offsetting differences in environmental regulation will only serve to diminish gains from trade, or preclude mobile factors of production from locating where they are most productive[18]. Consequently, the demand for policies to 'level the playing field' such as harmonisation of environmental standards or trade measures to offset these differences are branded as veiled protectionism[19]

If assumptions underlying the conclusions from the first best world are violated, non-optimal policies may be pursued by welfare-maximising governments. In theoretical models, it has been shown that under certain circumstances eco-dumping and ERTB become possible.

There are two kinds of models used to demonstrate eco-dumping and ERTB: International trade models where *goods are traded and factors are immobile*. In those models, environmental regulation defines the competitiveness of sectors producing internationally traded goods. Furthermore, we have *international trade models where factors are mobile*

15 E.g. fiscal externalities, i.e. governments setting taxes to affect trade flows or factor movements; or exchange rate externalities, i.e. government manipulating their currencies to affect trade flows or factor movements.

16 E.g. Bhagwati & Srinivasan [1996], Siebert [1996] and Subramanian [1992]. A first best world in the context of international trade theory is characterised by many small countries with welfare-maximising governments and no distortions apart from environmental externalities which are internalised by optimal environmental policy (see for example Feess [1998, ch.10] and Rauscher [1997, ch.5]).

17 Such a result has been derived for example by van Long & Siebert [1989] and Oates & Schwab [1988] in models where countries compete for mobile factors of production and by Rauscher [1993a&1994] in models where goods are traded.

18 Siebert [1996, 2/3]: "*Trade measures against less strict environmental policy elsewhere are not justified. If firms in other countries are facing less strict environmental rules, they can exploit that competitive advantage.*" And: "*...an artificial harmonisation of environmental policy instruments and standards would cause an inefficient factor allocation and would result in smaller ... gains from trade.*"

19 Subramanian [1992, 151]: "*...in relation to domestic environmental problems .... the use of trade measures is flawed because it is largely protectionist in intent. They are aimed at negating the very source of competitive advantage which could legitimately be conferred by differences in environmental endowments, pollution assimilation capacities and social preferences regarding environmental outcomes.*" See also Hoekman & Leidy [1992, 241].

and countries compete for these mobile factors of production. In these models, environmental regulation determines rates of return on factors, and hence incentives for factor relocation.

Since we shall develop a model where goods rather than factors are mobile, we summarise the results of the first modelling approaches in detail; the results of factor mobility models are only briefly summarised.

TRADE MODELS

It has been shown that modifications of the first best assumptions can provide theoretical frameworks in which both eco-dumping and (sometimes) ERTB become possible[20]: If countries are large, domestic environmental policy measures can affect the terms of trade. If the market structure is oligopolistic, domestic environmental policy can be used strategically. Finally, if governments are subject to regulatory capture by polluting industries, domestic environmental policy can be used to confer benefits to interest groups.

Terms of trade effects of environmental policy have been addressed by Krutilla, [1991] Markusen [1975] and Rauscher [1991b, 1995d, 1994 & 1997].

Krutilla [1991] shows in a partial equilibrium model that large countries can affect their terms of trade by the choice of environmental policy. In particular, he shows that a country importing a good whose PPM causes environmental pollution engages in eco-dumping while a country exporting such a good sets a NIMBY policy to improve its terms of trade.

Rauscher [1991b] shows in a Ricardo-Viner model where the environment is modelled as a sector specific factor of production that a country importing the environment-intensive good reduces stringency of environmental policy to improve its terms of trade[21]. Rauscher [1995d] analyses terms of trade effects of environmental regulation in more detail. He finds that the country relatively scarcely endowed with the environmental production factor will engage in eco-dumping to improve its terms of trade, while the country relatively well endowed with the environmental production factor will do the opposite, i.e. engage in a NIMBY policy. Thus, he finds that while terms of trade considerations may result in eco-dumping,

[20] These modifications can be subsumed under non-optimal policy interventions and second best considerations.

[21] In Rauscher's [1991b] Ricardo-Viner model environmental regulation is sought as an emission permit rather than a tax. Hence, the quantity of emissions is increased to yield a terms of trade improvement.

they will never yield an ERTB with lower than optimal environmental quality in both countries.

Rauscher [1994] investigates an alternative definition of eco-dumping, namely a differential, i.e. laxer, treatment of an export sector compared with a sector whose goods are only domestically consumed. He uses a modified Heckscher-Ohlin model[22] where input of an environmental factor of production causes a negative production externality both in the export and the non-tradables sectors. He finds his earlier result that eco-dumping does not generally yield a terms of trade improvement confirmed; in particular, a favourable treatment of the tradables sector (i.e. lower environmental standards for the export sector than for the sector serving only the domestic market) does not generally produce the desired effect of an improvement in the terms of trade[23]. Yet, depending on parameter constellations, scenarios where eco-dumping improves the terms of trade are also possible.

Rauscher [1997, ch.5] replicates the results from Rauscher [1991b,1994&1995d] in a Heckscher-Ohlin-Samuelson model with production and consumption externalities.

Markusen [1975] shows that the optimal environmental tax in the presence of global environmental distortions for a large country includes a terms of trade term which is positive if the good is exported and negative if it is imported.

Strategic environmental policy has been addressed by Barrett [1994c], Conrad [1993&1996], Kennedy [1994], Rauscher [1994, 1995c&d] and Walz & Wellisch [1997].

Barrett [1994c] shows in a partial equilibrium Cournot model where firms from two countries compete in a third market that governments have an incentive to reduce taxes on environmental externalities associated with production to improve the relative position of the domestic duopolist on the third market. If such an eco-dumping policy is undertaken unilaterally, increase in market share and hence profits for the domestic firm offsets losses from inefficient environmental policy. However, if both duopolists'

22 Apart from the existence of a negative environmental production externality, the main difference of Rauscher's model compared with the generic Heckscher-Ohlin-Samuelson model is that three goods are produced by two economies, whereby each economy produces two goods: one exclusively for the domestic market and one that is both exported and consumed domestically. The third good is imported. Hence, there is no import-competing sector.

23 Owing to the specific assumption that there is no import-competing sector, Rauscher [1994, 823] finds a tendency towards stricter environmental standards. Yet if this assumption were relaxed, the policy outcome would again depend on the relative endowments of the two economies with the environmentally polluting factor of production.

governments engage in eco-dumping, both countries' welfare deteriorates since profits decline and environmental quality deteriorates[24].

Conrad [1993&1996] finds similar results when negative environmental externalities are global. He shows in a partial equilibrium model that governments both unilaterally and bilaterally have an incentive to relax environmental policy to help their domestic duopolist to increase market share on the third market if no other policy instruments, i.e. abatement subsidies or input subsidies, are available. Rauscher [1995c] derives the same result in a similar model. He stresses that the globality of the environmental externality adds to the rent-capture effect in depressing the environmental tax below its Pigouvian level.

Kennedy [1994] finds similar results in a model where the good whose production causes negative environmental externalities is consumed in the two countries hosting the firms with market power. The presence of intra-industry trade adds a (positive) pollution-shifting effect to the (negative) rent-capture effect on the tax. However, the latter effect always dominates the former; therefore, both countries engage in eco-dumping.

Rauscher [1995d] analyses the effects of strategic trade policy on environmental policy in the Ricardo-Viner model mentioned above. If governments are constrained to support domestic dupolists in a third market by varying environmental tax rates, the most likely outcome is eco-dumping. Yet the opposite, i.e. a NIMBY policy, is also possible. The same result is derived in the above-mentioned Heckscher-Ohlin variant (Rauscher [1994]). To investigate the effects of strategic trade policy, the assumption that the export good is consumed domestically is dropped and it is assumed that the export sector has market power. Rauscher [1994] shows that it is likely that governments do apply laxer environmental standards for the export sector, yet, depending on parameter specifications, the opposite outcome is also possible.

Effects of regulatory capture in open economies on environmental policy-making have been analysed by Hillman & Ursprung [1992&1993],

[24] Necessary elements of Barretts [1994c] model are a small number of firms (i.e. an oligopolistic market structure) who compete in a Cournot fashion only on third markets. If the number of firms is large, the terms of trade argument enters government's decision to reduce the incentive to engage in eco-dumping; if competition is Bertrand, the opposite result occurs; if competition takes place also in domestic markets, the interests of domestic consumers enters government's environmental policy decision and an increase in the environmental tax becomes attractive to reduce market power and the price for domestic consumers.

Hoekman & Leidy [1992&1994], Rauscher [1994,1995b,1995d&1997] and Ursprung [1992][25].

Hoekman & Leidy [1992&1994] explore the political economy dimensions of the social choice of domestic environmental policy instruments in an open economy framework. They demonstrate that political obstacles blocking the introduction of efficient environmental policies are generally aggravated by open economy effects of environmental regulation. As a result, the pressure for eco-dumping[26] is expected to increase as shown in a partial equilibrium graphical analysis[27].

Rauscher [1995d] analyses the effect of regulatory capture by owners of a polluting, sector-specific factor in the Ricardo-Viner model mentioned above. If this factor profits from low environmental regulation and the government wishes to support its owners, eco-dumping is implemented. If such biased policy-making is prevalent in all countries, the outcome will be an environmental race towards the bottom. Rauscher [1994] examines the same issue in the modified Heckscher-Ohlin model outlined above when the export sector influences the environmental policy decision. His result is that under regulatory capture laxer environmental standards for the export sector are likely, yet - depending on parameter constellation - not the only possible outcome (Rauscher [1994]).

In Rauscher [1995b&1997], a partial equilibrium model where various interest groups are apt to influence political decision-making is analysed. He shows that in small countries the policy bias is such that factor owners of polluting factors lobby for lower environmental taxes (or laxer pollution standards), while environmentalists prefer the opposite. If environmental policy-makers are influenced in large countries, regulatory capture may aggravate or counteract the effect of terms-of-trade-improving environmental policy.

Ursprung [1992] analyses environmental policy-making in an open economy from a political economy point of view. He shows in a graphic analysis of a Heckscher-Ohlin-Samuelson model that the level of environmental protection tends to be inadequate, i.e. too low, if producers competing on international markets gain regulatory capture. Furthermore, it

[25] Hillman & Ursprung [1992&1993] consider the influence of environmental concerns on the political determination of trade policy while all others consider - exclusively or inclusively - also the influence of producer and factor owner lobbies whose profits or returns are reduced by environmental policy. Our focus is the latter, therefore Hillman & Ursprung's work is neglected in this survey.

[26] We interpret the quest of producer lobbies for inefficient environmental policy instruments as a demand for eco-dumping.

[27] The partial equilibrium graphical analysis is undertaken in Hoekman & Leidy [1994]; in their earlier contribution [1992] the argument is made verbally.

is argued that the policy instruments chosen under regulatory capture are inefficient.

FACTOR MOBILITY MODELS

Models in which countries compete for internationally mobile factors of production can yield outcomes of eco-dumping (and possibly) ERTB if governments do not optimally tax mobile capital (Oates & Schwab [1988]), or the labour market does not clear (Revesz [1994] & Wilson [1996]), or governments compete for location of a small number of firms (Markusen et al. [1992], Motta & Thisse [1994], Rauscher [1995b]).

Oates & Schwab [1988] analyse **non-optimal taxation of the mobile factor** in a model of inter-jurisdictional competition. They show that environmental regulation will be socially optimal as long as the mobile factor (capital) is not taxed. Yet, if governments have an incentive to follow an (suboptimal) policy of taxing mobile capital, the capital flight induced by the capital tax will be counteracted by reducing the environmental tax burden on the mobile factor[28]. This results in eco-dumping and an ERTB[29]. However, a scenario with the opposite, i.e. a NIMBY policy, is also possible.

In the presence of **unemployment**, inflow of mobile factors will be sought by governments to increase employment. If this can be achieved by reducing the burden of environmental regulation on mobile factors, the outcome will be an ERTB[30]. These are the findings from Revesz' [1994] construction of an ERTB that exemplifies the argument for the 'jobs vs. environment' punch-line often used by the opposition against strict environmental regulation[31].

[28] The reason for such sub-optimal taxation could be that public goods are under-provided and hence additional funds have a high marginal rate of return; see Wilson [1996, 407pp].

[29] Moreover, if public goods are under-provided, the environmental tax is set too low even in the absence of capital taxation since the optimal tax rate would lead to a shift of capital abroad, thereby reducing the environmental tax base; see Wilson [1996, 407pp].

[30] Wilson [1996, 413/14] reaches a similar conclusion if there are unemployment and environmental taxes.

[31] However, attracting mobile factors of production by means of low pollution requirements is not the most efficient policy to correct for labour market distortions. To explain why governments may not resort to wage or capital subsidies, one can advance Magee et al's [1989] optimal obfuscation theory. Governments may resort to eco-dumping if the associated costs are less transparent to the general public than direct subsidies. See Wilson [1996, 414/415].

In a model where two **governments interact with a small number of firms** (one or two), Markusen et al. [1992] find the following result when governments compete for investment of the polluting firm(s): while the location of the firm generates benefits in the form of oligopoly rents for the host country, it also confers a positive externality to the other in the form of consumer surplus from exports. Depending on the relative magnitude of the effects of the pollution externality, the rents and the consumer surplus externality, inter-jurisdictional competition may lead either to a ERTB or a NIMBY policy in which each jurisdiction prefers the other to host the firm. Similar models have been investigated by Motta & Thisse [1994] when the firm is already established and by Rauscher [1995b] when many governments compete for the firm, and by Hoel [1997]. Their results are analogous to Markusen et al.'s, namely that assumptions regarding the model parameters – specifically the severity of the pollution-induced disutility - may result in either an ERTB or a NIMBY type outcome.

Although all factor mobility models presented above can result in an ERTB, they cannot be seen to support such races as inherent to inter-jurisdictional competition since all rely on ad hoc assumptions why governments do not use optimal means of taxation or on a highly contrived market structure. Wilson [1996] in a survey of factor mobility models featuring ERTBs thus concludes that all models fail to justify convincingly why government policy is constrained by the absence of more direct means to attract mobile factors[32].

3. ECO-TARIFFS TO COUNTERACT ECO-DUMPING AND ERTB?

In the second best models explaining eco-dumping summarised above, tariffs (or other trade policy instruments) are not available to governments as additional policy instruments. Thus, environmental regulation was chosen to achieve two social goals: environmental protection **and** terms of trade improvement, strategic trade policy, or catering to special interest groups.

The question thus arises whether the availability of tariffs may improve environmental quality by preventing governments from resorting to eco-dumping in the pursuit of welfare-maximisation. If the use of tariffs can indeed achieve an improvement in environmental quality, the question arises whether welfare will be enhanced as well. We consider the availability of environmental tariffs in conjunction with the implementation of a domestic environmental tax.

[32] See Wilson [1996, 423].

TERMS OF TRADE CONSIDERATIONS

If terms of trade considerations cause governments to engage in eco-dumping, such policy will enhance social welfare within the country taking the measure since welfare gains from terms of trade improvements more than offset the loss of environmental quality. However, social welfare in the other countries decreases owing to a terms of trade deterioration. Global welfare is likely to fall because of the distortion having been introduced. Moreover, if the other country retaliates, a situation similar to an 'environmental tax war' occurs with the result that both countries' welfare decreases.

Krutilla [1991] finds that the availability of tariffs as policy instruments reduces the distorting effect of the terms of trade improvement sought by large countries. A correction of this deviation has welfare-improving effects. Similar results are derived by Markusen [1975] and Rauscher [1991b] in general equilibrium models where pollution spills across borders. The availability of a second policy tool improves welfare of the country now able to pursue its goals (environmental protection and terms of trade improvement) with two instruments. Environmental regulation will serve to internalise the external effect while the tariff is the 'optimal' tariff that serves to maximise welfare through terms of trade.

In this context, this study attempts to develop and extend Krutilla's [1991], Markusen's [1975] and Rauscher's [1991b] results in a Heckscher-Ohlin-Samuelson general equilibrium model with local pollution, and to isolate the environmental and (global) welfare implications if either one or two large countries use taxes and tariffs to maximise their (national) welfare.

STRATEGIC TRADE POLICY

If undertaken unilaterally, eco-dumping to achieve strategic trade policy objectives is welfare-enhancing for the country whose government undertakes the measure. Although the support for the domestic oligopolist tends to reduce environmental quality, this effect is overcompensated by the rents accruing to the oligopolist. Yet, if other countries are assumed to react to such a policy, an ERTB occurs. Welfare losses from the decline in environmental quality are aggravated by a decline in duopoly rents.

As far as tariffs are concerned, the two countries exporting the good whose PPM pollutes the environment cannot implement eco-tariffs. However, the importing nation may levy a tariff.

In this context, the following questions are tackled in our study: Whether the importing country has an incentive to levy such a tariff, and what the environmental and welfare implications are if eco-tariffs were implemented.

If we extend our scope to trade instruments other than tariffs, Walz & Wellisch's [1997] results are relevant. They find that availability of export subsidies as policy instruments reduces eco-dumping, i.e. the environmental distortions introduced for strategic reasons. Using export subsidies instead of eco-dumping improves welfare. Hence, the question arises whether this result is likely to remain valid if general equilibrium repercussions are taken into account.

REGULATORY CAPTURE

Regardless of whether eco-dumping caused by regulatory capture is pursued unilaterally or by all countries, social welfare will always be less than it would be in the absence of regulatory capture. The very assumption underlying the approach is that governments, rather than maximising social welfare, follow a policy which is biased towards a specific sector or factor. Society 'pays' for the preferential treatment of a certain group by lower environmental quality. If undertaken unilaterally, eco-dumping will yield benefits to pressure groups; yet, if all countries follow the same policy, the resulting ERTB is a prisoners' dilemma and all societies would be better off if optimal environmental policies were introduced.

Shrybman [1992] argues that the pressure from lobbies against stringent environmental regulation and resulting inertia of governments to implement optimal policies is due to the fact that trade restrictions are currently not available to governments. Thus, the implementation of eco-tariffs would reduce industry objection against stringent standards and relieve countries of the pressure to engage in eco-dumping[33]. Shrybman's argument is corroborated by Hoekman & Leidy [1994] who show that environmental policy in open economies increases pressure for protection of affected industries. Such protection is often granted[34].

In this context, our study addresses the following questions: What are the environmental and welfare effects of substituting eco-tariffs for eco-dumping if this would be demanded by lobby groups affecting the political decision-making process. Furthermore, if eco-tariffs are levied to off-set

[33] See Shrybman [1992, 100/1].

[34] "*Industries facing the highest pollution abatement costs are among those most frequently seeking and receiving protection in industrialised countries.*" (Hoekman & Leidy [1994, 243]).

competitiveness effects of internationally differing environmental policy measures, do they provide incentives for countries with lower environmental standards to improve environmental regulation?

4. SUMMARY AND CONCLUSIONS

Our survey of empirical evidence regarding eco-dumping and ERTB shows that there is little indication that differences in the stringency of environmental regulation across countries seriously harms competitiveness of industries subject to higher environmental standards. However, many experts agree that the current level of environmental regulation is below the optimum. Hence, it could be that governments are reluctant to implement more stringent policies for fear of negative welfare effects or because they are subject to regulatory capture[35]. Therefore, it may even be that eco-dumping causes environmental standards to be too low to impact trade flows[36].

Our survey of theoretical explanations for eco-dumping and ERTB shows that there is evidence that in specific circumstances – e.g. terms of trade-related or in case of imperfect competition - such a policy might be followed by welfare-maximising governments. Furthermore, if governments do not actually attempt to maximise social welfare but are subject to regulatory capture by industries or factors whose profits or returns are reduced by environmental policy, eco-dumping and ERTB are a possible outcome.

Our discussion of possible effects of the availability of eco-tariffs as additional policy instruments in the context of the scenarios that may result in eco-dumping shows that it is by no means clear whether such tariffs will indeed relieve the pressure from governments to engage in eco-dumping and therefore improve environmental quality. Furthermore, even if they are apt to relieve countries from the pressure to engage in eco-dumping, their effects upon national and global welfare remain to be determined.

Chapters 4, 5 and 6 of this study take up some of these questions. In chapter 4, we develop a general equilibrium model to analyse effects of government policy to increase welfare through terms of trade improvement. In chapter 5, we investigate the question of strategic trade policy by means of manipulation of an environmental tax. In chapter 6, we take up the question of regulatory capture in a general equilibrium model.

[35] Lax environmental standards can also result in autarky or in sectors producing non-tradables. However, different reasons are then found for such low standards.

[36] This depends on technological parameters such as supply and demand elasticities and substitution elasticities.

Chapter 3

An International Trade Model with Pollution and Eco-tariffs

To approach the question whether tariffs may serve as environmental policy instruments, this chapter develops a theoretical framework in which issues regarding trade and environmental policy can be incorporated.

We set forth a general equilibrium model where two sectors produce two goods using two factors of production. Society enjoys consumption of the two goods, yet is vexed by environmental pollution, generated by use of capital in one of the sectors. Government levies a Pigouvian tax to internalise the externality. For a first exposition, we assume that the country under consideration is small and the environmental problem is of a domestic kind, i.e. polluting emissions do not cross borders. We develop a Heckscher-Ohlin-Samuelson model in which no incentive exists to deviate from a socially optimal environmental policy, i.e. an eco-tax at its Pigouvian level. We analyse effects of trade liberalisation and determine the optimal trade policy if government chooses a Pigouvian tax. Furthermore, we determine effects of suboptimal environmental and trade policy.

1. MODEL

We consider a (small) country ('home') where two goods (x and y) are produced and consumed and an environmental externality is present.

For **production** of the goods x and y two factors (capital k and labour l) are used. The production side of the economy is concave; both goods are produced with non-increasing returns to scale, i.e. for $\kappa \geq 1$

$$f(\kappa k^x, \kappa l^x) \leq \kappa f(k^x, l^x), \qquad \text{and} \qquad h(\kappa k^y, \kappa l^y) \leq \kappa h(k^y, l^y) \qquad (3\text{-}1)$$

x is the capital-intensive good. Environmental degradation is caused by polluting smoke s, generated by capital input in the x sector. This PPM pollution is the sole source of environmental degradation; neither labour input in the x sector nor production of y nor consumption of either good affect environmental quality.

Let superscripts refer to sectors and subscripts denote partial derivatives. Thus k^x and l^x are input factors employed in the polluting sector; its output is

$$x = f(k^x, l^x) \tag{3-2}$$

Similarly, the y sector's output is given by

$$y = h(k^y, l^y) \tag{3-3}$$

Since total factor endowment is fixed at k respectively l, and factors are fully employed (3-3) reads

$$y = h(k-k^x, l-l^x) \tag{3-3'}$$

$f(\bullet)$ and $h(\bullet)$ are increasing and concave functions of capital respectively labour, i.e.

$$f_k, f_l, h_k, h_l > 0, \; f_{kk}, f_{ll}, h_{kk}, h_{ll} < 0, \; \text{and } f_{kk}f_{ll} - f_{kl}^2, h_{kk}h_{ll} - h_{kl}^2 \geq 0 \tag{3-4}$$

Regarding the polluting smoke emissions, we assume the following simple linear relationship between capital input in the x sector and smoke 'output', i.e. emissions

$$s = k^x \tag{3-5}$$

Welfare w of society consists of consumption utility u and pollution disutility v. For simplicity, we let the welfare function be separable in consumption of x and y, denoted by (c^x, c^y) and emissions

$$w = u(c^x, c^y) - v(s), \tag{3-6}$$

whereby $u(\bullet)$ is increasing in the two goods and strictly concave. Denoting derivatives by goods' quantities in subscripts, we thus have

$$u_x, u_y > 0, \qquad u_{xx}, u_{yy} < 0 \quad \text{and} \quad u_{xx}u_{yy} - u^2_{xy} > 0 \tag{3-7}$$

$v(\bullet)$ is increasing in smoke and strictly convex. Simplifying notation by writing $v(k)$ rather than $v(s)$ and denoting derivatives by dashes we have

$$v' > 0, \qquad \text{and } v'' > 0 \tag{3-8}$$

Additive separability of the welfare function implies that both aspects of welfare are superior.

In the **international trade equilibrium**, the value of imports equals the value of exports. The country under consideration is trading goods x and y and normalising over the price of x the relative price level is given by

$$p = p^y/p^x \tag{3-9}$$

and the trade equilibrium by

$$c^x + pc^y = x + py \tag{3-10}$$

with (3-2) and (3-3') (3-10) becomes

$$c^x = f(k^x,l^x) + p\,h(k\text{-}k^x,l\text{-}l^x) - pc^y \tag{3-10'}$$

(3-6) now reads

$$w = u(f(k^x,l^x) + ph(k\text{-}k^x,l\text{-}l^x) - pc^y,\ c^y) - v(k^x) \tag{3-11}$$

The assumption that consumers maximise utility and producers profit yields the following first order conditions (FOCs) in the absence of environmental regulation:

$$f_k - ph_k = 0 \tag{3-12}$$

$$f_l - ph_l = 0 \tag{3-13}$$

$$u_y - pu_x = 0 \tag{3-14}$$

We assume that government maximises social welfare by internalising the negative environmental externality. Internalisation is pursued by **environmental regulation** in the form of a ('green') tax g. Since the environmental externality is caused by capital input in the x sector, g is levied on k^x. Its optimal value is derived by differentiating (3-11) with respect to (w.r.t.) g. At the optimum, this partial derivative has to be zero.

$$\frac{dw}{dg} = (u_x(f_k - ph_k) - v')\frac{dk^x}{dg} + (u_x(f_l - ph_l)\frac{dl^x}{dg} + (u_y - pu_x)\frac{dc^y}{dg} \overset{!}{=} 0 \quad (3\text{-}15)$$[1]

We observe that the second and third term in (3-15) are zero, if utility and profit-maximisation is pursued. We thus have

$$\left(f_k - ph_k - \frac{v'}{u_x}\right)\frac{dk^x}{dg} = 0.$$

FOC (3-12) is hence now given by

$$f_k - (v'/u_x) - ph_k = 0 \quad (3\text{-}12')$$

Therefore, factor prices for k differ between the two sectors[2]. This difference is the environmental tax g given by

$$g = v'/u_x \quad (3\text{-}16)$$

which corresponds to a Pigouvian tax levied on k^x.

To present results of profit-maximising behaviour and the **equilibrium in the production sector**, if a tax is levied on k^x, we assume that $f(\bullet)$ and $h(\bullet)$ display constant returns to scale (CRS), i.e. the special case in which the equality in (3-1) holds[3]. If x and y are produced by linearly homogeneous production functions, we can express the production sector of our model in the intensive form, in which factor intensities are the dependent variables of the production functions for x and y which we denote by $\varphi(\bullet)$ and $\xi(\bullet)$ in the intensive form:

$$\tilde{x} = \tilde{l}^x \varphi(\tilde{k}^x), \text{ with } \tilde{x} = x/l,\ \tilde{l}^x = l^x/l, \text{ and } \tilde{k}^x = k^x/l^x \quad (3\text{-}17)$$

[1] We drop the term *dp/dg* since policy measures in small countries do not affect the world price level by assumption.

[2] In our model, this factor price differential corrects an (environmental) distortion. However, analytically it is similar to factor price distortions analysed in the 1970s.

[3] In the remainder, we will go back and forth between assumption of CRS and the weaker non-increasing returns to scale. As a rule, we use CRS whenever the less restrictive assumption does not lend itself to interpretable results.

$$\tilde{y} = \tilde{l}^{y} \xi(\tilde{k}^{y}), \text{ with } \tilde{y} = y/l,\ \tilde{l}^{y} = l^{y}/l, \text{ and } \tilde{k}^{y} = k^{y}/l^{y} \tag{3-18}$$

Full employment implies in the presence of the environmental tax:

$$\tilde{k} = \tilde{l}^{x}\tilde{k}^{x} + \tilde{l}^{y}\tilde{k}^{y}, \quad \text{with } \tilde{k} = k/l, \quad \text{and} \tag{3-19}$$

$$1 = \tilde{l}^{x} + \tilde{l}^{y} \tag{3-20}$$

Maximisation of (3-17) and (3-18) under constraints (3-19) and (3-20) yields the following two FOCs, where derivatives are denoted by dashes:

$$\frac{\varphi' - g}{\xi'} = p \tag{3-21}$$

$$\frac{f - \varphi'\tilde{k}^{x}}{h - \xi'\tilde{k}^{y}} = p \tag{3-22}$$

To examine the effects of environmental regulation on society's production possibilities, we combine and rearrange (3-21) and (3-22) to yield the ratio of the marginal products of capital and labour in both industries:

$$\left(\frac{\varphi' - g}{\varphi - \tilde{k}^{x}\varphi'}\right) = \left(\frac{\xi'}{\xi - \tilde{k}^{y}\xi'}\right) \tag{3-23}$$

The bracketed terms in (3-23) indicate the slope of the production isoquants for x and y. In the absence of environmental regulation, slopes are equal at the equilibrium point. The Edgeworth-Bowley box diagram in Figure 3-1 illustrates effects of environmental regulation for production efficiency loci. Since x is the capital-intensive good, the contract curve cc in the absence of environmental regulation lies below the diagonal. If there is no environmental regulation, x and y production isoquants *ip(x)* and *ip(y)* are tangential on cc. Introducing a tax on k^x changes the position of the contract curve. Furthermore, production isoquants are no longer tangential on the new efficiency locus.

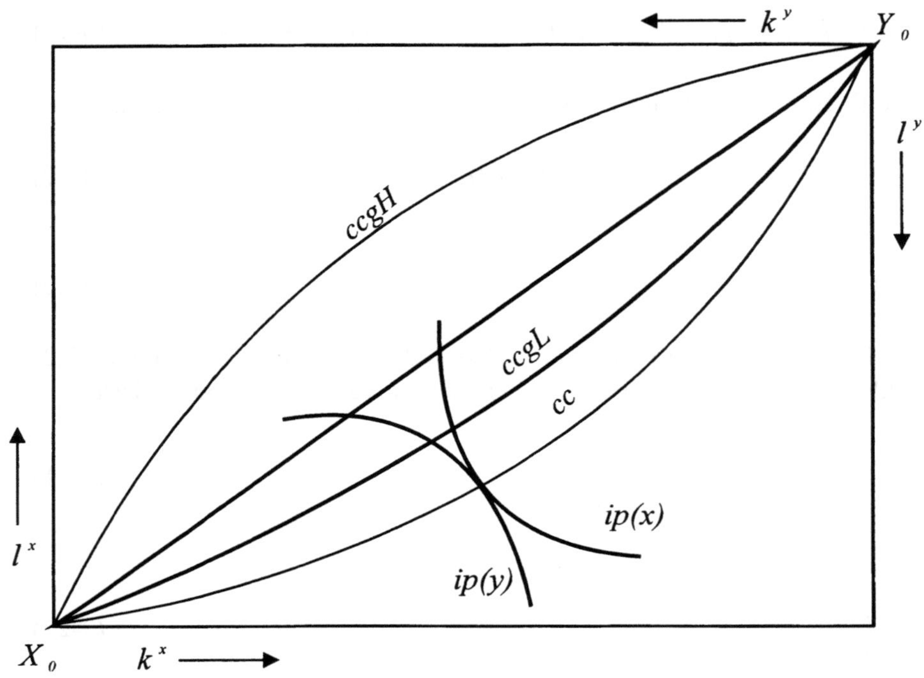

Figure 3-1. Effect I of the Environmental Tax *g*: Change of the Contract Curve

We observe that environmental regulation changes the position of the efficiency locus, whereby three cases are possible:

- If the Pigouvian tax is positive but relatively low, the contract curve *ccgL* is shifted towards the diagonal (except at endpoints), i.e. the difference in the factor intensities in the two sectors is reduced, yet not reversed. *x* remains the capital-intensive good.
- If the Pigouvian tax is high, the contract curve *ccgH* is shifted over the diagonal, i.e. factor intensities are reversed. In that case, *y* becomes capital-intensive as a consequence of environmental regulation[4].
- Finally, if a negative tax would be levied on capital use in the *x* sector, the contract curve would be moved further to the south east (not shown). Such a subsidy on capital in the *x* sector would enhance capital intensity of *x*.

Furthermore, we observe that the (absolute) slope of *x* isoquant is greater than the slope of.

[4] We assume throughout our study that factor intensities are not reversed by environmental regulation.

From figure 3-1 it is the *y* isoquant at the new efficiency locus resulting from environmental regulation obvious that the tax affects the production possibility frontier.

Figure 3-2 illustrates the consequences of environmental regulation for the transformation curve and for the consumption utility society can derive from its production possibilities.

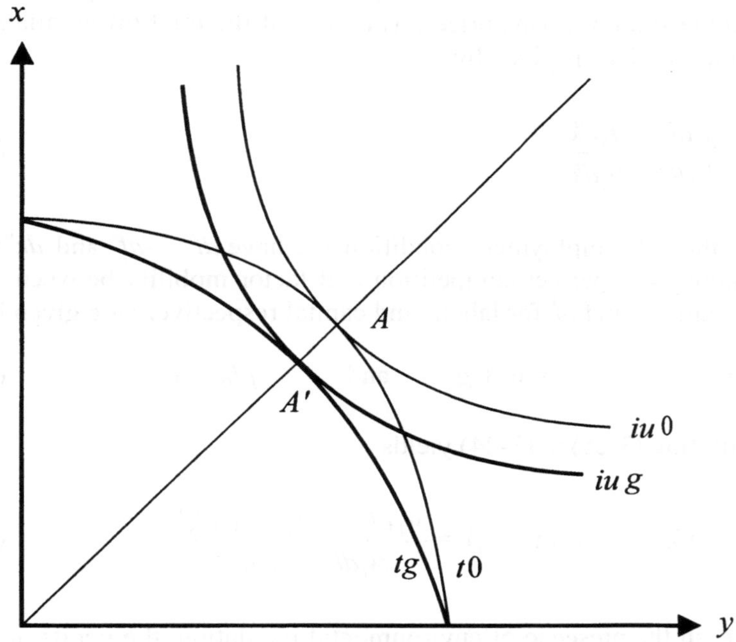

Figure 3-2. Effect II of the Tax *g*: Shrinkage of the Production Possibility Space

We observe that

- the transformation curve in the presence of environmental regulation *tg* lies inside *t*0, the production possibility frontier in the absence of environmental policy (shrinkage effect). It should be further noted that the shape of *tg* does not necessarily remain concave to the origin[5].
- at end points, the two production possibility frontiers coincide which reflects the fact that for complete specialisation, environmental regulation by means of a tax has no allocative effect.

[5] On the question of the slope of the production possibility frontier in the presence of taxes that distort the factor market see Bhagwati & Srinivasan [1971], Herberg & Kemp [1971] and Jones [1971]. For graphic representations of the effects of the environmental tax *g* on capital in the *x* sector, we shall assume that the shape of the production possibility frontier does in fact remain concave to the origin.

– unless we have a corner solution, production with the tax yields lower consumption utility. This is illustrated by the fact that consumption utility indifference curve *iug* tangential to *tg* corresponds to a lower utility level than *iu0*, the utility indifference curve tangential to *t0*.

Furthermore, we can derive that in the presence of environmental regulation the slope of the production possibility frontier in equilibrium does not equal the ratio of goods prices. The ratio of the total differentials of the production functions is given by

$$\frac{dx}{dy} = \frac{f_l dl^x + f_k dk^x}{h_l dl^y + h_k dk^y} \qquad (3\text{-}24)$$

From the full employment condition we have $dl^y = -dl^x$ and $dk^y = -dk^x$. Furthermore, with perfect competition and factor mobility between sectors, factor rewards ω^l and ω^k for labour and capital respectively are given by:

$$f_l,\ ph_l = w_l, \qquad f_k = w_k + g, \qquad \text{and} \qquad ph_k = w_k \qquad (3\text{-}25)$$

Substituting (3-25) in (3-24) yields

$$\frac{dx}{dy} = -p\beta, \qquad \text{with} \qquad \beta = \frac{w_k dl^x + (w_k + g)dk^x}{w_l dl^x + w_k dk^x} \qquad (3\text{-}26)$$

Hence, in the presence of environmental regulation, the goods prices are not tangent to the production possibility frontier. Furthermore, since $\beta > 1$, the slope of the relative price vector p in equilibrium is less than the slope of the production possibility frontier in absolute terms.

Allocative effects of environmental regulation are hence also determined by the fact that the price-vector is not tangent to the production possibility frontier in equilibrium. This is illustrated in figure 3-3 which shows the effects of this non-tangency in the production possibility space:

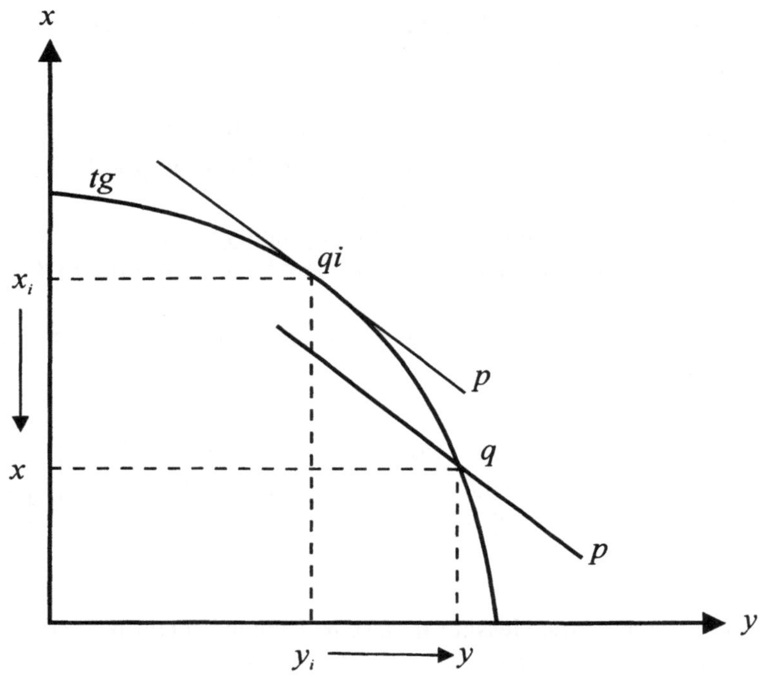

Figure 3-3. Effect III of the Tax g: Non-tangency of the Price-vector

We observe that

- since the price vector *p* is not tangential to the production possibility frontier *tg* in the presence of environmental regulation, the actual production point *q* will lie to the south-east of the imaginary production point *qi* which would be realised if *p* was tangential to *tg*.
- therefore, production shifts away from *x* towards *y*.
- this reduces - again ceteris paribus - input factors in the *x* sector, and hence pollution.
- in the absence of an environmental tax, the market allocation does not yield production at the welfare optimal level since the cost associated with the externality is not reflected, and the market price thus distorted.
- correction of the price (and production) distortion restores the optimality of the allocation.

2. EFFECTS OF TRADE LIBERALISATION AND TRADE POLICY

We shall first determine the effects of trade liberalisation for a small country. Furthermore, we derive the optimal tariff on the good whose PPM pollutes the environment for a small country.

For the sake of convenience, the following analysis shall be restricted to interior solutions. Therefore, equilibria can be derived from the FOCs given by (3-12'), (3-13), and (3-14).

Total differentiation of the FOCs yields the following linear equation system:

$$\begin{pmatrix} u_{yy} - 2pu_{xy} + p^2 u_{xx} & g(u_{xy} - pu_{xx}) & 0 \\ g(u_{xy} - pu_{xx}) & g^2 u_{xx} + u_x(f_{kk} - ph_{kk}) - v'' & u_x(f_{kl} + ph_{kl}) \\ 0 & f_{kl} - ph_{kl} & f_{ll} - ph_{ll} \end{pmatrix} \begin{pmatrix} dc^y \\ dk^x \\ dl^x \end{pmatrix} = \begin{pmatrix} u_x dp \\ u_x h_k dp \\ h_l dp \end{pmatrix}$$

Linear Equation System 3-1

The determinant of the Hessian matrix in Linear Equation System 3-1 is negative, if $(f_{kk}+ph_{kk})(f_{ll}+ph_{ll}) > (f_{kl}+ph_{kl})^2$, and $(u_{yy}-2pu_{xy}+p^2u_{xx})u_{xx} > (u_{xy}-pu_{xx})^2$. These conditions are fulfilled by virtue of concavity of the production side of the economy and the utility function.

Applying Cramer's Rule to the above system yields the following comparative static results, well-known from the pure theory of international trade[6]:

$$\frac{dk^x}{dp} < 0, \qquad \text{and} \qquad \frac{dl^x}{dp} < 0 \tag{3-27}$$

If preferences across trading societies are similar, increase of the relative price for y and changes in the industry structure according to (3-27) take place in a labour-abundant country. According to the Heckscher-Ohlin Theorem, a labour-abundant country hence exports y following a trade liberalisation. Therefore, the effects of a trade liberalisation regarding factor allocation and welfare for a labour-abundant country are:

- increase of production of y, and a shift of capital and labour into the y sector
- reduction of pollution, owing to the shift of capital out of the x sector
- an increase of welfare because $v(k)$ is reduced.

6 See for example Markusen et al. [1995, 98pp] or Gandolfo [1994, 76pp].

Consumption utility, however, is due to decrease if a labour-abundant country liberalises trade. This is illustrated in figure 3-4 which shows the effect of trade liberalisation in the production possibility space. Since a labour-abundant country faces an increase in the relative price if it opens up to trade, the free trade price vector p_F is steeper than the autarky price vector p_A. Consumption and production points which coincide in autarky (c_A=q_A) diverge if goods are traded. A labour-abundant country expands its production of y and exports the difference between production and consumption (y - cy = Ex), while it imports x.

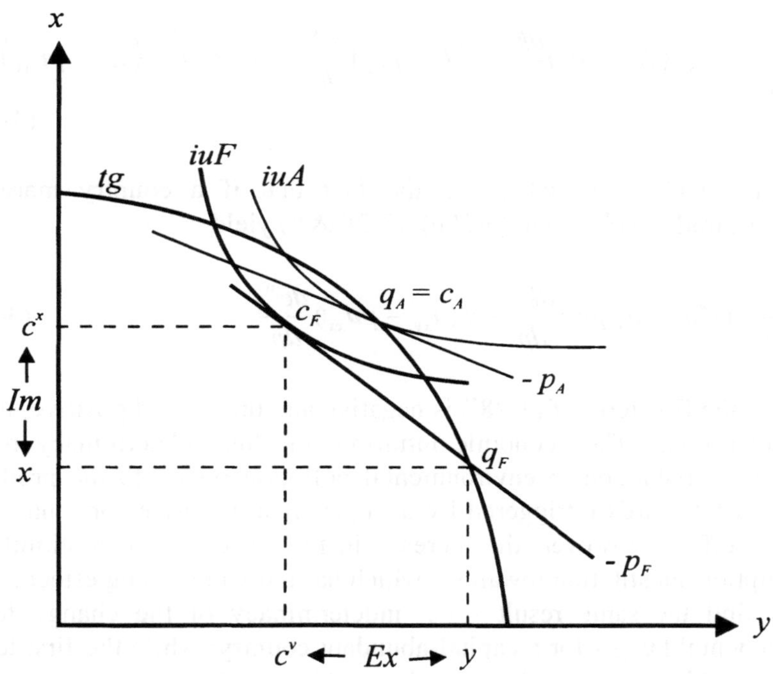

*Figure 3-4.*Effect of Trade-liberalisation on Production Possibility Space

We observe that consumption utility declines for a labour-abundant country as a result of trade liberalisation; utility indifference curve under free trade (*iuF*) is at a lower level than *iuA*, the utility indifference curve in autarky. It should be kept in mind, however, that in relatively capital-abundant countries trade liberalisation stimulates production of x and hence pollution.

Trade liberalisation also affects environmental regulation. For a labour-abundant country, the comparative static effects of trade liberalisation on the Pigouvian tax g are given by:

$$\frac{dg}{dp}=\frac{d(v'/u_x)}{dp}=\frac{(dv'/dp)u_x-(du_x/dp)v'}{u_x^2} \quad \lessgtr 0 \tag{3-28}$$

since

$$\frac{dv'}{dp}=\frac{dv'}{dk^x}\frac{dk^x}{dp}=v''\frac{dk^x}{dp}, \qquad \text{and} \tag{3-28a}$$

$$\frac{du_x}{dp}=u_{xx}\left[(f_k-ph_k)\frac{dk^x}{dp}+(f_l-ph_l)\frac{dl^x}{dp}+\left(h-c^y\right)\right]+\left(u_{xy}-pu_{xx}\right)\frac{dc^y}{dp} \tag{3-28b}$$

Using FOCs (3-12'&13) and the fact that if a country marginally liberalises trade $(h\text{-}c^y) = 0$ in (3-28b), (3-28a&b) yield

$$\frac{dg}{dp}=(v''u_x-u_{xx}gv')\frac{dk^x}{dp}-v'(u_{xy}-pu_{xx})\frac{dc^y}{dp} \tag{3-28'}$$

Since the first term of (3-28') is negative and the second positive, its sign is undetermined. The economic intuition for this indeterminacy runs as follows: the reduction in environmental pollution owing to the production substitution towards y triggered by a higher relative price for y has a tax-reducing effect. However, the increase in the price of y also stimulates a consumption substitution towards x which has a tax increasing effect[7].

We find the same result - i.e. indeterminacy of the change for the environmental tax g - for a capital-abundant country: while the first term in (3-28') would be positive, the second would be negative.

If countries liberalise trade, they can also pursue **trade policy**. We assume that governments command an import tariff as trade policy instrument. For a welfare-maximising government of a small, labour-abundant country, which internalises the environmental externality by setting g at the Pigouvian level, the optimal tariff on its import good x is given by differentiating (3-11) w.r.t. τ, whereby τ is the relative price of x including the tariff. This is the FOC for a welfare optimum; i.e. it has to equal zero.

[7] We observe opposite effects yet the same indeterminacy in a capital-abundant country.

$$\frac{dw}{d\tau} = (u_x(f_k - ph_k) - v')\frac{dk^x}{d\tau} + (u_x(f_l - ph_l)\frac{dl^x}{d\tau} + (u_y - pu_x)\frac{dc^y}{d\tau} \overset{!}{=} 0 \quad (3\text{-}29)$$[8]

If a tariff is levied on x, the FOCs (3-12'), (3-13) and (3-14) are given by

$$f_k - g - (p/\tau)h_k = 0 \quad (3\text{-}30)$$

$$f_l - (p/\tau)h_l = 0 \quad (3\text{-}31)$$

$$u_y - (p/\tau)u_x = 0 \quad (3\text{-}32)$$

Using these FOCs and the assumption that government charges a Pigouvian tax - i.e. $g = v'/u_x$ - in (3-29) yields the following expression:

$$p\left(\frac{1}{\tau} - 1\right)\left(h_k\frac{dk^x}{d\tau} + h_l\frac{dl^x}{d\tau} + \frac{dc^y}{d\tau}\right) = 0 \quad (3\text{-}33)$$

Therefore, if trade takes place[9], the optimal τ is given by

$$\tau = 1 \quad (3\text{-}34)$$

We can hence conclude with:

Proposition 3-1: *Trade liberalisation in a small country changes environmental quality and may change environmental policy. If an optimal environmental policy is pursued, optimal trade policy calls for a zero tariff.*

(a) If the country is labour-abundant, environmental pollution decreases as a consequence of trade liberalisation.

(b) Internalisation of the environmental externality in a labour-abundant country reinforces specialisation.

(c) If the country is capital-abundant, the opposite of (a) & (b) holds.

(d) In both capital and labour-abundant countries, the effect of trade liberalisation on the optimal environmental tax is undetermined.

[8] We drop the term $dp/d\tau$ since policy measures in small countries do not affect the world price level by assumption.

[9] We observe that with the full employment condition implying $dk^x/d\tau = -dk^y/d\tau$ and $dl^x/d\tau = -dl^y/d\tau$ we have $h_k(dk^x/d\tau) + h_l(dl^x/d\tau) + (dc^y/d\tau) = d(c^y-h)/d\tau$. Therefore, the equality in (3-33) is also fulfilled if $d(c^y-h)/d\tau = 0$, which would imply that no trade takes place.

(e) A welfare-maximising government of a labour-abundant country in which the environmental externality is internalised by a Pigouvian tax on k^x will not charge a tariff on x.

3. EFFECT OF NON-OPTIMAL ENVIRONMENTAL AND TRADE POLICY

We shall first elaborate on effects of suboptimal environmental policies; i.e. a reduction of the environmental tax below the Pigouvian level, or an increase above it for small countries. Furthermore, we shall examine the effects of an eco-tariff, i.e. a tariff on the good whose PPM pollutes the environment for a small country.

If government pursues **suboptimal environmental policy**, i.e. sets a tax which differs from the Pigouvian tax on capital, it can either engage in

eco-dumping, i.e. set the tax below the Pigouvian level ($g < v'/u_x$),

or pursue a

NIMBY policy, i.e. set the tax above the Pigouvian level ($g > v'/u_x$).

Allocative effects of suboptimal environmental policies are as follows: If government pursues an eco-dumping policy we observe a shift of labour and capital from the *x* into the *y* sector; if government pursues a NIMBY policy, we opposite factor movement results.

By virtue of the fact that governments are deviating from the optimal policies, welfare consequences of both eco-dumping and NIMBY are negative. In particular we find:

- if the tax is increased above its optimal level (NIMBY), the resulting environmental quality enhancement is more than offset by a decrease in consumption welfare owing to a reduced production efficiency.
- if the tax is reduced below its optimal level (eco-dumping), the opposite occurs; i.e. the production increase is more than offset by the deterioration of environmental quality.

If countries engage in trade, we find furthermore

- if the government of a labour-abundant country engages in eco-dumping (or the government of a capital-abundant country engages in NIMBY), trade flows are reduced compared with the Pareto optimum, and
- if the government of a labour (capital)-abundant country engages in NIMBY (or the government of a capital-abundant country engages in eco-dumping), trade flows increase.

If government of a small, labour-abundant country pursues **suboptimal trade policy** by levying a tariff on its import good, allocative effects resemble those of eco-dumping. The tariff protects the x sector, therefore capital and labour is shifted from the y into the x sector. Welfare effects of a deviation from the optimal (zero tariff) policy are negative as long as government pursues an optimal environmental policy. The environmental deterioration resulting from the tariff dominates the increase in consumption utility[10].

We can now look at **policy interdependencies** between trade and environmental policy measures. If a suboptimal environmental policy is pursued, the optimal, welfare-maximising eco-tariff is no longer zero. It is found by differentiating (3-11) w.r.t. τ which again yields (3-29)

$$\frac{dw}{d\tau} = (u_x(f_k - ph_k) - v')\frac{dk^x}{d\tau} + (u_x(f_l - ph_l)\frac{dl^x}{d\tau} + (u_y - pu_x)\frac{dc^y}{d\tau} \overset{!}{=} 0 \quad (3\text{-}29)$$

We substitute the FOCs (3-30), (3-31), and (3-32) whereby suboptimal environmental policy implies that $g \neq v'/u_x$. This yields the following expression for the optimal tariff[11]

$$\tau = \left(1 + \left(\frac{v'}{u_x} - g\right)\frac{dk^x}{d(c^y - h)}\right)^{-1} \quad (3\text{-}35)$$

Inspection of (3-35) reveals that an eco-tariff ($\tau > 1$) will be levied by a labour-abundant country where the tax is set above the Pigouvian level[12].

If a labour-abundant country levies a tariff on its import good, its optimal environmental policy is still given by the Pigouvian tax on capital in the x sector. The tariff affects this tax, yet the direction of the change is undetermined:

[10] If the tax is set too high, the tariff would bring pollution closer to its optimal level and the environmental effect would be positive; see Rauscher [1991b, 20]. The increase in consumption utility is illustrated in figure 3-4; as the tariff shifts p_F towards p_A, consumption occurs on a higher utility indifference curve.

[11] We use again the full employment condition in the way described in footnote 11 above.

[12] In the other three constellations (labour-abundant country where a tax below the Pigouvian tax is chosen, capital-abundant country with a tax higher or lower than the Pigouvian level) the suboptimal environmental policy also implies that $\tau \neq 1$. However, optimal policy choices are different, namely: a labour-abundant country in which eco-dumping is pursued subsidises imports; a capital-abundant country with a tax below the Pigouvian level taxes exports; a capital-abundant country in which the tax is set above the Pigouvian level subsidises exports.

$$\frac{dg}{d\tau} = \quad \lessgtr 0^{13} \tag{3-36}$$

Proposition 3-2: *Deviation from the Pigouvian tax and the optimal (zero) tariff reduces welfare in small countries. If a suboptimal environmental policy is pursued, an eco-tariff yields welfare improvement for a labour-abundant country in which government pursues a NIMBY policy.*

4. CONCLUSIONS

The preceding section showed that tariffs levied upon environmentally harmfully produced goods are not suitable to improve welfare in a small country where an optimal (Pigouvian) environmental tax is implemented as pollution is 'protected' alongside with production of x. Thus, if a situation is to be found in which tariffs may be environmental policy instruments, one or more of the above assumptions have to be relaxed respectively changed.

If the assumption of optimal environmental policy is relaxed, we showed in the preceding section that trade restrictions in form of eco-tariffs are welfare-improving for a labour-abundant country, if its environmental policy is too stringent, i.e. if a NIMBY policy is pursued. However, we elaborated in chapter 2.2 that environmental regulation is generally below the optimal level. If that is the case, an eco-tariff ($\tau > 1$) is not implemented to support domestic environmental policy. Therefore, if eco-tariffs are to come into play at all, we have to add yet another step. A possible tack is to investigate whether the absence of tariffs might be the reason for low eco-taxes or even an ERTB. If this is the case, we can further examine whether adding tariffs as policy instruments might increase environmental quality.

The following chapters present three stories in which the fact that economies are bound by multilateral trade rules to refrain from tariffs causes suboptimal environmental policy. We investigate whether a waiver of these rules, i.e. a reinstitution of tariffs, might be beneficial for the environment. Our conjecture is that if the deviation from a (Pigouvian) optimal environmental policy is caused by trade issues, trade policy measures should indeed relieve the problem of suboptimal environmental policy and possibly also increase welfare.

[13] Again, we have two opposite forces at work: the increase in pollution, and the production substitution towards x tend to increase g, while consumption substitution towards y which becomes relatively cheaper owing to the tariff has a tax-reducing effect.

Chapter 4

Tariffs to Avoid Eco-dumping for Terms of Trade Reasons

Krutilla [1991] shows in a partial equilibrium framework that the ability to influence terms of trade may induce governments to deviate from the optimal (Pigouvian) environmental policy. In certain cases, environmental standards are set below the Pigouvian level for open economy reasons, i.e. to improve terms of trade[1]. Furthermore, Krutilla argues that environmental policies would not be used to improve terms of trade, if governments could use tariffs. In particular, a country engaging in eco-dumping to improve its terms of trade could increase welfare, if instead it could levy a tariff on imports of the 'dirty' good while environmental regulation was set at the Pigouvian level[2].

We modify our Heckscher-Ohlin-Samuelson model from chapter 3 to address similar issues in a general equilibrium context. Specifically, we analyse effects of government policy to increase welfare through terms of trade improvement. If this is a reason for eco-dumping or even an ERTB, we further examine whether availability of eco-tariffs might serve to enhance welfare.

In this setting, home is modelled as a large country which faces either a conglomerate of small countries, the 'rest of the world', or another large country, 'foreign'. While the rest of the world does not coordinate policies vis-à-vis home, foreign reacts to home's policy choices.

[1] This is also derived by Rauscher [1994] in a general equilibrium model; Markusen and Rauscher [1991b] find similar results for cross-border externalities.

[2] Both Markusen [1975] and Rauscher [1991b] find a comparable result in general equilibrium models which differ from ours in their structure where the environmental externality crosses borders.

1. ECO-DUMPING AND TERMS OF TRADE IMPROVEMENT

To find the optimal, welfare-maximising tax g on capital for a large country, we differentiate (3-11) w.r.t. g and set it equal to zero[3]:

$$\frac{dw}{dg} = \left[u_x(f_k - ph_k) - v'\right]\frac{dk^x}{dg} + \left[u_x(h - c^y)\right]\frac{dp}{dg} \overset{!}{=} 0$$

For the optimal tax on capital, this yields

$$g = \frac{v'}{u_x} + (c^y - h)\frac{dp}{dg}\frac{dg}{dk^x} \qquad (4\text{-}1)$$

The optimal tax on capital for a large country is hence composed of the Pigouvian part (v'/u_x) by which the environmental externality is internalised, and the second part ($g - v'/u_x$) by which the world price, i.e. terms of trade effect of the tax on capital is taken into account.

We shall investigate sign and effect of the latter part of the optimal tax on capital in two circumstances, namely (i) when home can improve its terms of trade by an adequate choice of its environmental policy, while its (small) trading partners cannot, and when (ii) two large countries interact, both choosing their environmental policy to improve terms of trade.

LARGE HOME COUNTRY FACING ATOMISTIC COUNTRIES IN THE REST OF THE WORLD

We assume that the countries making up the rest of the world are small, and hence cannot affect the world price level by their environmental policy choice. Furthermore, we assume that these small countries do not coordinate their policies. Hence, they set their tax at the optimal level for a small country, i.e. the Pigouvian rate derived in chapter 3. In addition, we assume that all countries making up the rest of the world are identical and can be aggregated. Denoting the rest of the world's variables by capital letters, their environmental tax is given by

$$G = V'/U_X \qquad (4\text{-}2)$$

[3] We drop terms which become zero when FOCs are taken into account.

To perform comparative statics, we totally differentiate the followin FOCs which are conditions for optimal production and consumpt decisions in home and in the rest of the world, and the balanced tr identity:

$$f_k - g - ph_k = 0 \qquad (4\text{-}$$

$$f_l - ph_l = 0 \qquad (3\text{-}1$$

$$u_y - pu_x = 0 \qquad (3\text{-}1$$

$$F_K - (V' / U_X) - pH_K = 0 \qquad (3\text{-}$$

$$F_L - pH_L = 0 \qquad (3\text{-}$$

$$U_Y - pU_X = 0 \qquad (3\text{-}$$

$$c^y + C^Y - h - H = 0 \qquad (3\text{-}$$

Total differentiation of these FOCs yields the following system of lir equations :

$$\left(\begin{array}{cccc}
u_{yy}-2pu_{xy}-p^2u_{xx} & 0 & (u_{xy}-pu_{xx})(\frac{v'}{u_x}+g) & 0 \\
0 & 0 & f_{kl}+ph_{kl} & 0 \\
(u_{xy}-pu_{xx})\frac{v'}{u_x} & 0 & u_{xx}(\frac{v'}{u_x}+g\frac{v'}{u_x})+u_x(f_{kk}+ph_{kk})-v'' & 0 \\
1 & 1 & h_k & H_K \\
0 & U_{YY}-2pU_{XY}+p^2U_{XX} & 0 & (U_{XY}-pU_{XX}) \\
0 & 0 & 0 & F_{KL}+pH_{KL} \\
0 & (U_{XY}-pU_{XX})\frac{V'}{U_X} & 0 & U_{XX}G^2+U_X(F_{KK}
\end{array}\right.$$

Linear Equation System 4-1

$$
\begin{pmatrix}
0 & 0 & -u_x \\
f_{ll}+ph_{ll} & 0 & -h_l \\
u_x(f_{kl}+ph_{kl}) & 0 & -u_x h_k \\
h_l & H_L & 0 \\
0 & 0 & -U_X \\
0 & F_{LL}+pH_{LL} & -H_L \\
0 & U_X(F_{KL}+pH_{KL}) & -U_X H_K
\end{pmatrix}
\cdot
\begin{pmatrix}
c^y \\ dC^Y \\ dk^x \\ dK^X \\ dl^x \\ dL^X \\ dp
\end{pmatrix}
=
\begin{pmatrix}
0 \\ 0 \\ u_x dg \\ 0 \\ 0 \\ 0 \\ 0
\end{pmatrix}
$$

The reason for this indeterminacy are several effects, partly offsetting each other:

Substitution effect: reducing the tax leads to factor substitution in the x sector in favour of capital which ceteris paribus leads to a decrease in labour demand in the x sector.

Output effect: reduction of production cost for x leads to an output expansion of x, increasing factor demand for both capital and labour in the x sector.

Price effect: decline in relative world price for x leads to an output contraction of x, reducing factor demand for capital and labour in the x sector.

To illustrate these effects, we use results derived by Magee [1971] in the CRS form of the model. Following his approach we determine comparative static effects of eco-dumping for labour demand in the x sector in two steps. First, we perform comparative statics at constant world prices. Then we determine the effect of a change in relative world prices induced by eco-dumping in home.

Effect of eco-dumping for factor intensities if relative product prices are held constant are given by[5]:

$$\left(\frac{d\tilde{k}^x}{d(-g)}\right)_{\bar{p}} < 0, \qquad \text{and} \qquad \left(\frac{d\tilde{k}^y}{d(-g)}\right)_{\bar{p}} < 0 \qquad (4\text{-}10\&11)$$

The intuition for these results is as follows: From (4-5) we know that a decrease in the tax below the Pigouvian level leads to an excess demand for capital (substitution effect) and an expansion of output in the x sector. This triggers a decrease in the wage-rental ratio which in turn favours a substitution of labour for capital in both sectors. As a result, capital intensity in both sectors declines. Therefore, at constant prices, output and substitution effect lead to a shift of both labour and capital into the x sector.

Figure 4-1 illustrates the effects of eco-dumping if world prices remain constant: Eco-dumping leads to an outward movement of the production possibility frontier (except at endpoints); i.e. a reversal of the process described in chapter 3.1 and illustrated in Figure 3-2. Furthermore, the angle between the production possibility frontier and the price vector narrows. The latter effect is obvious, if we recall the connection between the slopes of the production possibility frontier and the price vector:

[5] See Magee [1971, 628].

$$\frac{dx}{dy} = -p\beta \tag{3-26}$$

and inspect how the β value changes with g

$$\beta = \frac{w_l dl^x + (w_k + g)dk^x}{w_l dl^x + w_k dk^x}, \qquad \frac{d\beta}{d(-g)} = -\frac{dk^x}{w_l dl^x + w_k dk^x} < 0$$

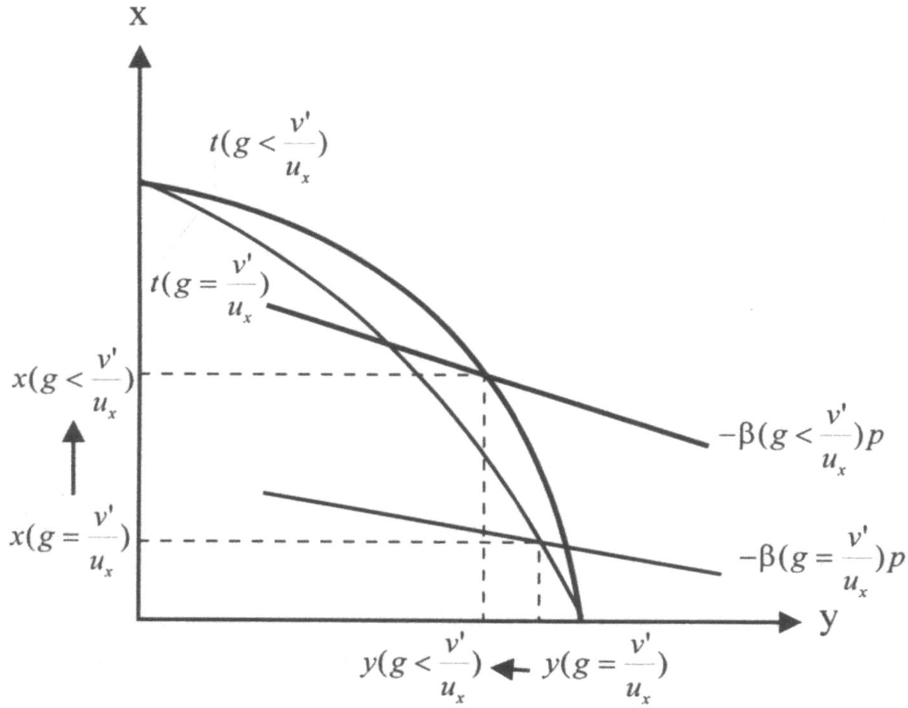

Figure 4-1. Effect of Eco-dumping in the Production Possibility Space: At Constant World Prices

We observe an increase in total (value) amount of production in home, whereby production of y decreases and production of x increases. Because of eco-dumping, the tax falls below the efficient Pigouvian level and the new allocation is therefore no longer Pareto optimal.

To complete the investigation of comparative statics for l^x, we determine the effects of the price effect of eco-dumping on $\tilde{k}^x$ and $\tilde{k}^y$. According to Magee [1971, 631], they are given by

$$\frac{d\tilde{k}^x}{dp} > 0, \quad \text{and} \quad \frac{d\tilde{k}^y}{dp} > 0 \qquad (4\text{-}12\&13)$$

The intuition runs as follows: the increase of p induced by eco-dumping triggers an expansion of the y sector (price effect mentioned above). Since y is produced relatively capital-intensively, there will be an excess demand for labour. As a result, the wage-rental ratio appreciates which in turn leads to factor substitution towards capital in both sectors. As a result, capital intensity in both sectors increases. Therefore, the price effect leads to an expansion of y output and a shift of both labour and capital into the y sector.

Figure 4-2 illustrates the effects of eco-dumping through its effect on world prices. The angle between the price vector and the production possibility frontier remains unchanged, yet the slope of the price vector changes.

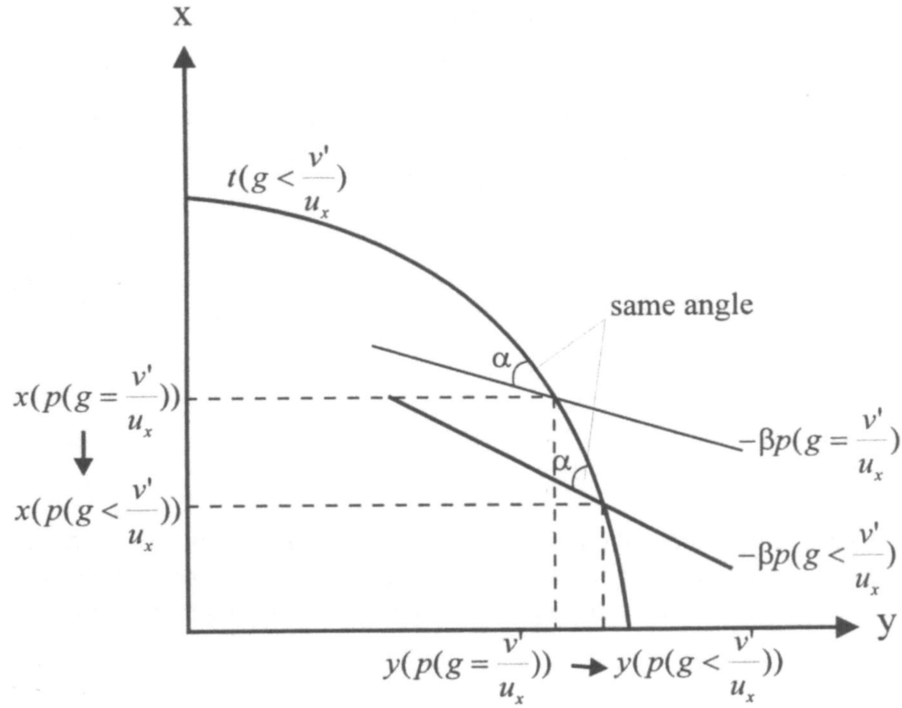

Figure 4-2. Effect of Eco-dumping in the Production Possibility Space II: Change in World Prices

We observe an expansion of y output and decline of x output in home.

We have argued that the net effect of factor substitution and output expansion of x on labour demand in the x sector is positive. The price effect of eco-dumping reduces labour demand in the x sector. If the latter effect were to dominate the former, the result would somewhat resemble the Metzler paradox known from the tariff literature[6].

If we exclude the 'eco-dumping Metzler paradox', $d\tilde{k}^y / d(-g) < 0$ even if the effect of the tax reduction on world prices is taken into account. Hence:

$$\frac{dl^x}{d(-g)} > 0, \qquad \text{and} \qquad \frac{df(k^x, l^x)}{d(-g)} > 0 \qquad \text{(4-14\&15)}$$

As regards allocative consequences of eco-dumping in home, we can hence conclude that capital input in the x sector and environmental pollution increase, andlabour input and output in the x sector increase, except in special cases when the price effect induced by eco-dumping reverses the output effect of the tax reduction.

Effects of eco-dumping in the **rest of the world**: In the capital-abundant rest of the world, the decrease of the relative world price of x following home's eco-dumping has the following effects[7]:

$$\frac{dK^X}{d(-g)} = \left(\frac{dK^X}{dp}\right)\left(\frac{dp}{d(-g)}\right) < 0, \qquad \text{and} \qquad \text{(4-16)}$$

$$\frac{dL^X}{d(-g)} = \left(\frac{dL^X}{dp}\right)\left(\frac{dp}{d(-g)}\right) < 0 \qquad \text{(4-17)}$$

Hence, environmental quality improves because less smoke is emitted.

Furthermore, the Pigouvian tax charged in the rest of the world is affected by home's eco-dumping, although the effect is undetermined:

6 Developed by Metzler [1949]; see for example Gandolfo [1994, 115pp]. The Metzler paradox captures the fact that the imposition of an import tariff by a large country may lead to such a pronounced reduction in the relative world price of its importable that the protective effect of the tariff would in fact be overcompensated.

7 Again we apply Cramer's rule to the system of linear equations 4-1 to find $dK^X/d(-g)$ and $dL^X/d(-g)$.

$$\frac{d(V'/U_X)}{d(-g)} \lessgtr 0^8 \qquad (4\text{-}18)$$

If it so happens that the tax in the rest of the world declines, the effects of eco-dumping on K^X, L^X and p are partly offset.

NIMBY POLICY: RATIONALE AND EFFECTS

By increasing production cost in its export sector, a capital-abundant country shifts its export supply curve and import demand curve which increases the relative price to its benefit. Such a policy compares to the profit-maximising behaviour of a monopolist or monopsonist. However, since perfect competition prevails in the export sector and consumers are atomistic, government regulation in the form of a NIMBY policy is needed to realise the welfare gain. A more stringent tax scheme contracts the production possibility frontier at home.

Effects of NIMBY in **home**: Effects of a NIMBY policy, i.e. if home chooses ($g > v'/u_x$), are just the reverse of eco-dumping effects. Hence, for a capital-abundant home country we have:

$$\frac{dk^x}{dg} < 0, \qquad \text{and} \qquad \frac{dl^x}{dg} < 0^9 \qquad (4\text{-}9\&14)$$

which implies an improvement of environmental quality.

Effects of NIMBY in the **rest of the world**: In the rest of the world, which would now be labour-abundant, the decrease in the terms of trade following home's NIMBY policy has the following effects on factor demands:

$$\frac{dK^X}{dg} > 0, \qquad \text{and} \qquad \frac{dL^X}{dg} > 0 \qquad (4\text{-}16'\&17')$$

Consequently, environmental pollution increases. The Pigouvian tax $G = V'/U_X$ in the rest of the world may increase or decrease as a result of home's NIMBY policy:

[8] Again, the influences on the tax offset each other: pollution reduction and production substitution towards y, as well as the terms of trade decline reduce the tax; consumption substitution towards y increase it. However, since we have two tax-reducing effects and only one which increases the tax, a tax decrease seems more likely.

[9] If the Metzler paradox is excluded.

$$\frac{d(V'/U_X)}{dg} \lessgtr 0 \quad (4\text{-}19)$$[10]

If the total effect is a tax reduction, the NIMBY effect is partly offset.

We summarise with:

Proposition 4-1: *Unilateral eco-dumping (NIMBY) policy by a labour (capital)-abundant country improves its welfare, although environmental quality is suboptimally low (high) as a consequence.*

(a) Eco-dumping is a terms-of-trade-improving and thus welfare-enhancing policy for a country importing the good whose PPM pollutes the environment. Welfare gains from terms of trade improvement, however, are reduced by a decline in environmental quality. A country exporting the polluting good pursues NIMBY to improve its terms of trade. Welfare gains are enhanced by an improvement of environmental quality.

(b) Thus, a unilateral NIMBY policy exploits the 'victims' by exploiting market power on the world market and by shifting polluting production abroad. A unilateral eco-dumping policy exploits the market power, yet the 'victims' enjoy a cleaner environment as a consequence of environmental policy used to improve terms of trade.

(c) As regards the (Pigouvian) tax in the rest of the world, the effect of either eco-dumping or NIMBY by home is indeterminate.

LARGE HOME COUNTRY FACING A LARGE TRADING PARTNER

We now assume that home's trading partner is a large country ('foreign'). Foreign is able to affect its terms of trade. Its environmental policy is given by (4-20), which is similar to (4-1)

$$G = \frac{V'}{U_X} + (C^Y - H)\frac{dp}{dG}\frac{dG}{dK^X} \quad (4\text{-}20)$$

Owing to our assumption of symmetry in the model, use of environmental policy to improve terms of trade by foreign compares to such use by home. Furthermore, if we confine ourselves to two countries, trade

[10] The terms of trade decline and consumption substitution towards x reduce G; the pollution increase together with the production substitution towards x increase it. We thus have again the opposite mechanism described for eco-dumping in home above.

flows mirror each other. Hence, home's import good originates from foreign's export sector and vice versa. Similarly, with only two goods, the terms of trade are linked through reciprocity, which implies that opposite policies are pursued to improve them. Two (symmetric) cases are possible:

Table 4-1: Factor Abundance and Terms-of-Trade-Improving Environmental Policy

Case 1 (Home Reduces, Foreign Increases the Tax)		
	Home	**Foreign**
Abundant Factor	Labour	Capital
Export Good	y	x
Terms of Trade	p	$1/p$
Terms-of-Trade-Improving Policy	Eco-dumping	NIMBY
Case 2 (Home Increases, Foreign Reduces the Tax)		
Abundant Factor	Capital	Labour
Export Good	x	y
Terms of Trade	$1/p$	p
Terms-of-Trade-Improving Policy	NIMBY	Eco-dumping

Thus, home engages only in eco-dumping only in case 1. Consequently, eco-tariffs should only be scrutinised regarding their usefulness to avoid eco-dumping for such a constellation. However, foreign's response to eco-dumping is a NIMBY policy; therefore, an ERTB will not occur.

In case 1, we recall comparative static results for home (eco-dumping Metzler case excluded) derived in (4-9) and (4-14):

$$\frac{dk^x}{d(-g)} > 0, \qquad \text{and} \qquad \frac{dl^x}{d(-g)} > 0 \qquad \text{(4-9'\&14')}$$

Similarly, we have in foreign:

$$\frac{dK^X}{dG} < 0, \qquad \text{and} \qquad \frac{dL^X}{dG} < 0 \qquad \text{(4-21\&22)}$$

The following table summarises total effects of such an 'environmental policy war':

Table 4-2: Effects of an Environmental Policy War

	dp	dk^x	dK^X	dl^x	dL^X
Effect of Home's Policy ($g - v'/u_x < 0$)	**> 0**	**> 0**	**> 0**	**< 0**	**< 0**
Effect of Foreign's Policy ($G - V'/U_X > 0$)	**< 0**	**> 0**	**> 0**	**< 0**	**< 0**
Sign of Total Effect	$\lessgtr$ **0**	**> 0**	**> 0**	**< 0**	**< 0**

The following effects result from home's and foreign's attempt to change the relative price level each in the opposite direction:

- Similar to a tariff war, it cannot be determined whether the relative price increases or declines. Home's policy works towards an increase, foreign's against.
- Both countries' policies increase capital and labour employed in the *x* sector at home and decrease capital and labour employed in the *x* sector in foreign.
- Pollution increases at home and decreases in foreign. The environmental quality part of welfare increases in foreign and decreases at home.
- Resources are shifted into the respective sector where the two countries have a comparative disadvantage. Effect is a reduction in trade flows.

The outcome of an environmental policy war is a Nash equilibrium in eco-dumping and NIMBY policy. At the new equilibrium, both countries are likely to be worse off, i.e. their welfare level decreases. We base this conclusion on results from the optimal tariff literature. If two countries engage in a tariff war, a decline in global welfare results since trade flows and gains from trade are reduced. However, nothing can be said about the distribution of these losses, i.e. it is possible that one or both countries lose[11]. If the choice variable is the environmental tax, however, the two countries cause two distortions: suboptimal environmental quality and a distortion in factor markets. In an environmental tax war, it is thus more likely that both countries end up at a lower welfare level than in a tariff war, although a definite statement cannot be made.

Nash equilibrium for an environmental tax war in close reference to a tariff war is illustrated in figure 4-3, where offer curves and trade indifference curves are depicted[12]. Home's (foreign's) export offer curve in the absence of eco-dumping (NIMBY) is denoted by *eo* (*EO*); the corresponding welfare indifference curves by *wi* and *WI*; trade flows by *x* and *y*, and the resulting relative world price by *p*. If home and foreign engage in eco-dumping or NIMBY, their export offer curves are denoted by *eo(ed)* and *EO(NI)*; trade flows by *x(ed,NI)* and *y(ed,NI)*.

[11] This was first noted by Johnson [1953/54] who showed that depending on the shape of export offer curves and tariff reaction functions, one country may be better off at the Nash equilibrium in terms-of-trade-improving tariffs.

[12] A representation with offer curves and trade indifference curves is commonly used in the context of large economies, trading two goods without the additional feature of environmental externalities. Baumol & Oates [1988, 270] use a similar illustration for the case where harmful environmental pollution is associated with the production of one of the tradable goods.

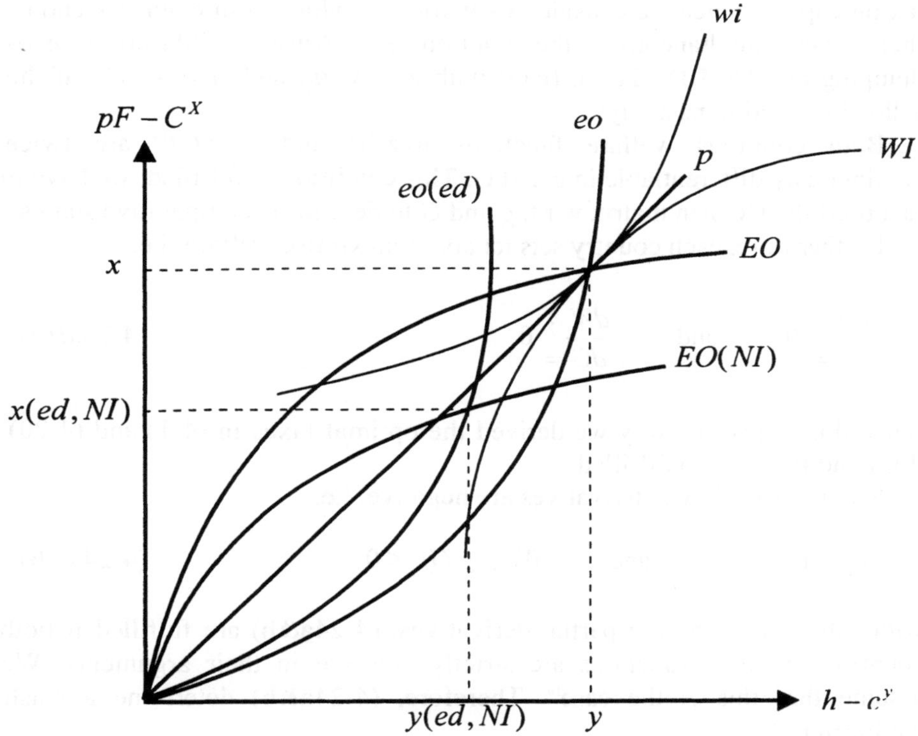

Figure 4-3. Nash Equilibrium in Eco-dumping and NIMBY in the Goods Space

We observe that if both countries vary their environmental taxes to improve their terms of trade, the trade flows *x(ed,NI)* and *y(ed,NI)* are lower than in the absence of eco-dumping and NIMBY.

At the new equilibrium, tangential welfare indifference curves (not shown) for both countries are at a lower level compared with the original equilibrium. Thus, both countries are worse off if they engage in an environmental tax war.

So far, we have portrayed the result of non-cooperative choice of environmental policies in reference to an (optimal) tariff war. However, an alternative presentation recurs to industrial organisation and the methods of non-cooperative game theory applied to it.

Nash equilibrium in eco-dumping and NIMBY: Each country or government, maximises welfare for its citizens, taking the other country's policy as given. Since home and foreign are duopolists/duopsonists on their im- and export markets, governments can affect welfare by choice of their tax on capital. Since we consider a situation in which both countries choose their taxes simultaneously, the solution is a Nash equilibrium in eco-dumping and NIMBY, i.e. in (g,G) with $g < v'/u_x$ and $G > V'/U_X$ if the following conditions apply:

Both countries welfare functions $w(g,G)$ and $W(g,G)$[13] are twice continuously differentiable in g and G. This condition is fulfilled; we have in fact used the Hessian matrix w.r.t. g and G to determine comparative statics.

Furthermore, each country sets its tax to maximise welfare, i.e.

$$\frac{dw}{dg} \stackrel{!}{=} 0, \qquad \text{and} \qquad \frac{dW}{dG} \stackrel{!}{=} 0 \qquad \text{(4-23a\&b)}$$

Since this is just the way we derived the optimal taxes in (4-1) and (4-20), this condition is also fulfilled.

Second partial own derivatives are negative, i.e.

$$w_{-g-g}(g,G) < 0 \qquad \text{and,} \qquad W_{GG}(g,G) < 0 \qquad \text{(4-24a\&b)}$$

with subscripts denoting partial derivatives. (4-24a&b) are fulfilled if both countries' welfare functions are strictly concave in their arguments. We assume that this is the case[14]. Therefore, (4-24a&b) determine a Nash equilibrium[15].

To characterise the Nash equilibrium, we define $r(G)$ as the best action of home given that foreign chooses G, and $R(g)$ as foreign's best action given that home chooses g. (4-23a&b) then become

$$r = w_{-g}(r(G),G) = 0, \qquad \text{and} \qquad R = W_G(R(g),g) = 0 \qquad \text{(4-25a\&b)}$$

Reaction functions $r(\bullet)$ and $R(\bullet)$[16] are unique, owing to our assumption of strict concavity of w and W in their arguments.

To gain insight regarding the slopes of the reaction function and stability of the Nash equilibrium, we need to determine the sign of $r(\bullet)$ and $R(\bullet)$. We

[13] For simplicity we drop all other arguments of the welfare functions; small caps denote home's welfare function, large caps foreign's.

[14] This assumption is needed to ensure that second order conditions which contain third derivatives are satisfied.

[15] See Tirole [1988, 207].

[16] The term reaction function is somewhat misleading since we consider simultaneous moves and countries have thus no chance to react to their trading partner's choices. The concept behind the term is that reaction functions represent choices that would be made, if rules of the games were such that sequential moves were allowed (compare Tirole [1988, 208] and Rasmusen [1989, 78]).

hence totally differentiate (4-25a&b), denoting first derivatives of the reaction functions by dr and dR:

$$dr = \frac{w_{-gG}(r(G),G)}{-w_{-g-g}(r(G),G)}, \quad \text{and} \quad dR = \frac{W_{G-g}(R(g),g)}{-W_{GG}(R(g),g)} \qquad \text{(4-26a\&b)}$$

For the sign (sg) of (4-26a&b) we find that with (4-24a&b) denominators of (4-26a&b) are always positive. Hence

$$\text{sg}(dr) = \text{sg}(w_{-gG}), \qquad \text{and} \qquad \text{sg}(dR) = \text{sg}(W_{G-g})$$

We note that the sign of the slope of the reaction functions depends on the cross-partial derivatives of countries' welfare functions; i.e. the derivatives of marginal welfare w.r.t. the other country's choice of the tax. $r(\bullet)$ and $R(\bullet)$ slope upwards if

$$w_{-gG}, W_{G-g} > 0$$

and downwards if

$$w_{-gG}, W_{G-g} < 0.$$

Welfare effects of home's eco-dumping and foreign's NIMBY are negative for their trading partner; we assume that this applies also to marginal welfare. With this assumption, we find that reaction functions slope downwards which indicates that eco-dumping and NIMBY policy are strategic substitutes[17]. Therefore, an increase of home's eco-dumping activity induces an increase in foreign's NIMBY policy.

To ensure that the Nash equilibrium is stable[18], an additional assumption regarding relative slopes of the reaction functions is needed. Stability of the Nash equilibrium requires that reaction functions intersect only once, for which a sufficient condition is that the absolute value of the own derivatives (denominators in (4-26a&b) are greater than the absolute values of the cross derivatives (numerators in (4-26a&b)). We assume that this is the case.

We can now depict the Nash equilibrium in (g,G) in figure 4-4. The Nash equilibrium $NE(g,G)$ in eco-dumping and NIMBY is given by the

[17] The distinction of strategic choice variables in strategic substitutes if reaction curves slope downwards, and strategic complements if they slope upwards has been introduced by Bulow et al. [1985]. This terminology refers to production and utility functions, in which factors or goods are complements, if a decrease in the price of one factor or good increases demand for another, and substitutes if the opposite holds.

[18] For stability of Nash equilibrium compare Tirole [1988, 226]

intersection of *R(g)* and *r(G)*. *wi(g,G)* and *WI(g,G)* are home's and foreign's welfare indifference curves associated with *NE(g,G)*.

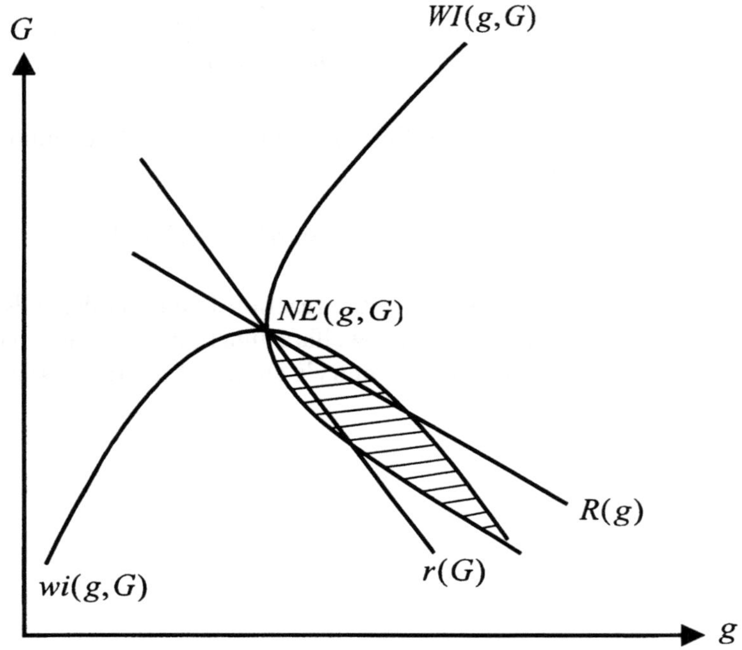

Figure 4-4. Nash Equilibrium in Eco-dumping and NIMBY in the Tax Space

We observe that:

- since iso-welfare lines *wi* and *WI* intersect, we have a core (shaded area) with potential for Pareto improvements,
- home's welfare would improve if foreign was to lower its tax,
- foreign's welfare would improve if home was to raise its tax.

Such an increase of home's tax rate and a reduction of foreign's might be possible if the two countries were to bargain, i.e. to cooperate. Since cooperation is not forthcoming, the jointly suboptimal tax policy with home eco-dumping and foreign engaging in a NIMBY policy will be implemented.

We summarise with:

Proposition 4-2*: An environmental tax war probably reduces welfare in both countries, though not symmetrically.*

(a) If two large countries trying to exploit their market power on the im- and export market use environmental policy to improve terms of trade, the home country importing the good whose production causes environmental

pollution pursues an eco-dumping policy while foreign engages in NIMBY policy. Consequently, environmental pollution increases at home and is reduced in foreign.

(b) Hence, we shall ***not*** *witness an ERTB if the objective is terms of trade improvement.*

(c) Welfare effects of such a policy are likely to be negative for both countries since the terms-of-trade-improving policies reduce trade, cause factor market distortions and cause suboptimal environmental policy. If the countries were to set their environmental policies cooperatively, a Pareto improvement would result.

2. ECO-TARIFFS AND TERMS OF TRADE IMPROVEMENT

As shown above, the objective of manipulating the environmental tax is a modification of relative world prices. The causal chain runs from input prices via goods prices to quantities demanded and supplied. Obviously, a trade tax, i.e. a tariff, should set off a similar chain reaction, albeit starting at the second link. To determine whether availability of an eco-tariff yields welfare improvement, we thus endow policy makers at home with two instruments, namely an eco-tax g and an eco-tariff[19].

To find the optimal welfare-maximising tax and tariff combination, we differentiate (4-11) w.r.t. the tax g and τ[20].

$$\frac{dw}{dg} = (u_x(f_k - ph_k) - v')\frac{dk^x}{dg} + u_x(f_l - ph_l)\frac{dl^x}{dg} + u_x(h - c^y)\frac{dp}{dg} + (u_y - pu_x)\frac{dc^y}{dg} \overset{!}{=} 0 \tag{4-27}$$

$$\frac{dw}{d\tau} = (u_x(f_k - ph_k) - v')\frac{dk^x}{d\tau} + u_x(f_l - ph_l)\frac{dl^x}{d\tau} + u_x(h - c^y)\frac{dp}{d\tau} + (u_y - pu_x)\frac{dc^y}{d\tau} \overset{!}{=} 0 \tag{4-28}$$

[19] Note that home imports x if an eco-tariff, i.e. $\tau > 1$, can be charged.

[20] Again we neglect terms which upon plugging in the FOCs become zero.

Substituting with the following FOCs in the presence of a tariff

$$f_k - g - (p/\tau)h_k = 0 \tag{3-30}$$

$$f_l - (p/\tau)h_l = 0 \tag{3-31}$$

$$u_y - (p/\tau)u_x = 0 \tag{3-32}$$

and rearranging yields the following two equations:

$$\left(g-\frac{v'}{u_x}\right)\frac{dk^x}{dg}+(h-c^y)\frac{dp}{dg}+p\left(\frac{1}{\tau}-1\right)\left(h_k\frac{dk_x}{dg}+h_l\frac{dl_x}{dg}+\frac{dc^y}{dg}\right)=0 \tag{4-27'}$$

$$\left(g-\frac{v'}{u_x}\right)\frac{dk^x}{d\tau}+(h-c^y)\frac{dp}{d\tau}+p\left(\frac{1}{\tau}-1\right)\left(h_k\frac{dk_x}{d\tau}+h_l\frac{dl_x}{d\tau}+\frac{dc^y}{d\tau}\right)=0 \tag{4-28'}$$

Assuming that

$$g = v'/u_x \tag{4-29a}$$

it follows from (4-27') that

$$\tau = \left(1+\left(\frac{dp}{p}\right)\frac{(c^y-h)}{d(c^y-h)}\right)^{-1} \tag{4-29b}$$

To verify that (4-29a&b) imply an optimal tax-tariff combination, we devide (4-27') by (4-28').

$$\frac{dp}{dg}\Big/\frac{dp}{d\tau} = \frac{d(h-c^y)}{dg}\Big/\frac{d(h-c^y)}{d\tau} \tag{4-30}$$

(4-30) is obviously fulfilled. Therefore, (4-29a&b) yield an optimal tax and tariff combination. We observe that (4-29a) is the Pigouvian tax for a small country and (4-29b) implies the optimal tariff which would maximise welfare in a large country with no environmental problem[21]. Assuming that w is strictly concave in g and τ (4-29a&b) is the only tax-(implied) tariff combination[22] maximising (4-11). We shall investigate the sign and effect of τ in the next sections.

LARGE HOME COUNTRY FACING ATOMISTIC COUNTRIES IN THE REST OF THE WORLD

Again the countries making up the rest of the world set their policy as described for small countries, i.e. they charge Pigouvian taxes to internalise the externality.

$$G = V' / U_X \tag{4-2}$$

To perform comparative statics, we totally differentiate the following 7 FOCs which are conditions for optimal production and consumption decision in home and foreign and the balanced trade identity:

$$f_k - (v' / u_x) - (p/\tau)h_k = 0 \tag{3-30'}$$

$$f_l - (p/\tau)h_l = 0 \tag{3-31}$$

$$u_y - (p/\tau)u_x = 0 \tag{3-32}$$

$$F_K - (V' / U_X) - pH_K = 0 \tag{4-4}$$

$$F_L - pH_L = 0 \tag{4-5}$$

$$U_Y - pU_X = 0 \tag{4-6}$$

[21] This can be verified by deriving the optimal tariff for a welfare function of the following type $w = u(f(k^x,l^x) + ph(k-k^x,l-l^x) - pc^y,\ c^y)$, i.e. without the environmental welfare component $v(\bullet)$ which corresponds to the optimal tariff derived e.g. in Gandolfo [1994,165].

[22] Since τ is - strictly speaking - not a tariff but the sum of the relative price of x, our numéraire good, and the tariff, g and τ are in fact an optimal tax-(implied)tariff combination. However, for simplicity, we may sometimes blur this distinction verbally.

$$
\left(\begin{array}{cccc}
-(1+\tau)u_{yy}-(2+\tau)pu_{xy}-p^2u_{xx} & 0 & ((1+\tau)u_{xy}-pu_{xx})\dfrac{v'}{u_x} & 0 \\
0 & 0 & (1+\tau)f_{kl}+ph_{kl} & 0 \\
(u_{xy}-pu_{xx})\dfrac{v'}{u_x} & 0 & \left(\dfrac{v'}{u_x}\right)^2 u_{xx}+u_x((1+\tau)f_{kk}+ph_{kk})-(1+\tau)v'' & 0 \\
1 & 1 & h_k & H_K \\
0 & U_{YY}-2pU_{XY}+p^2U_{XX} & 0 & (U_{XY}-pU_{XX})\dfrac{V'}{U_X} \\
0 & 0 & 0 & F_{KL}+pH_{KL} \\
0 & (U_{XY}-pU_{XX})\dfrac{V'}{U_X}. & 0 & U_{XX}G^2+U_X(F_{KK}+pH_{KK})-
\end{array}\right.
$$

$$^{y} + C^{Y} - h - H = 0 \qquad (4\text{-}7)$$

otally differentiating these FOCs yields the Linear Equation System

$$\begin{pmatrix} 0 & 0 & 0 & -u_x \\ \tau)f_{ll}+ph_{ll} & 0 & 0 & -h_l \\ \text{-}\tau)f_{kl}+ph_{kl}) & 0 & 0 & -u_x h_k \\ h_l & & H_L & 0 \\ 0 & & 0 & -U_X \\ 0 & & F_{LL}+pH_{LL} & -H_L \\ 0 & & U_X(F_{KL}+pH_{KL}) & -U_X H_K \end{pmatrix} \begin{pmatrix} c^y \\ dC \\ dk^x \\ dK^X \\ dl^x \\ dL^X \\ dp \end{pmatrix} = \begin{pmatrix} -(u_y+(1+\tau)u_{xy}-pu_{xx})d\tau \\ -f_l d\tau \\ -(f_k u_x+(1+\tau)f_k u_{xx} f-v')d\tau \\ 0 \\ 0 \\ 0 \\ 0 \end{pmatrix}$$

near Equation System 4-2

o find the trade policy instrument used by home's government to mise welfare, we apply Cramer's rule to Linear Equation System 4-2 to mine the effect of τ on the world price level p:

$$\frac{dp}{d\tau} > 0 \qquad (4\text{-}31)^{23}$$

ıspecting (4-29b) and recalling that $(c^y\text{-}h) > 0$ if home is a labour-dant, y exporting country, and $(c^y\text{-}h) < 0$ if home exports x, we observe

> 1 if home is labour-abundant, and
< 1 if home is capital-abundant.

ence, an x-importing country levies an eco-tariff while an x exporting try restricts trade by an export tax.

TARIFFS: RATIONALE AND EFFECTS

ationale for eco-tariffs is similar to the eco-dumping policy rationale ribed above. The labour-abundant home country shifts its import ınd and export supply curve, thereby increasing its terms of trade.

fficient condition for this apart from concavity of the social utility function and the oduction side of the economy is: $-f_k u_x - (1+\tau) f_k u_{xx} f - v_k < 0$.

Comparative static effects of an eco-tariff in home on input movements between sectors are indeterminate in general. The reason for this indeterminacy are two effects of τ, working in opposite directions:

Protective effect: the tariff reduces ceteris paribus the domestic price level which stimulates factor movement into the sector protected by τ.

World price effect: the contraction of home's import demand caused by the tariff increases the world price level which reverses the factor movement into the x sector.

Figure 4-5 illustrates these two effects. From the production point A in the absence of the tariff, production would move to B if the world price effect was 0. When we take the world price effect into account, we arrive at production point C.

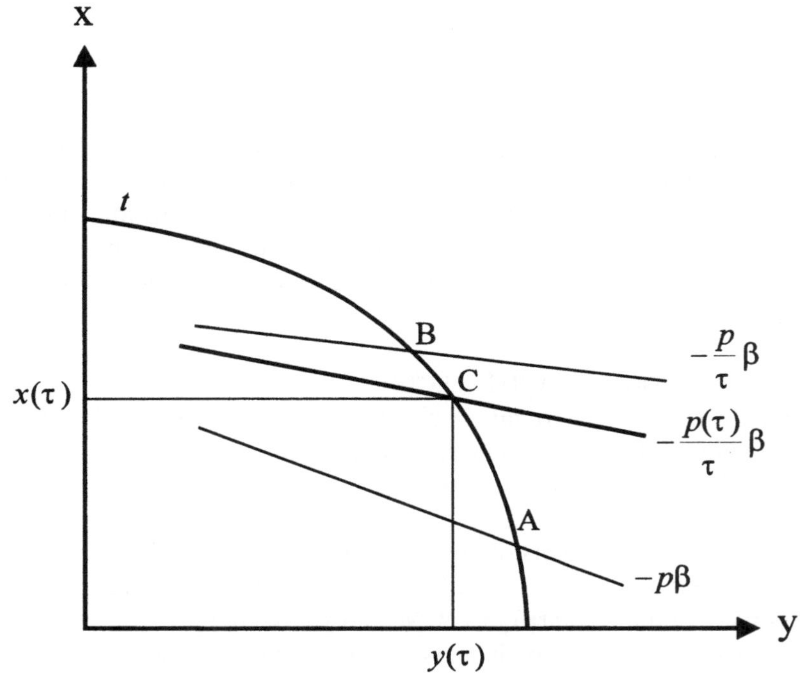

Figure 4-5. Effect of an Eco-tariff in Home: Protective and Price Effect

The fact that a tariff triggers a protective, and a world price effect affecting production structure in the country setting the tariff in opposite directions, is a well-known result in international trade theory. If the latter effect dominates, we observe the Metzler paradox. If we exclude the Metzler paradox, effects of an eco-tariff for factor allocation are as follows:

$$\frac{dk^x}{d\tau} > 0, \qquad \text{and} \qquad \frac{dl^x}{d\tau} > 0$$

In the capital-abundant rest of the world, the decrease in the relative world price of x reduces production of x and hence pollution. As regards factor allocation, we find:

$$\frac{dK^X}{d\tau} < 0, \qquad \text{and} \qquad \frac{dL^X}{d\tau} < 0$$

Finally, the eco-tariff also affects the Pigouvian tax charged in the rest of the world. However, the sign of the change cannot be determined:

$$\frac{dG}{d\tau} \lessgtr 0$$

Offsetting effects from the eco-tariff for G are similar to those isolated in (4-18) – reduction in pollution, production substitution towards y and the terms of trade effect work to reduce the tax, while consumption substitution towards y as an increasing effect. Since more downward than upward forces are at play we conclude that a tax decrease is somewhat more likely than an increase.

EXPORT-TAX: RATIONALE AND EFFECTS

Rationale for the export tax is similar to the NIMBY policy rationale described above. The capital-abundant country shifts its import demand and export supply curve which increases the price of x, thereby increasing its terms of trade.

Comparative static effects of an export tax in home are indeterminate for which the reason is very similar to the one advanced above for indeterminacy of the eco-tariff effect. We now have the

direct tax effect: the tax increases ceteris paribus the price level for domestic producers which stimulates factor movement into the y sector, and the

world price effect: the contraction of home's export supply caused by the export tax decreases the world price level which reverses the factor movement into the y sector.

If the direct tax effect dominates the world price effect, i.e. if we neglect an export-tax Metzler paradox, we find the following comparative static effects of the export tax for home's factor demands:

$$\frac{dk^x}{d(-\tau)} < 0, \qquad \text{and} \qquad \frac{dl^x}{d(-\tau)} < 0$$

As factors are moving out of the x sector, environmental pollution is reduced.

In the labour-abundant rest of the world, the increase in the relative world price of x stimulates production of x and an increase in polluting emissions. For factor allocation we find:

$$\frac{dK^x}{d(-\tau)} > 0, \qquad \text{and} \qquad \frac{dL^x}{d(-\tau)} > 0$$

Again, the effect of the trade policy instrument used by home on the rest of the world's environmental tax G is undetermined:

$$\frac{dG}{d(-\tau)} \lessgtr 0$$

LARGE HOME COUNTRY FACING A LARGE TRADING PARTNER

We now consider the case when both a labour-abundant home country and its large trading partner 'foreign' can alter their terms of trade. As regards foreign's policy options, we exclude that it can levy a tariff on y or tax x exports[24]. A counterpart to home charging an import tariff on x is therefore a NIMBY policy pursuit by foreign in.

Using results from chapter 3, we know that comparative static results of a (unilateral) NIMBY policy in foreign are:

$$\frac{dK^X}{dG} < 0, \qquad \text{and} \qquad \frac{dL^X}{dG} < 0$$

Effects in home are given by:

$$\frac{dk^x}{dG} = \left(\frac{dk^x}{dp}\right)\left(\frac{dp}{dG}\right) < 0, \qquad \text{and} \qquad \frac{dl^x}{dG} = \left(\frac{dl^x}{dp}\right)\left(\frac{dp}{dG}\right) < 0$$

[24] Reason could be provisions in a trade regime, or the domestic policy situation.

Thus, if home uses trade policy in form of an eco-tariff and foreign its environmental tax G to improve terms of trade, the following table summarise total effects of such an 'eco-tariff and environmental policy war':

Table 4-3: Effect of an Environmental Tax and Tariff War

	dp	dk^x	dK^X	dl^x	dL^X
Effect of Home's Policy ($d\tau$)	>0	>0	<0	>0	<0
Effect of Foreign's Policy ($d\widehat{G}$)	<0	>0	<0	>0	<0
Sign of total Effec	$\lessgtr 0$	>0	<0	>0	<0

The following effects result from home's and foreign's attempt to change the relative price level each in the opposite direction:

- Effect on the price level is undetermined since home tries to decrease the relative price level, while foreign tries to increase it.
- Both countries' policies work towards increasing capital and labour employed in the *x* sector in home; and towards decreasing capital and labour employed in the *x* sector in foreign.
- Environmental pollution increases in home, and decreases in foreign. Welfare effects from environmental quality are thus negative at home and positive in foreign.
- Resources are shifted into the respective sector in which the two countries have a comparative disadvantage. Effect is a reduction in trade flows, which reduces gains from trade.

We summarise with:

Proposition 4-3: *A unilateral eco-tariff improves welfare in a labour-abundant country. A capital-abundant country charges an export tax to maximise welfare. If there is retaliation, welfare consequences are likely to be negative.*

(a) A unilateral eco-tariff is terms-of-trade-improving and welfare-enhancing for a labour-abundant country. Environmental quality deteriorates absolutely, yet remains optimal in the Pigouvian sense. Welfare in the rest of the world is reduced since terms of trade decline, yet environmental quality increases.

(b) A unilateral export tax is terms-of-trade-improving and welfare-enhancing for a capital-abundant country. Environmental quality improves and remains optimal in the Pigouvian sense. Welfare in the rest of the world is reduced owing to terms of trade decline and deterioration of environmental quality.

(c) If two large countries interact, and only the labour-abundant one can use a trade policy instrument, it charges an eco-tariff. Its trading partner pursues a NIMBY policy. Global welfare effects of such policies are negative

since trade flows are reduced. If home charges an eco-tariff, pollution increases in home; while it is reduced in foreign.

3. COMPARISON OF ECO-DUMPING AND ECO-TARIFFS FOR TERMS OF TRADE REASONS

For home, the objective of engaging in eco-dumping or charging an eco-tariff is a change in the relative price level to improve its terms of trade. The effects of eco-dumping and the eco-tariff, on the relative world price and intersectoral factor allocation are therefore similar, i.e. both policy measures trigger a move of endogenous variables in the same direction. However, trade policy instruments affect import demand or export supply directly, while a change in the environmental tax affects them only indirectly. In the next two sections, we shall elaborate the welfare implications of this difference.

UNILATERAL TERMS OF TRADE IMPROVEMENT

The sign of comparative static effects of eco-dumping and an eco-tariff are similar as can be seen in the following table:

Table 4-4: Comparison of Unilateral Eco-dumping and Eco-tariff

	dp	dk^x	dK^X	dl^x	dL^X
Eco-dumping	>0	>0	<0	>0	<0
Eco-tariff	>0	>0	<0	>0	<0

Qualitatively, there is hence no difference between the two policies. However, the impetus of eco-dumping and the eco-tariff on the relative world price and intersectoral input allocation in home and foreign differs. While the comparative static effect of reducing g has a more pronounced effect for k^x than increasing τ, the opposite is true for p, l^x, K^X, and L^X. A minute tracing of the causal chains triggered by eco-dumping or an eco-tariff elucidates this observation:

Eco-dumping: reducing g increases ceteris paribus k^x, capital allocated in the x sector. Furthermore, it reduces production cost for x in home, which increases domestic supply of x - thereby also increasing l^x, labour allocated in the x sector - while it reduces supply of y. This is tantamount to a contraction of home's import demand and export supply. This in turn triggers an increase in the relative world price p, which reduces K^X and L^X, capital and labour allocated in the rest of the world's x sectors.

Eco-tariff: charging an eco-tariff ceteris paribus reduces the relative domestic price level, which triggers output expansion of the x sector, i.e. and increase of k^x and l^x, and an output reduction of y, i.e. a contraction of home's export supply. The relative increase of the price for x reduces demand for x in home, which hence reduces import demand. The latter is exacerbated by the fact that more x is supplied domestically. Contraction of export supply and import demand increase the relative world price p, thereby reducing K^X and L^X, factors allocated in the rest of the world's x sectors.

We note that the contraction of export supply and import demand, triggering the terms of trade improvement for home and the changes of intersectoral factor allocation in the rest of the world, are more directly achieved by an eco-tariff for two reasons:

– the eco-tariff changes the domestic price level for consumers and producers, and
– the tax reduction changes the domestic producer price level through change of the input price for only one factor.

Therefore, an eco-tariff achieves a more pronounced reduction of the relative world price level - i.e. an improvement of home's terms of trade - than eco-dumping. Welfare gains from terms of trade improvement are thus higher for home if it levies an eco-tariff. For the rest of the world, however, the opposite is true. Furthermore, if home engages in eco-dumping instead of charging an eco-tariff, environmental quality is at a suboptimal level.

TERMS OF TRADE IMPROVEMENT WITH RETALIATION

Again, marginal allocative effects of both scenarios - eco-dumping in home, NIMBY in foreign, and eco-tariff in home, NIMBY in foreign - are similar:

Table 4-5: Comparison of an Environmental Policy and an Environmental Tax and Tariff

	dp	dk^x	dK^X	dl^x	dL^X
Eco-dumping - NIMBY	$\lessgtr 0$	> 0	< 0	> 0	< 0
Eco-tariff - NIMBY	$\lessgtr 0$	> 0	< 0	> 0	< 0

Qualitatively, there is hence no difference between the environmental policy war and the eco-tariff and environmental policy war.

To discern possible differences, we recur to our analysis of the Nash equilibrium of the environmental tax war elaborated above. We compare the Nash equilibrium in (g,G) with the Nash equilibrium which results if foreign uses the tax only, and home the tax and a trade policy instrument. Derivation of the Nash equilibrium of a tax and tax/tariff war is slightly more involved since we now have four dimensions rather than just two: each country chooses a tax/tariff vector whereby foreign's tariff is constrained to zero, which leaves us de facto with three dimensions. To reduce the problem to the usual two dimensions which can be visualised graphically, we consider a (hypothetical) two part game: in a first part, both countries set their trade policy; in the second part, they simultaneously determine their environmental taxes[25].

We find the following conditions for a Nash equilibrium in tax and tax/tariff[26]:

Part I - Trade Policy Choice: Given home's welfare function w(g,τ,G) is twice continuously differentiable in τ, the tariff is chosen to maximise welfare, i.e.

$$\frac{dw}{d\tau} \stackrel{!}{=} 0 \tag{4-32}$$

We assume that the second partial own derivative in τ is negative, i.e.

$$w_{\tau\tau}(g,\tau,G) < 0 \tag{4-33a}$$

Part II - Environmental Policy Choice: We denote home's and foreign's welfare function in the second stage by $w(g(\tau),G)$ and $W(g(\tau),G)$ and assume that they are twice continuously differentiable in g and G. Taxes are chosen such that

$$\frac{dw}{dg} \stackrel{!}{=} 0, \qquad \text{and} \qquad \frac{dW}{dG} \stackrel{!}{=} 0 \tag{4-34\&23b}$$

(4-34&23b) are fulfilled if w and W are strictly concave in their arguments which we assume. Therefore, (4-34&23b) determine a Nash equilibrium in $g(\tau)$ and G.

[25] Compare the two-stage Cournot game in capacities and quantities in Tirole [1988, 228pp].

[26] Note that the following game is still thought of as a one-period game in which both governments simultaneously determine tax or tax **and** tariff. A non-zero tariff can only be chosen if the good is imported: if a tariff is chosen, the tax is set at the Pigouvian level.

Furthermore, we assume that second partial own derivatives are negative, i.e.:

$$w_{gg}\,(g(\tau),G) < 0, \qquad \text{and} \qquad W_{GG}\,(g(\tau),G) < 0 \qquad \text{(4-34b\&c)}$$

(4-34b&c) are fulfilled if w and W are strictly concave in their arguments which we assume[27]. Therefore, (4-34a&b) determine a Nash equilibrium in $g(\tau)$ and G.

Reaction functions are now $r(G)$ and $R(g(\tau))$. (4-34a&b) then become

$$r = w_g\,(r(G),G) = 0, \qquad \text{and} \qquad R = W_G\,(R(g(\tau),g) = 0 \qquad \text{(4-35a\&b)}$$

Again, reaction functions $r(\bullet)$ and $R(\bullet)$ are unique, owing to strict concavity of w and W in their arguments.

To determine comparative static effects, we have to find the sign of the slopes of $r(\bullet)$ and $R(\bullet)$. Differentiating (4-35a&b) yields

$$dr = \frac{w_{\tau G}(r(G),G)}{-w_{\tau\tau}(r(G),G)}, \quad \text{and} \quad dR = \frac{W_{G\tau}(R(\tau),\tau)}{-W_{GG}(R(\tau),\tau)} \qquad \text{(4-36a\&b)}$$

If we assume that home's and foreign's policy choices have a negative impact on marginal welfare of their respective trading partner, $r(\bullet)$ and $R(\bullet)$ slope downwards[28].

We can now depict the Nash equilibrium in eco-tariff and NIMBY in figure 4-6. Rather than in the tax-tariff space, we depict it in the tax-tax space to compare the Nash equilibrium in eco-tariff and NIMBY with $NE(g,G)$, the Nash equilibrium in eco-dumping and NIMBY. The Nash equilibrium in eco-dumping and NIMBY $NE(g,G)$ is given by the intersection of $r(G)$ and $R(G)$; $wi(g,G)$ and $WI(g,G)$ are home's and foreign's welfare indifference curves associated with $NE(g,G)$. The equilibrium is therefore $NE(g(\tau),G)$, the Nash equilibrium in home's eco-tax g if it can charge the optimal tariff τ, and foreign's NIMBY response to $g(\tau)$. It is given by the intersection of $R(g(\tau))$ and $r^{\tau}(G)$, foreign's reaction curve which traces the tax foreign charges in response to home's tax-tariff combination, and home's reaction curve which traces the tax home charges in response to foreign's NIMBY policy if it can levy an eco-tariff. $wi(g(\tau),G)$ and $WI(g(\tau),G)$ are home's and foreign's welfare indifference curves associated with $NE(g(\tau),G)$.

27 See above; this implies that third derivatives are 'well-behaved'.

28 See above; we also assume that the necessary conditions for stability of the Nash equilibrium hold.

From (4-30a&b), we know that the optimal tax-tariff combination for home is the Pigouvian tax and an eco-tariff > 0. Therefore, if we contrast $r^{\tau}(G)$ with $r(G)$, home's reaction function when it cannot levy a tariff and hence engages in eco-dumping, we observe that home chooses a higher tax if it can levy the tariff. Availability of an eco-tariff hence shifts home's reaction curve to the right. Furthermore, we know that home's eco-dumping and foreign's NIMBY policies are strategic complements. Therefore, if we compare foreign's reaction curve $R(g(\tau))$ to $R(g)$, its reaction curve to home's tax choice in the absence of an eco-tariff, we notice that foreign chooses a lower tax if home reduces its eco-dumping. Home's eco-tariff hence shifts foreign's reaction curve downwards.

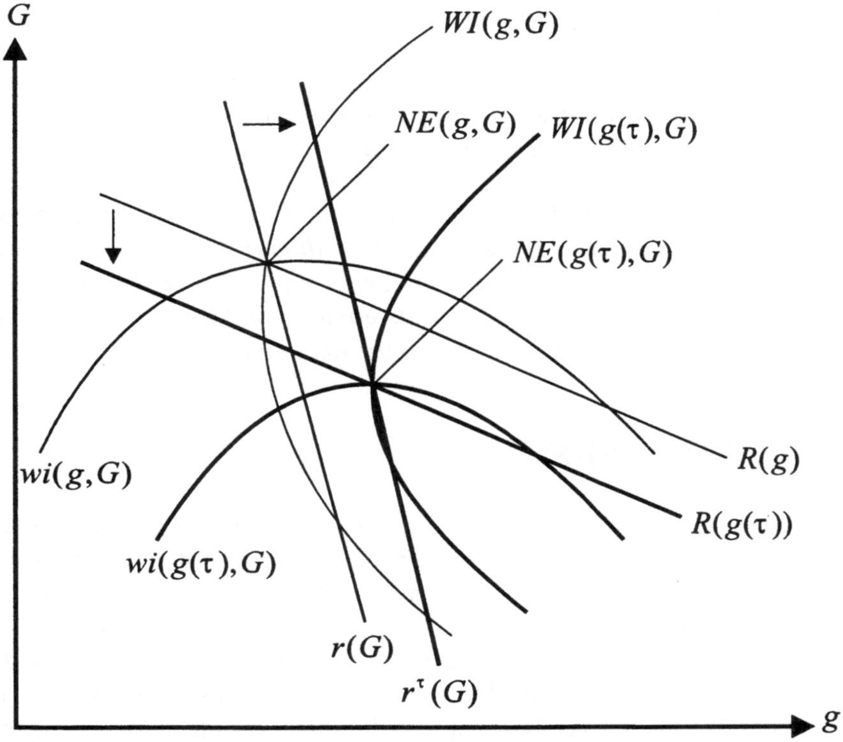

Figure 4-6. Comparison of Nash Equilibria in Eco-dumping & NIMBY, and Eco-tariff & NIMBY

We observe that

- the availability of an eco-tariff for home shifts the Nash equilibrium to the south-east from $NE(g,G)$ to $NE(g(\tau),G)$.
- $NE(g(\tau),G)$ may hence lie in the core described by $wi(g,G)$ and $WI(g,G)$ of $NE(g,G)$. This implies that both home and foreign are on higher

welfare levels if home can charge an eco-tariff, i.e. $wi(g(\tau),G)$ lies inside $wi(g,G)$ and $WI(g(\tau),G)$ lies inside $WI(g,G)$.
- the global welfare improvement is by no means certain; if foreign's reaction curve is shifted further down, only home's welfare improves while foreign's declines if home charges both a tax and a tariff.

We summarise with:

Proposition 4-4: *If used unilaterally, the eco-tariff yields higher welfare benefits for home compared with eco-dumping while the opposite is true for the rest of the world. If there is a policy war, the tariff is again better for home; welfare implications for foreign are less clear.*

(a) If home uses a tariff for unilateral terms of trade improvement, both the terms of trade improvement will be higher and the negative environmental consequences lower than if it has to resort to eco-dumping. However, in the rest of the world the loss implied by terms of trade deterioration is lower if home eco-dumps than if it levies a tariff on x.

(b) If there is retaliation, home will again achieve its terms of trade improvement more effectively and without negative environmental effects if it levies a tariff. Foreign will be worse off from the point of view of its terms of trade if a tax and tariff war breaks out rather than a tax-tax war. However, since the optimal level of NIMBY policy for foreign is lower if home uses an eco-tariff than in the tax-tax situation, its environmental quality is closer to the optimum and hence welfare higher in the tax and tariff war.

4. CONCLUSIONS

If (some) trading countries are large, we find that a labour-abundant country engages in eco-dumping to improve its terms of trade. However, since capital-abundant countries' terms of trade are improved by the opposite policy measure, we will not witness an ERTB. If an eco-tariff can be levied, it will be used instead of eco-dumping by labour-abundant countries since its effect on the world price is more direct and less environmentally disruptive. If a capital-abundant country can use a trade instrument to maximise welfare, it chooses an export tax on x.

If an eco-tariff were to be sanctioned, and used unilaterally, it will not yield a Pareto improvement. The country or countries which levy an eco-tariff instead of pursuing an eco-dumping policy benefit from the tariff. However, welfare in the rest of the world declines. Nevertheless, the net effect may still be positive. However, if two large countries interact and use trade and environmental policy to improve their terms of trade, sanctioning of an eco-tariff might yield a Pareto improvement.

Chapter 5

Tariffs to Avoid Eco-dumping for Strategic Trade Policy Reasons

Walz & Wellisch [1997] show in a partial equilibrium framework that the existence of oligopolistic export markets may induce governments to deviate from the optimal (Pigouvian) environmental policy. This results in eco-dumping for open economy reasons, i.e. to shift oligopoly rents[1]. Furthermore, Walz & Wellisch [1997] argue that environmental policies would not be used for strategic reasons if governments could use a trade instrument. In particular they show that a country or countries engaging in strategic environmental policy would chose an export subsidy on the export good whose PPM causes environmental pollution, while environmental regulation would be set at the Pigouvian level.[2]

We modify our Heckscher-Ohlin-Samuelson model from chapter 3 to address similar issues in a general equilibrium context. Specifically, we analyse effects of a duopoly in the x market on government's environmental policy. If the duopoly causes eco-dumping or even a ERTB, we further examine whether availability of eco-tariffs might serve to enhance environmental quality and welfare.

1 Similar results have been found in several other partial equilibrium models. See for example Barrett [1994c] for domestic pollution; and by Conrad [1993&96], Kennedy [1994] and Rauscher [1995c] for global pollution. Verdier [1993] and Ulph [1992] show that an inefficient environmental regulation instrument is chosen for rent-shifting purposes. Rauscher [1994&1995d] finds in general equilibrium models also a tendency towards eco-dumping for duopoly rent-shifting reasons.

2 Again in partial equilibrium models, Conrad [1993&96] finds similar results in the context of global pollution. He compares abatement subsidies and subsidies for the polluting input. He derives that only the latter restores the Pigouvian tax. Verdier [1993] and Ulph [1992] show that as a consequence of availability of export subsidies the efficient environmental control instrument is chosen.

In this setting, home is modelled as a country hosting a duopolist with market power on the world market. This producer faces competition by the second duopolist who is situated in foreign. Foreign either reacts to home's strategic policy or not.

1. STRATEGIC ENVIRONMENTAL POLICY

In order to consider strategic environmental policy, some modifications of our Heckscher-Ohlin-Samuelson model from chapter 3 are necessary. In accordance with the existing literature on the subject, we assume that the good whose PPM causes environmental pollution is produced by a sector with market power.

To adapt our model to analyse strategic environmental policies where x is no longer produced competitively, we change our definition of the relative price level which is now $p = p^x/p^y$.[3]

The balanced trade identity is then given by

$$pc^x + c^y = px + y$$

Rearranging and substituting production functions for x and yields

$$c^y = px + y - pc^x = pf(k^x, l^x) + h(k-k^x, l-l^x) - pc^x$$

Domestic welfare is therefore given by

$$w = u(c^x, pf(k^x, l^x) + h(k-k^x, l-l^x) - pc^x) - v(k^x) \quad (5\text{-}1)$$

As regards market structure of the x markets in home and foreign, we assume that duopoly prevails, i.e. the respective domestic monopolists face import competition. The market is characterised by quantity competition; i.e. the duopolists play a Cournot-Nash game. Hence, the relative world price p is not exogenous but determined by the total quantity of x produced in home and foreign. The welfare function (5-1) can thus be written as

3 Reason is that if there is an international oligopoly, strategic interaction determines quantities (Cournot competition) or price (Bertrand competition). To analyse government's role in this interaction, we need x in the expression for welfare.

$$w = u(c^x, p[f(k^x,l^x) + F(K^X,L^X)]f(k^x,l^x) + h(k\text{-}k^x,l\text{-}l^x) - p[f(k^x,l^x) + F(K^X,L^X)]c^x) - v(k^x) \tag{5-1'}$$

whereby $p[f(k^x,l^x)+F(K^X,L^X)]$ denotes the inverse demand function of the x market[4].

The quantity of x produced in home is given by maximisation of the producer's profit function,

$$\pi = p[f(k^x,l^x) + F(K^X,L^X)]f(k^x,l^x) - w_l l^x - (w_k+g)k^x \tag{5-2}$$

whereby we assume that government internalises the environmental externality by means of the tax g; w_k and w_l denote the rental rate of capital and the wage rate for labour respectively.

To find the FOCs for the profit-maximising level of output or capital and labour input for the x duopolists, (5-2) is differentiated w.r.t. factor demands, whereby the FOCs are zero at the optimum:

$$\frac{d\pi}{dk^x} = p_x f_k f(k^x,l^x) + pf_k - (w_k + g) \overset{!}{=} 0 \tag{5-3a}$$

$$\frac{d\pi}{dl^x} = p_x f_l f(k^x,l^x) + pf_l - w_l \overset{!}{=} 0 \tag{5-3b}$$

Using the convention to denote derivatives of univariate functions by a dash, p_x becomes p' and (5-3a&b) can be written to yield

$$f_k(p + p' f(k^x,l^x)) - g - w_k = 0 \tag{5-3a'}$$

$$f_l(p + p' f(k^x,l^x)) - w_l = 0 \tag{5-3b'}$$

The term $f_k\, p' f(k^x,l^x)$ by which the FOCs for a firm with market power differ from the competitive outcome has the following interpretation: Marginal output expansion has a negative effect for profit on inframarginal output since output expansion reduces p[5].

4 This form of the inverse demand function corresponds to the one derived in a partial equilibrium model. In a general equilibrium model where income effects enter the inverse demand function, the utility function has to be of the quasi-linear type to yield an inverse demand function similar to the partial equilibrium form.

5 See Tirole [1988, 218/219].

w_k and w_l are assumed to be determined by profit maximisation in the competitive y sector and given by

$$w_k = h_k, \qquad \text{and} \qquad w_l = h_l$$

Therefore, in a general equilibrium setting the FOCs determining factor inputs and thus the profit-maximising choice of the quantity of x are

$$f_k(p + p' f(k^x, l^x)) - g - h_k = 0 \tag{5-3a''}$$

$$f_l(p + p' f(k^x, l^x)) - h_l = 0 \tag{5-3b''}$$

Nash–Equilibrium: To determine the equilibrium on the market for x, we assume a symmetric duopoly, i.e. that foreign's x-producer faces a similar set of FOCs. We assume that the equilibrium is of a Cournot Nash type, i.e. that home's and foreign's duopolists simultaneously determine quantities of x and X supplied by choosing k^x, l^x and K^X, L^X respectively taking the other producer's choices as given. Input decisions by the two duopolists yield a Nash equilibrium in x and X if the following conditions apply:

- both duopolists' profit functions $\pi(f(k^x,l^x), F(K^X,L^X))$ and $\Pi(f(k^x,l^x), F(K^X,L^X))$ are twice continuously differentiable in firms' choice variables. We have already taken first derivatives; regarding second derivatives, we assume that π_{kk} and π_{ll} and by virtue of symmetry Π_{KK} and Π_{LL} also exist;
- both duopolists choose capital and labour input to maximise profit, i.e.

$$\frac{d\pi}{dk^x} \overset{!}{=} 0, \qquad \text{and} \qquad \frac{d\pi}{dl^x} \overset{!}{=} 0 \tag{5-3a\&b}$$

for home's duopolist, and

$$\frac{d\Pi}{dK^X} \overset{!}{=} 0, \qquad \text{and} \qquad \frac{d\Pi}{dL^X} \overset{!}{=} 0 \tag{5-3c\&d}$$

for foreign's. Since this corresponds to our derivation of the profit-maximising factor inputs in (5-3a&b), and we furthermore assumed symmetry between home's and foreign's duopolists, this condition is fulfilled;

- second partial own derivatives are negative, i.e.

$$\pi_{kk} < 0, \qquad \text{and} \qquad \pi_{ll} < 0 \tag{5-4a\&b}$$

and

$$\Pi_{KK} < 0, \qquad \text{and} \qquad \Pi_{LL} < 0 \tag{5-4c\&d}$$

(5-4a,b,c&d) are fulfilled if both duopolists' profit functions are strictly concave in their arguments. We assume that this is the case.

Solving the four FOCs (5-3a,b,c&), we find Nash equilibrium values of k^x, l^x and K^X, L^X and therewith the Nash equilibrium pair of outputs (x,X).

To characterise the Nash equilibrium, we define $r(F(K^X,L^X))$ as the best action(s) for home's duopolist given that foreign's chooses the output associated with K^X and L^X, and $R(f(k^x,l^x))$ as the foreign duopolist's best action(s) given that home chooses k^x and l^x. With (5-3a,b,c&d), these reaction functions become

$$r = \begin{bmatrix} \pi_k(r(F(K^X,L^X)), f(k^x,l^x)) \\ \pi_l(r(F(K^X,L^X)), f(k^x,l^x)) \end{bmatrix} \tag{5-5a}$$

$$R = \begin{bmatrix} \Pi_K(R(f(k^x,l^x)), F(K^X,L^X)) \\ \Pi_L(R(f(k^x,l^x)), F(K^X,L^X)) \end{bmatrix} \tag{5-5b}$$

The two-dimensional reaction functions[6] $r(\bullet)$ and $R(\bullet)$ are unique, owing to the assumption of strict concavity of π and Π in their arguments.

Regarding comparative statics and stability of the Nash equilibrium, we recur to results from the industrial organisation literature: it is usually assumed that marginal profit of one duopolist is decreasing in the other one's quantity expansion[7]. Hence, reaction functions in a one-dimensional context of quantities are downward sloping, and choices of k^x, l^x and K^X, L^X are thus

6 The pair of reaction functions (5-5a&b) are somewhat unconventional since the bulk of the industrial organisation literature works with the assumption that firm's choice variables are quantities, and FOCs determining the Nash equilibrium therefore one dimensional for each firm (first derivative of profit w.r.t. a firm's own quantity), and the resulting Nash equilibrium two dimensional in the quantities chosen by each duopolist (see for example Rasmusen [1989, 76pp] or Tirole [1988, 218pp]). Throughout our investigation, we have assumed that producers' choice variables are capital and labour. Keeping this assumption, we hence derive two-dimensional reaction functions for each duopolist whose solution is a four dimesional Nash equilibrium in both duopolists' input choices. However, if factor prices are given, the resulting factor combination is unique, yielding a unique x output. We can depict reaction functions in a two dimensional output space.

7 See Tirole [1988, 218].

strategic complements. Furthermore, we add the assumption that the conditions for stability of the Nash equilibrium are fulfilled[8].

We can now depict this Nash equilibrium in quantities (x,X) in figure 5-1. The Nash equilibrium $NE(f(k^x,l^x),F(K^X,L^X))$ is given by the intersection of $R(f(k^x,l^x))$ and $r(F(K^X,L^X))$. $\pi(NE(f(k^x,l^x),F(K^X,L^X)))$ and $\Pi(NE(f(k^x,l^x),F(K^X,L^X)))$ are the domestic and foreign duopolists' iso-profit curves associated with $NE(f(k^x,l^x),F(K^X,L^X))$.

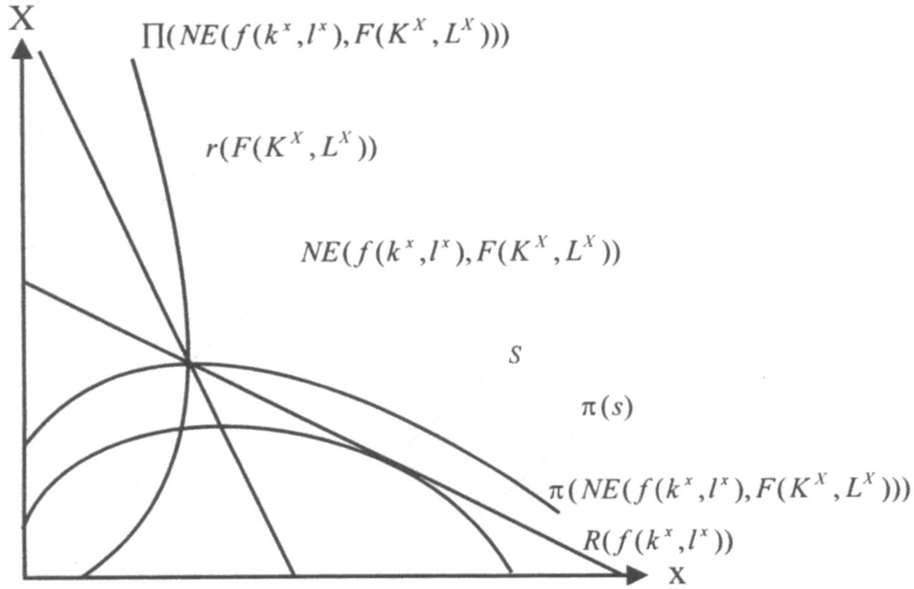

Figure 5-1. Nash Equilibrium in Quantities Chosen by Home's and Foreign's Duopolists

We observe:

- Since iso-profit curves $\pi(NE(f(k^x,l^x),F(K^X,L^X)))$ and $\Pi(NE(f(k^x,l^x),F(K^X,L^X)))$ intersect, we have a core with potential of profit increases for both duopolists.
- The domestic duoplist's profit would increase if the foreign duopolist would lower its output, and vice versa.
- At the point *S*, representing the point home could reach if it were a Stackelberg leader in a sequential game, the domestic duopolist's iso-profit curve $\pi(S)$ is tangential to the foreign duopolists reaction function. *S* lies to the south-west of $NE(f(k^x,l^x),F(K^X,L^X))$. This is the highest profit

8 A sufficient condition is that a decrease in one duopolist's output is not offset by the other's optimal reaction to yield an aggregate output increase; see Tirole [1988, 220].

the domestic duopolist could attain, given the foreign duopolist's presence.

ECO-DUMPING FOR STRATEGIC REASONS

We now determine the level of home's environmental tax g.

If government sets its environmental policy to maximise welfare by taking into consideration the strategic choices by foreign's duopolist, its objective is to maximise

$$w = u(c^x, p[f(k^x,l^x) + R(f(k^x,l^x))]f(k^x,l^x) + h(k-k^x,l-l^x) - p[f(k^x,l^x) + F(K^X,L^X)]c^x) - v(k^x) \qquad (5\text{-}1'')$$

which differs from (5-1') by the expression for the foreign duopolist's output. If government intervenes knowing that it can alter the strategic output choices on the x market, the decisions by the policy-maker regarding the environmental tax g and the output decision by the duopolists are part of a two-stage process. The solution to the Cournot Nash game between producers is anticipated by home's government and taken into consideration for the determination of the tax.

The socially optimal environmental tax is found by differentiating (5-1'') w.r.t. g and setting it equal to zero[9]:

$$\frac{dw}{dg} = u_y(f(k^x,l^x)-c^x)\frac{dp}{dg} + (u_x-pu_y)\frac{dc^x}{dg} + \{u_y[f_l(p+p'f(k^x,l^x))-$$
$$h_l + p'\,R'f_lf(k^x,l^x) - p'(f_l+R'f_l)c^x]\}\frac{dl^x}{dg} + \{u_y[f_k(p+p'f(k^x,l^x))-$$
$$h_k + p'\,R'f_kf(k^x,l^x) - p'(f_k+R'f_k)c^x] + v'\}\frac{dk^x}{dg} \overset{!}{=} 0 \qquad (5\text{-}6)$$

Upon inserting FOCs (5-3a''&b'') and the FOC resulting from utility maximisation by consumers

$$u_x - pu_y = 0$$

(5-6) yields for the optimal tax on capital:

9 The derivative of the univariate R is denoted by R'.

$$g = \frac{v'}{u_y} + (c^x - f(k^x,l^x))\frac{dp}{dg}\frac{dg}{dk^x} + p' f_k c^x + (p' f_l c^x)\frac{dl^x}{dg}\frac{dg}{dk^x} +$$

$$p'\ R' f_k(c^x - f(k^x,l^x)) + p'\ R' f_l(c^x - f(k^x,l^x))\frac{dl^x}{dg}\frac{dg}{dk^x} \qquad (5\text{-}7)$$

The optimal environmental tax g is hence composed of

- the Pigouvian part (v'/u_y) by which the environmental externality is internalised,
- the terms of trade improving part of the environmental tax which is captured in the second term in (5-7),
- terms three and four of (5-7) with which government takes into account the effect of the suboptimal quantities produced by a duopoly on consumer surplus, and
- a strategic part (the last two terms in (5-7) which reflect the effect of the tax for output decisions by the foreign duopolist.

Regarding the sign of the divergence of g from the Pigouvian tax we find for the first term that home's tax is reduced below the Pigouvian level if x is imported, and increased above the Pigouvian level if x is exported. Eco-dumping or NIMBY serve to improve home's terms of trade.

Regarding the signs of the last four terms in (5-7) which result from the fact that the x market is a duopoly; we find that

- the third and the fourth term are negative since $p' < 0$ (see above) and dk^x/dg, $dl^x/dg < 0$ (see chapter 4);
- the last two terms are negative if x is imported since $R' < 0$ owing to the fact that output is a strategic substitute in a Cournot Nash game.

Hence, if home exports x, the strategic aspects of government's choice of g causes eco-dumping, if we abstract from terms of trade considerations.

RATIONALE AND EFFECTS

Output expansion resulting from a tax below the Pigouvian level has a positive welfare effect through the increase in consumer rents associated with it, which more than offsets production costs of additional output. This effect is captured by the third and fourth term in (5-7).

The last two terms in (5-7) show the strategic effect of home's choice of its tax level. If home exports x, the output expansion in favour of home's duopolist resulting from the tax reduction increases profits with a positive welfare effect. This positive effect dominates the negative effect of domestic consumption increase of a good whose price is above the competitive level. If home imports x, these effects are reversed: the welfare loss associated with increased consumption at a price above the competitive level accruing partly in foreign, dominates the profit-shifting in favour of the domestic duopolist.

The strategic reduction of home's environmental tax below marginal damage affects FOCs (5-3a''&b'') according to

$$\frac{d\pi_k}{dg} = f_k\left(\frac{dk^x}{dg}+\frac{dl^x}{dg}\right)\left(p+p'f(k^x,l^x)\right) + h_k\left(\frac{dk^x}{dg}+\frac{dl^x}{dg}\right) - 1$$

$$+ f_k(p'+p'')\left[(1+R')\left(f_k\frac{dk^x}{dg}+f_l\frac{dl^x}{dg}\right)\right] + p'\left(f_k\frac{dk^x}{dg}+f_l\frac{dl^x}{dg}\right) \quad (5\text{-}8a)$$

$$\frac{d\pi_l}{dg} = f_l\left(\frac{dk^x}{dg}+\frac{dl^x}{dg}\right)\left(p+p'f(k^x,l^x)\right) + h_l\left(\frac{dk^x}{dg}+\frac{dl^x}{dg}\right)$$

$$+ f_l(p'+p'')\left[(1+R')\left(f_k\frac{dk^x}{dg}+f_l\frac{dl^x}{dg}\right)\right] + p'\left(f_k\frac{dk^x}{dg}+f_l\frac{dl^x}{dg}\right) \quad (5\text{-}8b)$$

With the assumption of negative second partial own derivatives (5-8a&b) are negative.

Therefore, eco-dumping chosen by government in the (first stage) policy-setting has a positive effect on marginal profit for home's duopolist. This affects the equilibrium quantities determined in the second stage when the duopolists enter into the Cournot Nash game. Eco-dumping lowers the marginal cost to the domestic duopolist which commits it to a reaction function according to which the domestic duopolist responds with a higher output level to the foreign firm's choice.

This is shown in figure 5-2: The tax reduction shifts the reaction function of the domestic firm from $r(F(K^X,L^X))$ to $r^{ED}(F(K^X,L^X))$. Thus, the Nash equilibrium is shifted from $NE(f(k^x,l^x),F(K^X,L^X))$ to $NE^{ED}(f(k^x,l^x),F(K^X,L^X))$.

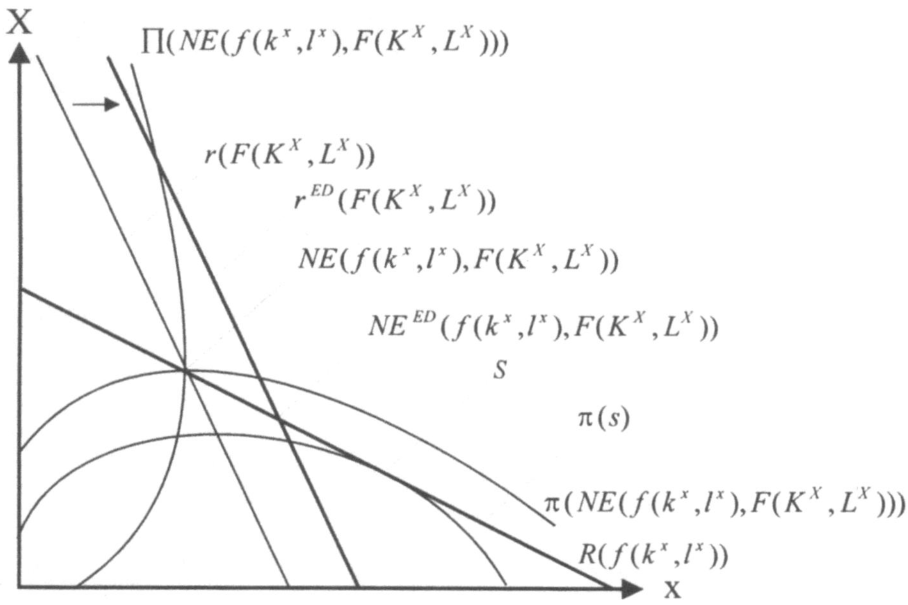

Figure 5-2. Nash Equilibrium in Quantities Chosen by Home's and Foreign's Duopolist with Eco-dumping in Home

We observe

- Eco-dumping by home's government yields a profit increase for the domestic duopolist since the foreign duopolist's output associated with $NE^{ED}(f(k^x,l^x),F(K^X,L^X))$ is lower than the one associated with $NE(f(k^x,l^x),F(K^X,L^X))$. Hence, home's duopolist's iso-profit curve associated with $NE^{ED}(f(k^x,l^x),F(K^X,L^X))$ (not shown) lies south of $\pi(NE(f(k^x,l^x),F(K^X,L^X)))$, i.e. at a higher profit level.
- The effect for the foreign duopolist's profit is just the reverse: its iso-profit curve associated with the $NE^{ED}(f(k^x,l^x),F(K^X,L^X))$ (not shown) lies east of $\Pi(NE(f(k^x,l^x),F(K^X,L^X)))$.
- While eco-dumping shifts the domestic duopolist's reaction function towards *S*, the highest possible profit it can attain, it does not move it all the way onto *S*.
-

The reason for the last observation is that eco-dumping is not costless, i.e. there are social trade-offs (environmental quality, consumption increase at a price above marginal cost, and terms of trade considerations) which are reflected in government's environmental policy choice, apart from the duopolist's profit.

Additional effects of eco-dumping in home are a decline in environmental quality, and increase in consumer surplus from inframarginal

x consumption at the new relative price p, and a loss in welfare caused by a consumption increase at a price above marginal cost. However, the total effect of eco-dumping for social welfare is positive if we abstract from terms of trade effects.

In foreign, environmental quality appreciates if production of x is curtailed because of home's eco-dumping. Furthermore, we have positive welfare effects from surplus of inframarginal x consumption, and negative effects from consumption increase (see above). If foreign imports x, home's eco-dumping has positive terms of trade effects for foreign. The total effect remains indeterminate.

Our analysis of unilateral eco-dumping is based on the assumption that foreign's government remains aloof to the strategic potential of its environmental policy choice. This rather artificial assumption is relaxed in the next section.

ERTB AS A RESULT OF STRATEGIC INTERACTION

We now assume that both countries' governments use their environmental policies to support their respective duopolist in order to maximise welfare.

The welfare-maximising tax in home is given by (5-7); for foreign it is given by

$$G = \frac{V'}{U_Y} + (C^X - F(K^X,L^X))\frac{dp}{dg}\frac{dg}{dK^X} + p' F_K C^X + (p' F_L C^X)\frac{dL^X}{dg}\frac{dg}{dK^X}$$

$$+ p' R' F_K (C^X - F(K^X,L^X)) + p' R' F_L (C^X - F(K^X,L^X)) \frac{dL^X}{dg}\frac{dg}{dK^X} \quad (5\text{-}9)$$

We have elaborated above that an x-importing country may but will not necessarily engage in eco-dumping to affect duopoly output. Hence, if the (trading) world consists of home and foreign exclusively, the effect of the duopolistic market structure will not induce eco-dumping in both countries in general[10].

If we assume that the trading world consists of more countries than home and foreign, and the duopolists serve these markets apart from catering to domestic demand, both duopolists can be exporters of x. In that case, the strategic choice faced by both governments is similar. Therefore, both

10 Again we abstract from terms of trade effects of the environmental tax.

home's and foreign's governments engage in eco-dumping, and we observe an ERTB.

RATIONALE AND EFFECTS

Both governments have the same objective, namely improving the position of their respective duopolist by choosing an environmental tax below the Pigouvian level. If the game is symmetric, the result of such interaction is an ERTB.

The positive effect of eco-dumping derived above is perceived by both countries, i.e. the low tax chosen by governments in the first (policy-setting) stage shifts both duopolists' reaction functions. The direction of the shift for home's duopolist was shown above; symmetrically foreign's duopolist's reaction function is shifted vertically, yielding a higher output level as a reaction to every output choice made by the domestic duopolist.

This is shown in figure 5-3. Bilateral eco-dumping yields reaction functions $r^{ED}(F(K^X,L^X))$ for home's and $R^{ED}(f(k^x,l^x))$ for foreign's duopolist. As in figure 5-2, $r^{ED}(F(K^X,L^X))$ lies to the right of $r(F(K^X,L^X))$. The foreign duopolist's reaction function is shifted vertically above from $R(f(k^x,l^x))$ to $R^{ED}(f(k^x,l^x))$. The Nash equilibrium of the resulting ERTB is given by $NE^{ERTB}(f(k^x,l^x),F(K^X,L^X))$ which lies to the north-east of $NE(f(k^x,l^x),F(K^X,L^X))$ and to the north-west of $NE^{ED}(f(k^x,l^x),F(K^X,L^X))$.

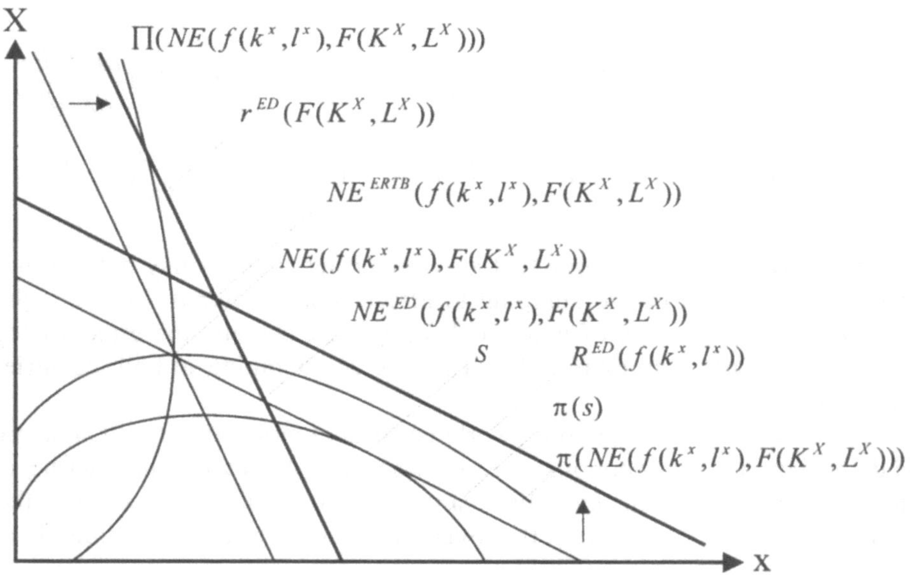

Figure 5-3. Nash Equilibrium in Quantities Chosen by Home's and Foreign's Duopolists with Eco-dumping in Home and Foreign

We observe

- The ERTB results in a lower level of profits for home's duopolist compared with both $NE(f(k^x,l^x),F(K^X,L^X))$ and $NE^{ED}(f(k^x,l^x),F(K^X,L^X))$.
- Effects for the foreign duopolist are a decline of profits compared with $NE(f(k^x,l^x),F(K^X,L^X))$ but an increase compared with $NE^{ED}(f(k^x,l^x),F(K^X,L^X))$.
- Total industry output increases which depresses aggregated duopoly profits.

The reason for this last observation is that both governments do not take into consideration welfare effects of their actions for the duopolist in the respective foreign country. Both governments' policy choice results in output expansion of the duopolist they are hosting and causes a negative externality for the other duopolist.

As regards environmental quality, the ERTB yields pollution above marginal damage in both countries. Since profits are not increased - which was one of the intended effects - bilateral eco-dumping is partly wasteful. However, the price decline yields also positive welfare effects since consumption rents from inframarginal consumption of *x* increases.

So far, we have abstracted from terms of trade effects and assumed that both home and foreign export *x* since these conditions ensure that (5-7&9) imply an ERTB. If we allow for terms of trade consideration to enter government's environmental policy decision or relax the assumption that*x* is exported, eco-dumping is no longer the only possible outcome. However, owing to the fact that

- welfare effects of eco-dumping for consumer rents from inframarginal consumption are always positive, and
- terms of trade effects and the strategic implications of *x* exports for home's optimal tax choice offset each other,

government is likely to choose a tax below the Pigouvian level even if terms of trade effects are reflected in the tax chosen for an *x* exporting country or if *x* is imported. However, the optimal tax will be higher, i.e. closer to the Pigouvian tax, owing to these effects.

We can summarise our results with

Proposition 5: *A duopoly on the market of the good whose PPM pollutes the environment causes governments to engage in eco-dumping to improve the strategic position of the duopolist they are hosting, if x is exported.*

(a) Unilateral eco-dumping by home's government shifts duopoly rents towards the domestic duopolist. This profit increase together with welfare gains for consumers of x stemming from the price reduction caused by eco-

dumping, dominates losses associated with environmental quality deterioration and with consumption expansion at a price above marginal cost if home exports x.

(b) Profits of the foreign duopolist drop as a consequence of unilateral eco-dumping by home; the resulting welfare loss is partly offset by an increase in consumer surplus and an increase in environmental quality.

(c) If both governments use environmental policy to affect the choices of their duopolist in the Cournot Nash game, an ERTB occurs if both countries export x. Effects are a decline in profits for both duopolists and in environmental quality in both countries. These negative welfare effects of the ERTB are partly offset by an increase in consumer rents caused by the drop in the relative price of x.

(d) If we relax the assumption that x is exported and consider the terms of trade effect of environmental policy, the above results may no longer be valid. However, they are still likely.

2. STRATEGIC ENVIRONMENTAL AND TRADE POLICY

As shown above, the objective of the reduction in the environmental tax is an increase in duopoly profit, increase in consumer rents and - although we have neglected it for most of the analysis - terms of trade improvement.

Trade policy in the form of

- import protection (i.e. a tariff),
- export promotion (i.e. an export subsidy),
- import promotion (i.e. an import subsidy), or
- export reduction (i.e. an export tax),

may achieve a similar result by affecting prices and the strategic positive of the duopolist.

To determine effects of availability of a trade policy, we again endow government with two instruments, namely the environmental tax g and a trade policy instrument levied on x.

To find the welfare-maximising environmental and trade policy combination, we differentiate (5-1'') w.r.t. g and τ, whereby τ is now the relative price of y including a tariff[1] and set it equal to zero:

11 Defining τ as the relative price of y including a tariff corresponds to the change of the reference good which we undertook to analyse effects of a duopoly on the x market. This does not contradict our statement above that the trade instrument is to be levied on x since in a general equilibrium model where prices are relative, we can always interpret whichever optimal τ we find in terms of the trade instrument it implies for x.

$$\frac{dw}{dg} = u_y(f(k^x,l^x)\text{-}c^x)\frac{dp}{dg} + (u_x\text{-}pu_y)\frac{dc^x}{dg} + \{u_y[f_l(p + p' f(k^x,l^x)) \text{-} h_l +$$
$$p'\ R' f_l f(k^x,l^x) \text{-}\ p'(f_l + R' f_l)c^x]\}\frac{dl^x}{dg} + \{u_y[f_k(p + p' f(k^x,l^x)) \text{-} h_k +$$
$$p'\ R' f_k f(k^x,l^x) \text{-}\ p'(f_k + R' f_k)c^x] + v'\}\frac{dk^x}{dg} \overset{!}{=} 0 \tag{5-10}$$

$$\frac{dw}{d\tau} = u_y(f(k^x,l^x)\text{-}c^x)\frac{dp}{d\tau} + (u_x\text{-}pu_y)\frac{dc^x}{dg} + \{u_y[f_l(p + p' f(k^x,l^x)) \text{-} h_l +$$
$$p'\ R' f_l f(k^x,l^x) \text{-}\ p'(f_l + R' f_l)c^x]\}\frac{dl^x}{d\tau} + \{u_y[f_k(p + p' f(k^x,l^x)) \text{-} h_k +$$
$$p'\ R' f_k f(k^x,l^x) \text{-}\ p'(f_k + R' f_k)c^x] + v'\}\frac{dk^x}{d\tau} \overset{!}{=} 0 \tag{5-11}$$

Substituting with the following FOCs in the presence of a tariff:

$$f_k((p/\tau) + (p/\tau)' f(k^x,l^x)) - g - h_k = 0$$

$$f_l((p/\tau) + (p/\tau)' f(k^x,l^x)) - h_l = 0$$

$$u_x - (p/\tau)u_y = 0$$

and rearranging yields the following two equations:

$$\left(g - \frac{v'}{u_y}\right)\frac{dk^x}{dg} + (f(k^x,l^x) - c^x)\frac{dp}{dg} + p\left(\frac{1}{\tau} - 1\right)\left(h_k\frac{dk^x}{dg} + h_l\frac{dl^x}{dg} + \frac{dc^x}{dg}\right)$$
$$+ \quad p'\left(\frac{1}{\tau} - 1\right)\left(f_l\frac{dl^x}{dg} + f_k\frac{dk}{dg}\right) \quad + \quad \left(p'R'f_l f(k^x,l^x) - p'f_l(1 + R')c^x\right)\frac{dl^x}{dg}$$
$$+\left(p'R'f_k f(k^x,l^x) - p'f_k(1 + R')c^x\right)\frac{dk^x}{dg} = 0 \tag{5-12}$$

$$\left(g-\frac{v'}{u_y}\right)\frac{dk^x}{d\tau} + (f(k^x,l^x)-c^x)\frac{dp}{d\tau} + p\left(\frac{1}{\tau}-1\right)\left(h_k\frac{dk^x}{d\tau}+h_l\frac{dl^x}{d\tau}+\frac{dc^x}{d\tau}\right)$$

$$+ \quad p'\left(\frac{1}{\tau}-1\right)\left(f_l\frac{dl^x}{d\tau}+f_k\frac{dk}{d\tau}\right) \quad + \quad \left(p'R'f_lf(k^x,l^x)-p'f_l(1+R')c^x\right)\frac{dl^x}{d\tau}$$

$$+\left(p'R'f_kf(k^x,l^x)-p'f_k(1+R')c^x\right)\frac{dk^x}{d\tau}=0 \tag{5-13}$$

Solving (5-12&13) for their two unknowns g and τ should yield the optimal tax-tariff combination if the x market is a duopoly.

However, the method used in chapter 3 above where we took an 'educated guess' that the optimal tax, if government can pursue terms of trade improvement by means of a tariff would be the Pigouvian tax, cannot be applied in the present context.

The reason is that government pursues more than two objectives with its choice of an environmental tax if the x market is a duopoly, namely

- internalisation of the environmental externality,
- terms of trade improvement,
- shifting profit to the domestic duopolist, and
- increasing consumer surplus.

Only if government commands policy instruments to address each of these objectives individually, will the environmental tax be set at the Pigouvian level. Adding the tariff as an additional instrument might, however, relieve the downward pressure on the environmental tax.

To find out whether this is indeed the case, we shall determine the tax in the presence of a tariff and investigate whether it will be higher or lower than g determined in (5-7).

(5-12) yields the following tax in the presence of a tariff:

$$g=\frac{v'}{u_y} + (c^x - f(k^x,l^x))\frac{dp}{dg}\frac{dg}{dk^x} + p'f_kc^x + (p'f_lc^x)\frac{dl^x}{dg}\frac{dg}{dk^x} +$$

$$p'\ R'f_k(c^x - f(k^x,l^x)) + p'\ R'f_l(c^x - f(k^x,l^x))\frac{dl^x}{dg}\frac{dg}{dk^x} -$$

$$p\left(\frac{1}{\tau}-1\right)\frac{d(c^x-f(k^x,l^x))}{dg}\left(\frac{dk^x}{dg}\right) - p'\left(\frac{1}{\tau}-1\right)\frac{df(k^x,l^x)}{dg}\left(\frac{dk^x}{dg}\right) \tag{5-14}$$

We observe that (5-14) is similar to (5-7), with the last two terms added to capture the tariff effect.

Inspecting (5-14) we find the following conditions for a tax-increasing effect of the trade instrument:

- the last term is positive if $\tau < 1$, which corresponds to a (border) subsidy for *y* or a (border) tax on *x;*
- the second to last term is positive if in an *x* exporting country $\tau > 1$ which corresponds to a tariff on *y*, or an export tax on *x*.

If we neglect terms of trade considerations, (5-14) implies that, if government sets an ex- or import tax to address the negative profit effect of a price decline triggered by output expansion, its environmental tax increases (last term).

However, we also observe that the effect of the trade policy instrument in (5-14) has ambiguous effects for *g*, if we take into account terms of trade effects of τ. An *x* exporting country would set a tariff on *y* (which corresponds to an export tax on x) to improve its terms of trade. An *x*-importing country would tax *y* exports (corresponding to a tariff on *x*). In both cases $\tau > 1$ which triggers an output expansion abroad. As a consequence, *g* is lowered (effect of the last term in (5-14) to offset the negative effect of terms of trade improvement for duopoly profits.

3. DISCUSSION

Our analysis in the preceding section shows that the above mentioned results from Walz & Wellisch [1997] cannot be generalised to apply in a general equilibrium context.

Walz & Wellisch [1997] derived the result that availability of trade instruments restores optimality of environmental regulation in a very specific model. In the context of a so-called third market model[12], they show that governments engage in eco-dumping to strategically alter the position of their duopolists[13]. If trade instruments are available, governments charge a Pigouvian tax, while subsidising exports of the duopolist to maximise domestic duopoly rents. Walz & Wellisch [1995] also undertake a welfare analysis, comparing the case of bilateral eco-dumping with bilateral tax-

12 Third market models are one of two variants of strategic trade policy models. Strategic trade policy refers to an area of international trade theory where economists have sought to incorporate imperfect competition into the formal analysis of trade and trade policy. In third market models, duopolists from two countries compete on a third (export) market. The alternative modelling approach is a so-called reciprocal market model in which duopolists situated in two different countries compete on segmented markets in these two countries (see Brander [1995]).

13 To derive their results, Walz & Wellisch [1997] further restrict the model by adding assumptions regarding functional forms.

cum-export-subsidy. Their result is that for home and foreign, the eco-dumping alternative welfare dominates the tax-cum-subsidy combination, i.e. the positive effects of reducing the environmental distortion is offset by the negative effect of reduced duopoly rents[14]. However, if welfare in the importing country is taken into account, this result is reversed, i.e. if consumption rent increase is included, world welfare is higher if governments can use both instruments[15].

By virtue of the partial equilibrium character of strategic trade and strategic environmental policy models, terms of trade effects which figure both in the optimal environmental tax we derived in (5-7) and in the tariff effect in (5-14) are neglected. Terms of trade considerations reduce the incentive for governments to implement policies which reduce the price of their export good. Therefore, terms of trade effects and the profit-shifting objective always imply opposite effects for the optimal policy if the duopoly good is exported[16].

Furthermore, by virtue of assumption that duopoly competition occurs exclusively on third markets, effects of government policy for domestic consumers are neglected.

Such effects are taken into account in reciprocal market models. Conrad [1996] analyses optimal environmental policy in a reciprocal market model. He finds that the effects of the tax for consumer surplus adds to eco-dumping, which ties with our results from above.

In a reciprocal markets model, both countries ex- and import the good produced by the two duopolists since markets are segmented. Hence, there is

14 Using an export subsidy while setting the tax at the Pigouvian level moves firms' reaction function further to the right towards their respective Stackelberg points (compare figure 5-2). Therefore, the Nash equilibrium output under bilateral tax-cum-subsidy is higher than under eco-dumping which implies that profits and duopoly rents are lower.

15 The basic idea for Walz & Wellisch's [1997] investigation is taken from Brander & Spencer [1983] who analyse a two-stage Cournot Nash game between two duopolists whose production entails R&D expenditure in the first stage, which determines output decisions in the second stage. To improve their strategic position vis-à-vis their rival, duopolists choose suboptimally high R&D levels. If government can subsidise R&D (in a policy-setting stage before duopolists make their choices), this distortion is aggravated by an R&D subsidy with which governments search to improve their duopolist's position on the imperfect export market. If governments also command a trade policy instrument, they will use an export subsidy to improve the strategic position of their duopolist, and an R&D tax to restore production efficiency. If both governments engage in a tax-cum-subsidy game, both countries will end up worse off because of the negative externality for rival duopolist entailed by the unilaterally optimal policy choices.

16 This is shown by Brander & Spencer [1985] in an extention of their [1983] paper. If terms of trade effects are taken into account, this reduces the incentive for governments to subsidise exports. However, an export subsidy - albeit at a lower level - remains government's optimal policy choice as positive welfare effects from duopoly profit increase dominate terms of trade related losses.

ample scope for trade instruments. However, Conrad does not analyse trade instruments in addition to environmental policy.

In a reciprocal markets model without environmental externalities, Brander & Spencer [1984] show that both countries' governments have an incentive to levy a tariff on imports since gains to the domestic duopolist and government revenue dominate loss of consumer rents.

Dixit [1984&88] extends Brander & Spencer's [1984] analysis to show that, if governments are not restricted to one trade policy instrument (i.e. a tariff) but can also subsidise exports, the policy equilibrium implies positive subsidies and tariffs.

The latter result indicates it is possible that for our tax-cum-trade policy scenario above, the policy equilibrium determined by (5-12&13) would consist of eco-dumping and a trade policy instrument.

Finally, we should note an important qualification applying to all results derived and discussed: They rest on the crucial assumption that competition is of the Cournot Nash type, i.e. in quantities rather than prices. Conjectural variation may upset all of these results[17].

4. CONCLUSIONS

We have shown that in a setting in which the market of the good whose PPM pollutes the environment is a duopoly, government has a number of different motives for choosing an environmental tax below the Pigouvian level. While eco-dumping is welfare-improving if undertaken unilaterally, rents are partly dissipated if it comes to an ERTB which entails suboptimally low environmental quality for both home and foreign.

However, trade instruments are not likely to restore optimality of environmental regulation, although an eco-tariff or an export subsidy may reduce the pressure for governments to engage in eco-dumping. Welfare effects from the additional trade policy instrument are not necessarily positive as Walz & Wellisch's [1997] result shows.

Against the background that eco-tariffs and export subsidies are banned by the GATT/WTO, our and earlier results seem to indicate that at least occasionally, i.e. in particular theoretical models, eco-tariffs and other trade instruments are shown to imply positive environmental effects. If such situations are found be practically relevant, a change of rules might be considered.

[17] Conjectural variation refers to a change in the variable assumed to be the producer's choice variable; the alternatives are usually price and quantity (compare Tirole [1988, 244]).

Of relevance in this context are changes which have been proposed for GATT/WTO rules on border tax adjustment, which currently restrict the adjustment of prices for exports (or imports) at the border. So far, only indirect taxes on products can be rebated. Hence, neither environmental taxes on PPMs nor on inputs would be considered for border tax adjustment. Proposals to change these rules to allow broader scope for border tax adjustment to compensate for international differences in environmental PPM taxes have been made.

Chapter 6

Tariffs to Counteract Eco-dumping Caused by Regulatory Capture

It has been argued by several economists[1] that regulatory capture by industries whose activities have negative environmental effects may induce governments to set too low environmental standards, in particular if the preservation of competitiveness of export or import-competing industries is at stake. If undertaken unilaterally, eco-dumping yields benefits for pressure groups[2].

Shrybman [1992] argues that objection against stringent environmental regulation and resulting reluctance of governments to implement optimal policies is due to the fact that trade restrictions are currently not available for governments to offset the advantage gained by countries which improve the competitiveness of their industries by setting low environmental standards. Thus, the implementation of eco-tariffs would reduce industry objection against stringent environmental policy, and hence relieve countries from the pressure to engage in eco-dumping[3].

We modify our Heckscher-Ohlin-Samuelson model from chapter 3 to address this issue in a general equilibrium context. Specifically, we analyse effects of government policy to increase welfare for producers of the good whose PPM pollutes the environment. Since this results in eco-dumping or an ERTB, we further examine whether availability of eco-tariffs might serve to enhance welfare.

1 Hoekman & Leidy [1992&1994], Klepper [1992], Ursprung [1992], VanGrasstek [1992].

2 Shown by Hoekman & Leidy [1994], and Rauscher [1997, ch.7] in partial equilibrium models, and Rauscher [1994&1995d], and Ursprung [1992] in general equilibrium models.

3 See Shrybman [1992, 100]: "*Restrictions on the use of import controls, together with pressure from the corporate sector to achieve a 'level playing field', create a powerful disincentive for ... countries to regulate.*"

In this setting, home is modelled as a country in which producers of the good whose competitiveness on international markets suffers from environmental regulation are able to influence political decision-making. Home is either a small or a large country. If it is large, its trading partners are either atomistic or one large foreign country.

1. ENVIRONMENTAL REGULATION UNDER REGULATORY CAPTURE

In order to consider environmental policy under regulatory capture, some modifications of our Heckscher-Ohlin-Samuelson model from chapter 3 are necessary[4]. Governments caring about the welfare of lobby groups maximise the following objective function

$$w^L = w + \ell \qquad (6\text{-}1)$$

We assume that producers of x are able to influence political decision-making; therefore, their welfare is captured in the political support function ℓ in (6-1) which enters government's objective function along with social welfare. If government is influenced by lobby of x producers, we assume that ℓ is given by

$$\ell = f(k^x, l^x)^5 \qquad (6\text{-}2)$$

and government's objective function becomes

$$w^L = u(f(k^x,l^x) + ph(k-k^x,l-l^x) - pc^y, c^y) - v(k^x) + f(k^x, l^x) \qquad (6\text{-}1')$$

ECO-DUMPING AND REGULATORY CAPTURE IN A SMALL COUNTRY

We assume that government uses environmental policy in form of the tax on capital to maximise w^L.[6].

---

4 We revert to the original model specification as developed in chapter 3, i.e. the numeraire is again good x.

5 The particular functional form of ℓ implies that welfare of producers in the x industry is simply given by their output. This assumption is made for simplicity; we discuss alternatives below.

The tax on capital chosen by a government influenced by lobby groups is denoted by g^L and given by differentiating (6-1') w.r.t. g^L and setting it equal to zero.

$$\frac{dw^L}{\mathrm{dg}^L} = \left[u_x(f_k - ph_k) + f_k - v'\right]\left(\frac{dk^x}{dg^L}\right) + \frac{df}{dg^L} \stackrel{!}{=} 0 \tag{6-3}$$

This yields for the tax on capital

$$g^L = \frac{v'}{u_x} - \frac{1}{u_x}\left(\frac{df}{dg^L}\frac{dg^L}{dk^x}\right) \tag{6-4}$$

The tax on capital if government is subject to regulatory capture is hence composed of

- the Pigouvian part (v'/u_x) by which the environmental externality is internalised, and
- the second part ($g^L - v'/u_x$) by which the effect of the tax on welfare for producers of x is taken into account.

To find out whether home engages in eco-dumping or a NIMBY policy, we have to determine the sign of the last term in (6-4), i.e.

$$\mathrm{sg}\left[-\frac{1}{u_x}\left(\frac{df}{dg^L}\frac{dg^L}{k^x}\right)\right]$$

($1/u_x$) is positive; (df/dg^L) and (dk^x/dg^L) are negative. We hence have

$$-\frac{1}{u_x}\left(\frac{df}{dg^L}\frac{dg^L}{k^x}\right) < 0 \tag{6-5}$$

Therefore, we find the following result regarding the effect of regulatory capture of producers of x:

$g^L < v'/u_x$ i.e. government engages in eco-dumping to maximise its objective function if producers of x affect the political decision-making process.

---

[6] The welfare effects are determined for unbiased social welfare, i.e. w without the political support function ℓ Welfare w^L including the political support function is referred to as biased welfare.

RATIONALE AND EFFECTS

The rationale for a government to reduce the environmental tax below the level found optimal in a small country in chapter is the influence of the x-producing lobby. One of the effects of eco-dumping is an increase of k^x and l^x and therefore x. It corresponds to the regulatory capture bias in government's objective function.

Further effects are

- increase of environmental pollution, and
- decrease of (unbiased) welfare.

Hence, the gain in welfare of producers of x comes at the expense of the rest of the society. Environmental quality is reduced and consumption utility is increased, whereby the former effect dominates the latter.

We should also note that if every small country is subject to regulatory capture, they all follow the same eco-dumping policy. Hence, if this is a world-wide phenomenon, no country gains market share and competitiveness for its x industry. However, global production is biased towards x at the expense of environmental quality.

ECO-DUMPING AND REGULATORY CAPTURE IN A LARGE COUNTRY

In chapter 4 we derived that large countries have either an incentive to engage in eco-dumping or NIMBY to improve their terms of trade, dependent on relative factor abundance. If in large countries governments are biased towards producers of x, we thus expect that eco-dumping for regulatory capture reasons

- is aggravated by terms of trade considerations in a labour-abundant country, and
- counteracted by terms of trade considerations in a capital-abundant country.

Government in a large country subject to regulatory capture by the x industry lobby sets the following tax on capital:

$$g^L = \frac{v'}{u_x} + (c^y - h)\left(\frac{dp}{dg^L}\frac{dg^L}{dk^x}\right) - \frac{1}{u_x}\left(\frac{df}{dg^L}\frac{dg^L}{dk^x}\right)$$

Therefore, both labour and capital-abundant countries engage in eco-dumping if

$$(c^y - h)\left(\frac{dp}{dg^L}\frac{dg^L}{dk^x}\right) - \frac{1}{u_x}\left(\frac{df}{dg^L}\frac{dg^L}{dk^x}\right) < 0 \qquad (6\text{-}6)$$

Assuming that $df/dg^L < 0$ (i.e. excluding the Metzler eco-dumping case), we observe that for a labour-abundant country all terms in (6-6) are negative. This implies eco-dumping in a labour-abundant country since the inequality in (6-6) shall always be fulfilled.

For a capital-abundant country the first term in (6-6) is positive. It engages in eco-dumping if (6-6) holds which implies that regulatory capture by producers of x reverses NIMBY for terms of trade reasons. However, even if the inequality (6-6) does not hold, the tax will be less than in the absence of regulatory capture.

RATIONALE AND EFFECTS

The rationale for a government to reduce the environmental tax below the level found optimal for a large country in chapter 4 is the influence of the x producer lobby. The effect of the reduction of the tax on factor allocation, i.e. an increase in capital and labour employed in the x sector caters to the interest of the x industry.

We found in chapter 4 that labour-abundant countries engage in eco-dumping for terms of trade reasons, while capital-abundant countries follow a NIMBY policy to improve their terms of trade. Hence, if government is subject to regulatory capture, eco-dumping policy in labour-abundant countries is reinforced, while NIMBY policy is reduced in capital-abundant countries for the sake of the lobbyists.

A further effect of the regulatory capture induced reduction of the environmental tax is an increase in environmental pollution.

Therefore, (unbiased) social welfare is lower in regulatory capture countries than in those where government is not influenced by lobbies[7].

Effects of regulatory capture in a large country on welfare in the rest of the world consisting of small countries are as follows:

– If a labour-abundant country is subject to regulatory capture, terms of trade in the rest of the world decline. If the rest of the world is also subject to regulatory capture, all governments engage in eco-dumping to reduce negative output effects for x producers. Environmental deterioration and (aggregated) terms of trade effects of such biased policies further reduce social welfare in the rest of the world.

[7] By definition, the policy choice in the absence of regulatory capture attains the welfare optimum. Since (unbiased) social welfare is single peaked, any deviation from the optimal policy choice implies a welfare loss.

- If a capital-abundant country is subject to regulatory capture and engages in eco-dumping, terms of trade in the rest of the world appreciate. However, if the rest of the world is also subject to regulatory capture, governments' biased policies offset this effect.

STRATEGIC INTERACTION OF LARGE COUNTRIES SUBJECT TO REGULATORY CAPTURE

If we analyse effects of regulatory capture in two large countries, two scenarios are possible:

- only one is subject to regulatory capture, while the other one chooses its environmental policy to maximise welfare, or
- both countries are subject to regulatory capture.
-

Unilateral regulatory capture: If in only one of two large countries producers of x affect environmental policy formation, two possibilities arise:

- the labour-abundant country is subject to regulatory capture, or
- the capital-abundant country is subject to regulatory capture.

Welfare effects of unilateral regulatory capture are illustrated in figure 6-1, depicting a Nash equilibrium in environmental taxes which we introduced in chapter 4[8]. In figure 6-1, small caps refer to a labour-abundant, large caps to a capital-abundant country. Policy biased towards x producers moves a capital-abundant country's reaction function downward from $R(g)$ to $R^L(g)$: at every level of its trading partner's tax choice, the tax chosen by a government subject to regulatory capture is lower than the choice of an unbiased regulator. Similarly, a labour-abundant country's reaction function is moved to the left from $r(G)$ to $r^L(G)$ if its government pursues environmental policy biased towards producers of x. Hence, if producers of x gain regulatory capture in a capital-abundant country, the Nash equilibrium is given by $NE(g,G^L)$ which lies to the south-east of $NE(g,G)$, the Nash equilibrium in eco-dumping and NIMBY which results from terms of trade considerations by two large countries. If the labour-abundant country is subject to regulatory capture, the Nash equilibrium is given by $NE(g^L,G)$ which lies to the north-west of $NE(g,G)$. Welfare indifference curves associated with $NE(g,G)$ are given by $wi(g,G)$ and $WI(g,G)$.

[8] We assume that all the necessary conditions for a Nash equilibrium in environmental taxes are fulfilled for taxes set under regulatory capture; therefore, the derivation of the Nash equilibrium in chapter 4 above applies.

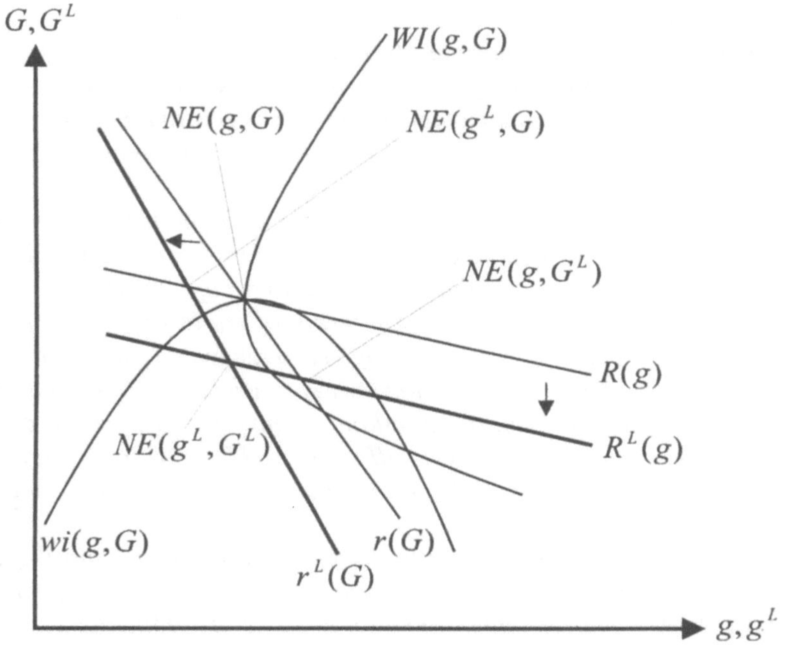

Figure 6-1. Nash Equilibrium in the Tax Space under Regulatory Capture

We observe that

- the downward shift of a capital-abundant country's reaction curve is welfare-improving for both countries if $NE(g,G^L)$ lies inside the core described by $wi(g,G)$ and $WI(g,G)$. The reason is that the labour-abundant country's terms of trade improve from the tax reduction abroad, while the capital-abundant country's welfare improvement is due to the reduction in the factor market distortion from too high a tax on capital.
- the opposite is true if a labour-abundant country is subject to regulatory capture, and reduces its tax even further (in that case, the Nash equilibrium $NE(g^L,G)$ lies outside the core). The reasons for the negative welfare effect are the decline of the capital-abundant country's terms of trade caused by eco-dumping abroad, together with the inefficiencies caused by the suboptimal tax in the labour-abundant country.
-

Bilateral regulatory capture: If both countries' environmental policy is influenced by producers of x, the resulting Nash equilibrium is given by $NE(g^L,G^L)$. Welfare effects depend on the relative strength of the resulting tax reductions. Scenarios in which both countries gain, both lose or one gains while the other loses, are all possible.

We summarise with

***Proposition 6-1**: Regulatory capture leads to eco-dumping and reduces welfare in small countries. If it happens in large countries, regulatory capture in a capital-abundant country reinforces eco-dumping for terms of trade reasons, while it reduces NIMBY for terms of trade reasons in a labour-abundant country.*

(a) If the trading world consists of small countries all subject to regulatory capture, they will be trapped in a welfare-reducing ERTB.

(b) If large countries are subject to regulatory capture, they reduce their tax below the level found optimal for terms of trade improvement. For a labour-abundant country, eco-dumping is aggravated while a capital-abundant country's environmental tax moves towards the Pigouvian level. It is not possible that the capital-abundant country will be worse off or the labour-abundant country better off. An ERTB is possible, if the environmental tax in the labour-abundant country drops below the Pigouvian level.

(c) Global welfare effects of regulatory capture in a capital-abundant country are positive. However, they are negative in a labour-abundant country. If both countries' environmental policies are influenced by lobbies, welfare effects are indeterminate.

2. ECO-TARIFFS AND REGULATORY CAPTURE

We now consider the case when governments subject to regulatory capture can use trade policy in addition to environmental policy to maximise the objective function w^L given by (6-1'). In particular, we investigate whether the availability of trade policy instruments in form of tariffs has a welfare-improving effect if governments are subject to regulatory capture.

For both small and large countries, we determine the optimal tariff and its welfare effects if there is eco-dumping for regulatory capture reasons. Furthermore, we examine whether availability of eco-tariffs reduces the pressure for eco-dumping in countries where governments are subject to regulatory capture. To that end, we determine the optimal tax-tariff combination and its welfare effects for a small country and discuss optimal policy instruments for large countries subject to regulatory capture.

2.1 Eco-tariffs and Regulatory Capture in a Small Country

Eco-tariffs when there is eco-dumping: If lobby groups are successful in reducing the tax below the Pigouvian level and the government subject to regulatory capture can also levy a tariff, the relative price including the tariff is denoted by τ^L and given by differentiating (6-1') w.r.t. τ^L and setting it equal to zero

$$\frac{dw^L}{d\tau^L} = [u_x(f_k - ph_k) - v'] \frac{dk^x}{d\tau^L} + [u_x(f_l - ph_l)] \frac{dl^x}{d\tau^L} +$$

$$(u_y - pu_x) \frac{dc^y}{d\tau^L} + \frac{df}{d\tau^L} \overset{!}{=} 0 \tag{6-7}$$ [9]

Substituting FOCs in the presence of a tariff

$$f_k - g - (p/\tau)h_k = 0 \tag{6-30}$$

$$f_l - (p/\tau)h_l = 0 \tag{6-31}$$

$$u_y - (p/\tau)u_x = 0 \tag{6-32}$$

and noting that eco-dumping implies that ($g \neq v'/u_x$), (6-7) yields the following result[10] for the tariff if government engages in eco-dumping

$$\tau^L = \left[1 + \frac{1}{p}\left(\left(\frac{v'}{u_x} - g\right)\frac{dk^x}{d(c^y - h)} - \left(\frac{1}{u_x}\right)\frac{df}{d(c^y - h)}\right)\right]^{-1} \tag{6-8}$$

Inspecting (6-8) we observe the following

- if there is eco-dumping, ($v'/u_x - g$) > 0. Therefore, the second term in (6-8) (the eco-dumping term) is positive if x is imported; it is negative if x is exported.
- The third term in (6-8) (the regulatory capture term) is negative if x is imported and positive if x is exported.

RATIONALE AND EFFECTS

We consider the effect of eco-dumping and regulatory capture on the trade policy instrument chosen by a country which imports x. In that case, eco-dumping causes government to lower the tariff since import stimulation

[9] Owing to our assumption that the country under consideration is small, the world price effect of the tariff is zero; for brevity we drop the relevant term.

[10] Some algebraic manipulations are necessary.

reduces domestic production of x and thus environmental pollution which is above the socially optimal level.

Regulatory capture, however, has the opposite effect: curtailing imports increases domestic production of x which caters to the interests of the lobby exercising regulatory capture.

The aggregated effect of eco-dumping and regulatory capture is thus indeterminate; a positive tariff is changed if

$$\left[\frac{1}{p}\left(\left(\frac{v'}{u_x}-g\right)\frac{dk^x}{d(c^y-h)}-\left(\frac{1}{u_x}\right)\frac{df}{d(c^y-h)}\right)\right]<0 \tag{6-9}$$

The effect for unbiased social welfare if (6-9) holds is negative since

- environmental pollution increases, and
- the tariff further distorts allocation in the economy[11].

If the eco-dumping term dominates in (6-8) and thus (6-9) does not hold, and government can hand out an import subsidy, unbiased welfare improves.

As regards the effect of the eco-tariff for the x-producing lobby group, it is positive if the regulatory capture term dominates the eco-dumping term; otherwise, they would be worse off if government was allowed to introduce an import subsidy.

OPTIMAL TAX AND TARIFF UNDER REGULATORY CAPTURE

If government of a small country subject to regulatory capture maximises its objective function (6-1') using environmental and trade policy, the optimal tax-(implied) tariff combination is found by differentiating (6-1') w.r.t. g^L and τ^L and setting both equations equal to zero[12]:

$$\frac{dw^L}{dg^L}=[u_x(f_k-ph_k)-v']\frac{dk^x}{dg^L}+[u_x(f_l-ph_l)]\frac{dl^x}{dg^L}+$$

$$(u_y-pu_x)\frac{dc^y}{dg^L}+\frac{df}{dg^L}\overset{!}{=}0$$

[11] Eco-dumping already causes a distortion.

[12] This optimum is constraint by the fact that we limit government in the choice of its instruments; the first best instrument to achieve a production expansion would be a subsidy.

$$\frac{dw^L}{d\tau^L} = [u_x(f_k - ph_k) - v']\frac{dk^x}{d\tau^L} + [u_x(f_l - ph_l)]\frac{dl^x}{d\tau^L} +$$

$$(u_y - pu_x)\frac{dc^y}{d\tau^L} + \frac{df}{d\tau^L} \overset{!}{=} 0$$

Substituting FOCs in the presence of a tariff (3-30), (3-31) and (3-32) given yields

$$\left(g^L - \frac{v'}{u_x}\right)\frac{dk^x}{dg^L} + p\left(\frac{1}{\tau^L} - 1\right)\left(\frac{d(c^y - h)}{dg^L}\right) + \frac{1}{u_x}\frac{df}{dg^L} = 0 \tag{6-10}$$

$$\left(g^L - \frac{v'}{u_x}\right)\frac{dk^x}{d\tau^L} + p\left(\frac{1}{\tau^L} - 1\right)\left(\frac{d(c^y - h)}{d\tau^L}\right) + \frac{1}{u_x}\frac{df}{d\tau^L} = 0 \tag{6-11}$$

Assuming that

$$g^L = v'/u_x \tag{6-12a}$$

if follows from (6-10) that

$$\tau^L = \left[1 - \frac{1}{p}\frac{1}{u_x}\frac{df}{d(c^y - h)}\right]^{-1} \tag{6-12b}$$

Dividing (6-10) by (6-11) yields under the assumption that ($g^L = v'/u_x$)

$$\frac{df}{dg^L} \Big/ \frac{df}{d\tau^L} = \frac{d(h - c^y)}{dg^L} \Big/ \frac{d(h - c^y)}{d\tau^L} \tag{6-13}$$

If (6-13) is fulfilled, (6-12a&b) imply an optimal tax and tariff combination. We observe that (6-12a) is the optimal (Pigouvian) tax for a small country whose government is not subject to regulatory capture. As regards the tariff, (6-12b) implies a higher than optimal tariff in small countries whose governments are not subject to regulatory capture if

$$-\frac{1}{p}\left(\frac{1}{u_x}\right)\frac{df}{d(c^y - h)} < 0 \tag{6-14}$$

We hence observe that a positive tariff is charged if x is imported; if it is exported, government hands out an export subsidy.

RATIONALE AND EFFECTS

We observe that regulatory capture in a small labour-abundant country increases the tariff above the optimal level in the absence of regulatory capture while the optimal tax is the Pigouvian one both with and without regulatory capture.

In comparison with the eco-tariff charged if there is eco-dumping, we note that the optimal tax-tariff combination implies a higher tax and a higher tariff for x-importing, small countries[13]. This is explained by the fact that protecting the x industry from international competition is more effective in expanding output than subsidising capital input. Therefore, only trade policy is used to cater to the special interest of the lobby group of x producers.

Therefore, the Shrybman [1992] conjecture cited above is correct: if governments subject to regulatory capture can use trade policy in addition to environmental policy, they do not engage in eco-dumping. However, this result depends on the particular functional form chosen for the political support function ℓ

As regards the effects on (unbiased) welfare of the availability of eco-tariffs, we observe

- a positive welfare effect from increased environmental tax,
- a negative welfare effect from price distortion caused by the tariff.

Therefore, although the availability of eco-tariffs causes a stricter environmental policy, it is not necessarily welfare-enhancing.

Finally, the ERTB which results from regulatory capture is not overcome if countries can charge eco-tariffs since only countries importing x can recurr to this instruments, while those exporting x still engage in eco-dumping. Therefore, we would observe a tax and tariff race.

[13] If we compare (6-9) with (6-14), we observe that the eco-dumping term is 0 if government can maximise its objective function without constraints.

2.2 Eco-tariffs and Regulatory Capture in a Large Country

ECO-TARIFFS WHEN THERE IS ECO-DUMPING

If the government of a large country is subject to regulatory capture and charges a tax below the Pigouvian level, the optimal tariff is given by differentiating the objective function (6-1') w.r.t. τ^L and setting it equal to zero.

$$\frac{dw^L}{d\tau^L} = \left[u_x(f_k - ph_k) - v'\right]\frac{dk^x}{d\tau^L} + \left[u_x(f_l - ph_l)\right]\frac{dl^x}{d\tau^L} + (u_y - pu_x)\frac{dc^y}{d\tau^L} +$$
$$\left[u_x(h - c^y)\right]\frac{dp}{d\tau^L} + \frac{df}{d\tau^L} \overset{!}{=} 0$$

Substituting FOCs in the presence of a tariff (3-30), (3-31) and (3-32) given above yields the following expression for the optimal tariff:

$$\tau^L = \left[1 + \frac{1}{p}\left(\left(\frac{v'}{u_x} - g\right)\frac{dk^x}{d(c^y - h)} + (c^y - h)\frac{dp}{d(c^y - h)} - \frac{1}{u_x}\frac{df}{d(c^y - h)}\right)\right]^{-1}$$
(6-15)

Inspecting (6-15) we observe that in labour-abundant countries the effect of eco-dumping - i.e. the second term in (6-15) - reduces the tariff, while the influence of the x-producing lobby captured in the fourth term in (6-15) reinforces the terms of trade effect (captured in the third term), thereby increasing the tariff.

RATIONALE AND EFFECTS

We consider the effect of eco-dumping and regulatory capture on the trade policy instrument chosen by a large labour-abundant country.

Similar to the forces at work in a small country, a tax below the Pigouvian level induces government to reduce environmental pollution by stimulating x imports, i.e. choosing a low tariff. The terms of trade effect of the tariff on the other hand stimulates protection; an effect further reinforced by regulatory capture since protection of the import-competing x industry serves the interest of the lobbyists.

If the regulatory capture term dominates the eco-dumping term, i.e.

$$\frac{1}{p}\left[\left(\frac{v'}{u_x}-g\right)\frac{dk^x}{d(c^y-h)}-\frac{1}{u_x}\frac{df}{d(c^y-h)}\right]<0 \qquad (6\text{-}16)$$

the tariff charged by a labour-abundant country where eco-dumping is prevalent and government subject to regulatory capture, is higher than the optimal one found in chapter 4 which maximises national (unbiased) welfare through manipulating the terms of trade.

Social welfare implications if an eco-dumping government levies a tariff are indeterminate for a labour-abundant country since

- terms of trade improve, yet
- environmental quality declines.

As regards global welfare implications, they are indeterminate: If eco-dumping is a world wide phenomenon, welfare loss owing to terms of trade decline in the rest of the world if a labour-abundant country charges a tariff is partly offset by environmental improvement. The reason is that the tariff causes output reduction and therefore environmental quality enhancement in the rest of the world.

OPTIMAL TAX AND TARIFF UNDER REGULATORY CAPTURE

If the government of a large country subject to regulatory capture maximises its objective function (6-1') using environmental and trade policy, the optimal tax-(implied) tariff combination is found by differentiating (6-1') w.r.t. g^L and τ^L and setting both equations equal to zero:

$$\frac{dw^L}{dg^L}=[u_x(f_k-ph_k)-v']\frac{dk^x}{dg^L}+[u_x(f_l-ph_l)]\frac{dl^x}{dg^L}+$$
$$(u_y-pu_x)\frac{dc^y}{dg^L}+[u_x(h-c^y)]\frac{dp}{dg^L}+\frac{df}{dg^L}\overset{!}{=}0$$

$$\frac{dw^L}{d\tau^L}=[u_x(f_k-ph_k)-v']\frac{dk^x}{d\tau^L}+[u_x(f_l-ph_l)]\frac{dl^x}{d\tau^L}+$$
$$(u_y-pu_x)\frac{dc^y}{d\tau^L}+[u_x(h-c^y)]\frac{dp}{d\tau^L}+\frac{df}{d\tau^L}\overset{!}{=}0$$

Substituting FOCs in the presence of a tariff (3-30), (3-31) and (3-32) given above yields

$$\left(g^L - \frac{v'}{u_x}\right)\frac{dk^x}{dg^L} + p\left(\frac{1}{\tau^L} - 1\right)\left(\frac{d(c^y - h)}{dg^L}\right) + \frac{1}{u_x}\frac{df}{dg^L} + (h - c^y)\frac{dp}{dg^L} = 0 \quad (6\text{-}17)$$

$$\left(g^L - \frac{v'}{u_x}\right)\frac{dk^x}{d\tau^L} + p\left(\frac{1}{\tau^L} - 1\right)\left(\frac{d(c^y - h)}{d\tau^L}\right) + \frac{1}{u_x}\frac{df}{d\tau^L} + (h - c^y)\frac{dp}{d\tau^L} = 0$$

Assuming that $g^L = v'/u_x$ it follows from (6-17) that

$$\tau^L = \left[1 + \frac{(c^y - h)}{d(c^y - h)}\frac{dp}{p} - \frac{1}{p}\frac{1}{u_x}\frac{df}{d(c^y - h)}\right]^{-1} \qquad (6\text{-}18)$$

Thus, if government of a large country subject to regulatory capture sets the Pigouvian tax, the resulting tariff differs from the optimal tariff for a large country (determined in chapter 4) by the regulatory capture term

$$-\frac{1}{p}\left(\frac{1}{u_x}\right)\frac{df}{d(c^y - h)} < 0 \qquad (6\text{-}14)$$

RATIONALE AND EFFECTS

The bias in government's objective function towards the x-producing industry increases the tariff in a labour-abundant country. Protection of the import-competing industry has a positive terms of trade effect and serves the interest of the lobby exercising regulatory capture.

In a capital-abundant country, terms of trade improvement and output stimulation in the x industry trigger opposite trade instruments; if the latter dominates, government hands out an export subsidy.

If government uses a tariff rather than eco-dumping to expand output of x, welfare effects are positive in a labour-abundant country. Both terms of trade improvement and production stimulation are better - i.e. less environmentally harmful - achieved by a tariff than by a suboptimal environmental tax. In a capital-abundant country, welfare effects of the second policy instrument are indeterminate.

In the rest of the world, home's tariff policy has a pollution reducing effect with positive welfare implications. Terms of trade effects, however, cause welfare in the rest of the world to decline if a labour-abundant country can charge a tariff while it increases if a capital-abundant country recurs to trade policy rather than manipulating its environmental policy.

STRATEGIC INTERACTION OF LARGE COUNTRIES SUBJECT TO REGULATORY CAPTURE

We analyse effects of availability of trade policy in addition to environmental policy if two large countries - of which one is subject to regulatory capture - interact strategically. These effects are illustrated in figure 6-2, depicting a Nash equilibrium in environmental taxes when tariffs are available to one government, introduced in chapter 4. We assume that the labour-abundant country (denoted by small caps and referred to as 'home') is subject to regulatory capture while foreign (the capital-abundant country denoted by large caps) is not.

We compare the Nash equilibrium in NIMBY and eco-dumping given by $NE(g^L,G)$ with the Nash equilibrium in NIMBY and tax/tariff $NE(g(\tau^L),G)$. $NE(g(\tau^L),G)$ is given by the intersection of $R(g(\tau^L))$ - foreign's reaction curve which traces the tax foreign's government charges in response to home's tax/tariff combination - and $r^\tau(G)$, denoting home's tax choice in response to foreign's if home can levy a tariff. $wi(g^L,G)$ and $WI(g,G)$ are home's and foreign's welfare indifference curves associated with $NE(g^L,G)$; $wi(g(\tau^L),G)$ and $WI(g(\tau^L),G)$ are indifference curves corresponding to $NE(g(\tau^L),G)$.

Choice of the Pigouvian tax triggers a reduction in foreign's since foreign is assumed to be not subject to regulatory capture and therefore considers taxes as strategic complements. Hence, home's reaction curve shifts to the right and foreign's downward.

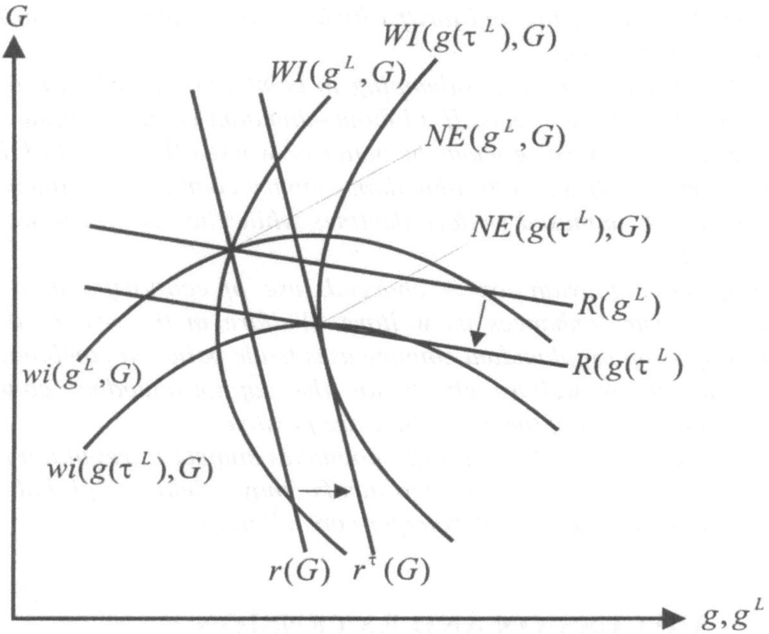

Figure 6-2. Comparison of Nash Equilibria in Eco-dumping and NIMBY, and Eco-tax/tariff and NIMBY if the Labour-abundant Country is subject to Regulatory Capture

We observe that:

- the availability of an eco-tariff for home shifts the Nash equilibrium to the south-east from $NE(g,G)$ to $NE(g(\tau),G)$;
- $NE(g(\tau),G)$ may hence lie in the core described by $wi(g^L,G)$ and $WI(g^L,G)$ of $NE(g^L,G)$. This implies that both home and foreign are on higher welfare levels if home can chose an eco-tariff;
- the global welfare improvement, however, is by no means certain; if foreign's reaction curve was shifted further downwards only home's welfare would improve, while foreign's would decline.

We summarise with

Proposition 6-2*: If governments subject to regulatory capture use trade policy in form of eco-tariffs in addition to environmental taxes, pressure to engage in eco-dumping is reduced. Welfare effects of the second policy instrument are indeterminate.*

(a) In small countries, we find that eco-tariffs in combination with eco-dumping reduce welfare for society. If the use of eco-tariffs restore the Pigouvian environmental policy, welfare effects may be positive. If all countries are subject to regulatory capture, we no longer observe an ERTB.

However, the race in tax and tariff which occurs instead has also negative welfare consequences.

(b) In large countries, eco-dumping in combination with eco-tariffs has indeterminate welfare effects. If a labour-abundant country engages in such a policy mix, its own society may be better or worse off; the rest of the world will be worse off. If a capital-abundant country combines eco-dumping and trade policy, its unbiased welfare declines while the rest of the world shall be better off.

(c) If the Pigouvian tax is charged, use of eco-tariffs in a labour-abundant country enhances its welfare. Welfare in the rest of the world declines. If a capita- abundant country uses trade policy in combination with the Pigouvian tax welfare effects for the capital-abundant country are negative; for the rest of the world they are positive.

(d) Strategic interaction of large countries subject to regulatory capture in environmental taxes and eco-tariffs may yield a global welfare improvement, depending on parameter constellations.

3. DISCUSSION AND EXTENSION

3.1 Regulatory Capture, Environmental and Trade Policy

The somewhat puzzling fact that the optimal policy of free trade is not pursued in practice even in the absence of all market imperfections[14] can be explained by the regulatory capture approach[15]. There is ample evidence to support the proposition that protectionist policies are rooted in domestic policy formation[16].

[14] In a first best world of small open economies, welfare-maximising governments have no reason to introduce trade restrictions - i.e. to deviate from optimal trade policy - if there are no market failures (see for example Krugman & Obstfeld [1997, 216pp]). Compare chapter 2 where we established a comparable result for environmental policy: in small open economies with no market failures other than an environmental externality governments have no reason to deviate from optimal environmental policy, i.e. a Pigouvian tax.

[15] The term 'regulatory capture' is not the only notion for the phenomenon that governments deviate from optimal policies because they are influenced by interest groups. Alternative terms are political economy approach or - when trade policy in particular is discussed - endogenous protection.

[16] See Rodrik [1995, 1480-1487] and Hillman [1989, 133-149], whose literature reviews include empirical parts in which they summarise evidence for trade protection across industries, countries and time.

The political economy perspective is based on the presumption that governments do not set their policies to maximise social welfare but rather the politician's objective function which we denoted by w^L in (6-1). w^L is biased towards interests of that social group which is able to capture the regulatory process. There are a number of approaches trying to explain how organised groups take action to influence government's trade policy to shift income in their favour[17].

The way we have integrated regulatory capture in our Heckscher-Ohlin-Samuelson model follows the political support function approach used by Hillman [1989]. In this approach, the policy maker is assumed to favour the interest of a particular industry, but is also assumed to care about the efficiency consequences of restricting trade[18]. Our model reflects this by assuming that government maximises an objective function which combines both social welfare w and interests of the x industry captured in $l = f(k^x, l^x)$.

Following the political support function approach, we assume that an industry rather than a factor gains regulatory capture. This seems to conflict with the insights from the Heckscher-Ohlin-Samuelson model for which the Stolper Samuelson effect[19] predicts that factors would form coalitions to seek (trade) protection. Hillman [1989,10], however, finds that empirical observations support that in general, industry-specific interest groups seek protection. This phenomenon is consistent with a Heckscher-Ohlin-Samuelson framework if we consider short-run implications: even if factors are mobile in the long run, there may be imperfect mobility in the short run. Hence, declining industries in particular would seek protection to postpone the (costly) factor reallocation[20].

If industries whose PPMs pollute the environment are subject to environmental regulation, such industries' output will contract in consequence. They are thus likely candidates to seek protection. Furthermore, there are reasons why industries subject to environmental regulation are particularly suited to gain regulatory capture: Since it is difficult to assess the true level of environmental damage, indirect subsidies

[17] Following Rodrik [1995], the various models are categorised as follows: tariff formation approach, political support function approach, median voter approach, campaign contributions approach, and political contributions approach.

[18] The policy maker hence maximises a function which trades off the gains from protection of the favoured industry against the losses to the general population. Politicians follow their self-interest in this approach. The industry captures the regulatory process either by contributing to politicians' campaign, thereby increasing the probability of reelection or simply by handing out bribes, thereby increasing politicians' income.

[19] Quote from Krugman & Obstfeld [1997, 70/71] or Gandolfo [1994, 112pp].

[20] Alternative explanations consistent with the Heckscher-Ohlin-Samuelson framework would be that factors are imperfectly substitutable or that regional interests are pursued by interest groups (see Hillman [1989, 14;26]).

can be easily hidden[21]. Moreover, even if direct subsidies were handed out to 'dirty' industries, such subsidies may be easier sold to the electorate than others since green policies are en vogue. Hence, although the political support function approach fails to model explicitly which industries are likely to gain regulatory capture, an argument can be made that industries subject to environmental regulation are likely to seek income redistribution by applying for trade protection[22].

In practice, however, we do not observe eco-tariffs since the international trade regime has banned tariffs as trade restrictions in most instances. The only exception are protective instruments if an industry is under pressure for reasons of unfair trade practices by importers or importing countries[23]. If an exporting firm is found to engage in dumping activities, the importing country may levy antidumping duties; if the exporting country engages in policies subsidising its export industries, the importing country may levy countervailing duties[24].

In the context of environmental policy, it is obvious that governments rather than specific firms engage in unfair trade practices. To countervail eco-dumping, countries would use conditional eco-tariffs corresponding to the countervailing duty concept used in other trade policy areas. Countervailing duties are motivated by the fear that international differences in the stringency of policy result in loss of competitiveness. If such differences are driven by competitiveness reasons they are seen as instances of unfair trade practices.

Applied to environmental regulation, lower standards in some countries may lead to a loss of competitiveness of affected industries in high standard countries. Such disadvantages could be coined as unfair and hence give rise to conditional eco-tariffs. We shall elaborate on tariffs as countervailing (eco) duties in the next section.

21 The principle of 'optimal obfuscation' proposed by Magee et al. [1989] supports this argument: Indirect policies such as environmental policy measures lend themselves to manipulation because their effects are not likely to be observed by those who bear the costs.

22 In this context, it may be puzzling that trade policy is sought to achieve income redistribution since trade policy is a rather inefficient means to attain this goal (see Dixit [1985]). Two tacks are suggested to reconcile the observed use of trade policy for redistribution with its economic inefficiency to achieve such a goal: it is possible that tariffs are preferred because their economic inefficiency makes them hard to use; alternatively, incomplete information may increase the attractiveness of tariffs for redistribution (see Rodrik [1995, 1470-1474]).

23 This refers to GATT/WTO regime; goods covered in special sub-agreements such as agricultural products and textiles may have considerable tariff or quota protection.

24 The use of such policies is labelled contingent protection because it is triggered by price and injury contingencies; see Markusen et al. [1995, 354].

3.2 Conditional Eco-tariffs and Regulatory Capture

We consider an eco-tariff which is conditional upon the stringency of environmental regulation in a country's trading partners. This tariff only applies if the environmental tax in exporting countries is below thethe level in the importing country. The objective of such a tariff would be to offset competitiveness effects from international differences in environmental regulation. We assume that the tariff setting country is large[25].

Effects of an conditional eco-tariff (if it is charged) in the rest of the world are identical to effects of an unconditional eco-tariff

- decline in their terms of trade,
- reduction in environmental pollution since price for and hence output of x declines in the rest of the world if home actually levies its conditional tariff.

We shall address

- further effects in the rest of the world depending on the size of the countries if home levies a conditional eco-tariff, and
- effects in the home country if it levies a conditional eco-tariff, depending on whether the tariff is actually implemented or not.

EFFECTS OF A CONDITIONAL ECO-TARIFF IN HOME'S TRADING PARTNERS

Home's tariff reduces x output in the rest of the world. If home's trading partners are small and subject to regulatory capture, the tariff increases pressure from the x lobby to further reduce environmental taxes.

Therefore, the tariff does not trigger a tax increase which would be necessary to achieve a waiver of home's tariff.

If home has a large trading partner, its reaction to home's conditional eco-tariff is an increase in the environmental tax since such an increase yields two terms of trade benefits for foreign:

- terms of trade improvement through the reduction in export supply, and
- terms of trade improvement since home has to waive its tariff.

We note that the assumption that small countries do not coordinate their policies is driving the result for small trading partners. A joint tax increase

[25] Since a small country cannot affect the world price level, the effect of a conditional eco-tariff charged by a small country is certainly nil; so we do not analyse this case further.

would have positive welfare consequences for small countries comparable to those for a large one.

EFFECTS OF A CONDITIONAL ECO-TARIFF IN HOME

To determine the effect of the conditional eco-tariff for home, we have to distinguish two cases, namely

- the environmental tax in the rest of the world is increased to avoid being subjected to the tariff and the tariff is hence removed, or
- the environmental taxes in the rest of the world are not increased and the tariff stays in place.

If tariff causes home's large trading partner to increase its tax, the effect in home is

- decline in its terms of trade, and
- reduction in *x* output, and hence pollution.

Hence, if home has to abandon its tariff, we expect its environmental tax to decline since:

- producers of *x* with lobby power exercise downward, and
- home engages in eco-dumping to improve its terms of trade since it can no longer rely on the tariff for terms of trade improvement.

If home's trading partner are small countries, the conditional eco-tariff has the same effects as an unconditional eco-tariff; it will not be abandoned.

4 Conclusions

We have shown that if government is subject to regulatory capture by producers of *x*, all governments in small countries engage in eco-dumping to maximise an objective function biased towards the *x* industry. Governments in large countries exporting *x* have to weigh the negative terms of trade effect of reducing the tax against positive effects for *x* output.

Effects of regulatory capture on unbiased social welfare are negative apart from a few special constellations.

Availability of an eco-tariff relieves importing countries' governments from the pressure to engage in eco-dumping with positive environmental effects. Whether the tariff increases (unbiased) welfare compared with eco-dumping in small countries is not sure. Large countries profit from the availability of the eco-tariff while their trading partners - small or large - suffer.

Furthermore, eco-tariffs cannot avoid ERTB since only countries which import x can levy them.

We also considered conditional eco-tariffs for large countries since competitiveness effects stemming from internationally differing environmental standards drive eco-dumping and ERTB. Such conditional eco-tariffs, however, do not seem to be a suitable concept to avoid eco-dumping and ERTB. If applied against small countries, they do not trigger a change in their environmental policies; their effect is similar to an unconditional tariff. If applied against a large country, they would be effective in changing their environmental policy; yet, a large x-importing country has no incentive to implement a conditional eco-tariff because of the negative terms of trade effect it implies[26].

Therefore, our assessment of eco-tariffs if countries are subject to regulatory capture is negative. They can neither prevent ERTB nor raise welfare.

Furthermore, the fact that governments are subject to regulatory capture indicates that the reason for eco-dumping is policy failure rather than the fact that countries trade with each other. Consequently, changing GATT rules to allow eco-tariffs is likely to result in the protection of ailing industries, rather than environmental protection.

Hence, we note that eco-dumping and tariffs (if they were allowed) would serve the purpose of protecting an industry for which the country does not have a comparative advantage. Consequently, offering x-importing countries a tariff to alleviate protectionism should not be part of policy recommendations to improve global welfare.

[26] Furthermore, there is little reason to presume that an x exporting country would not implement an environmental tax since this tax has positive environmental and terms of trade effects.

Chapter 7

The Role of Tariffs in Protecting Global Environmental Commons

The aim of this chapter is to set out and discuss the theoretical considerations that led to the claim that successful combat of degradation of global environmental commons may require the use of trade instruments. Furthermore, we raise open issues regarding eco-tariffs to protect global environmental commons which shall be addressed in chapters 8, 9 and 10.

Trade theory suggests that in the presence of externalities that are not internalised, global free trade will not be Pareto optimal[1]. To tackle such externalities, however, trade restrictions are in general less suitable than instruments addressing the externality directly at its source[2]. Optimal policies to combat global pollution therefore prescribe emissions taxes or other efficient policy instruments[3]. However, optimal policies require international cooperation which is difficult to attain.

It has been claimed that in the absence of international environmental cooperation, domestic measures to safeguard the global environment should be supported by trade instruments. In this context, it has been shown that eco-tariffs serve to internalise cross-border environmental spill-overs arising from PPMs of an import good. If cooperation cannot be attained, such eco-tariffs are parts of a successful protection of the global environment.

1 See Srinivasan [1993, 23].

2 Pareto optimality of the trade equilibrium rests on a number of assumption, of which the absence of distortions such as (uninternalised) externalities is one. If the distortion is not corrected, the resulting equilibrium price will not reflect all social cost, and the allocation will thus not be optimal, see Bhagwati [1987/1971].

3 See Snape [1992, 76].

Furthermore, since international cooperation on global environmental issues is difficult to obtain, the use of trade measures has been proposed to alter payoffs to make environmental cooperation easier to achieve.

1. GLOBAL COOPERATION AND LEAKAGE EFFECT

In the context of protection of the global environmental commons, international cooperation plays a central role since only cooperation between all countries who share and pollute the environmental commons can yield a Pareto optimal outcome[4]. The reason is that efficient internalisation of a global externality requires a uniform emission tax to be charged across all affected countries[5].

However, international cooperation is difficult to attain for a number of reasons:

- Countries may differ with respect to their preferences for global environmental quality. If they do, they favour different levels of pollution abatement, hence, different tax rates or other pollution control instruments which may be in the way of a cooperative solution[6].
- Countries have, in general, different income levels; they therefore value environmental quality-related to consumption utility differently. Consequently, they favour different levels of pollution abatement and different tax rates which complicates cooperation[7].
- Countries may disagree with the cost they have to incur in a globally cooperative environmental regime. If countries feel that their share of the cost is disproportionate, they do not agree with a cooperative solution of which such cost allocation would be part[8].

[4] See GATT [1992, 34], compare also Simonis & Weizsäcker [1990, 40/41], and Zimmermann [1992].

[5] Harm done by global emissions have an identical impact, regardless of where they are emitted; therefore, a tax internalising the negative externality would have to be uniform across the globe; compare Baumol & Oates [1988, 279] and Siebert [1995a, ch.13].

[6] Compare Blackhurst & Subramanian [1992, 256], GATT [1992, 35], and Siebert [1995a, 199].

[7] Compare Siebert [1995a, 199].

[8] Compare Blackhurst & Subramanian [1992, 256], GATT [1992, 34/35]. A further reason for failure of a global environmental agreement is difference in risk attitude towards a particular environmental problem or a different interpretation of scientific evidence pointing towards such risks (compare Blackhurst & Subramanian [1992, 256], GATT [1992, 35], and Siebert [1995a, 199].

- The number of countries which may form a stable coalition for cooperation on global environmental issues may be too small to comprise a large enough share of the world's polluters[9].

If for these reasons cooperation does not come about, countries are left to individual, uncoordinated actions to protect the global environmental commons. An individual country's effort to abate spill-over pollution, however, is a contribution to a global public good[10]. Therefore, countries have an incentive to free-ride on efforts of others to reduce pollution; the consequence is underprovision of the global public good, i.e. no abatement at all or too little emission reduction[11].

Furthermore, even if countries unilaterally internalise spill-over pollution, they will not take into account damages accruing outside their borders and therefore internalise too little of the global externality[12].

Finally, if unilateral efforts to reduce global emissions are considerable, reactions in other countries may offset the positive environmental effect for two reasons:

- governments in the rest of the world reduce their own efforts to internalise spill-over pollution if marginal damage from pollution is increasing, and
- if curtailing of emissions caused by the PPM of a particular good triggers a price increase of that good, countries in the rest of the world will have an incentive to expand production which will lead to an increase in emissions.

This last effect has been coined **emission leakage**: In the context of cross-border spill-overs of pollution, national environmental policy has its limits since part of the environmental problem is caused by activities outside national boundaries/jurisdiction. Moreover, effectiveness of national environmental policy measures may be (partly) offset by international trade flows. If a (large) country taxes environmentally harmful PPMs, the result is a relative price increase for the good whose PPM pollutes the global environment. This price increase stimulates production in other countries where comparable environmental policy measures are not in place. As a consequence, pollution of the global environmental commons increases,

9 See Barrett [1994a&b].

10 All countries - respectively their citizens - benefit from reduced pollution; they cannot be excluded from these benefits and there is no rivalry in the 'consumption' of a cleaner global environment; compare Blackhurst & Subramanian [1992, 258].

11 See Carraro & Siniscalco [1992, 384] and Pethig [1983, 59].

12 Compare Carraro & Siniscalco [1992, 385].

causing a world-wide welfare loss. This so-called leakage effect is explained by the fact that two - not just one - externalities are present, namely the PPM pollution in the country engaging in environmental policy and the cross-border externality caused by foreign emissions. In such a situation, free-trade may not be optimal since not all externalities are internalised if some countries fail to institutionalise an appropriate environmental policy[13].

2. TRADE INSTRUMENTS AS SECOND BEST MEASURES

If cooperation is not forthcoming, one or several countries might choose to take unilateral or non-universal measures as a first step while still striving for complete cooperation[14]. Within such a non-universal regime, trade instruments have been proposed as efficient instruments for countries to internalise environmental spill-over externalities if the following conditions hold simultaneously[15]:

- Physical environmental spill-overs arise in the production of an imported good, and
- policies to internalise the environmental externalities in the exporting country do not take into account the harm they cause outside its borders, and
- it is not possible to correct the externality at the source in the exporting country because national environmental jurisdiction halts at the border.

Furthermore, trade measures may be efficient instruments for an exporting country if domestic measures to internalise global environmental externalities are undermined by relocation of polluting activities (leakage effect)[16].

Most of the discussion on trade measures for global environmental protection has concentrated on the role of trade measures as incentives to

[13] Compare Helm [1996, 221/2]. For a compilation of leakage rate estimates in various static and dynamic general equilibrium models see Barker & Johnstone [1998]. Leakage rates found in different studies vary greatly; most static general equilibrium models find leakage rates of less than 10%; however, one result is as high as 80% (see Barker & Johnstone [1998, 95]). Results in dynamic general equilibrium models vary even more, namely from negative leakage to marginal rates of almost 100%; the majority of the models, however, predicts leakage rates below 30% (see Barker & Johnstone [1998, 95-97]).

[14] See Weizsäcker & Welsch [1991], Klepper [1994].

[15] See Baumol & Oates [1988], Srinivasan [1993], Lloyd [1992], Koopmann [1995].

[16] See Barrett [1994a], Mæstad [1998].

enforce and maintain the first best global environmental cooperation. However, there are a few authors who address the subject of trade measures as second best instruments for internalising global environmental pollution.

This literature can be subsumed under the following categories:

- analysis of tariffs to internalise global pollution generated abroad (Baumol [1971], Markusen [1975], Rauscher [1991b]);
- investigation of tariffs to avoid emission leakage (Mæstad [1998], Hœl [1993]);
- Examination of welfare effects if there is strategic interaction in eco-tariffs (Baumol & Oates [1988, ch. 16], Ludema & Wooton [1994]).

TARIFFS TO INTERNALISE GLOBAL POLLUTION

Environmental tariffs in the role of cross border instruments to internalise global externalities have first been introduced by Baumol [1971]. He shows that in the presence of international pollution problems, the theoretical argument for free trade is weakened in so far as a suitable tariff may improve the allocation of the world's resources[17]. The effect of such an eco-tariff is an improvement in resource allocation and thus an increase in global welfare through a reduction of imports whose PPM harms the global environment. Furthermore, as long as the exporting country does not implement an appropriate policy to internalise the externality, the importing country's 'tax cum tariff' scheme is the global optimum. Yet, if the country charging the tariff uses the trade instrument to maximise its gains from trade in addition to internalising the cross border externality, allocation ceases to be globally optimal.

Markusen [1975] develops a formal model in which Baumol's results are formalised. He shows that in the case of unilateral tackling of a global externality, the optimum can be achieved by a production tax for the polluting good together with a trade tax and a system of lump sum transfers[18]. The tariff that maximises social welfare consists of two terms:

[17] He graphically analyses a two-country two-commodity case where production of one good causes trans-border pollution of the global environment. The two countries engage in trade. If the exporting country does not implement a pollution tax (or other suitable instrument), the importing country can reduce pollution by charging a domestic tax and a tariff to internalise the externality.

[18] He considers two economies, each producing and trading two commodities. Production of one good gives rise to global pollution, causing disutility for the population in both countries. The government in one of the countries ('home') is assumed to maximise social welfare by means of a tax structure. The tax

one is the optimal tariff that maximises a large country's benefits from international trade (hence the implicit assumption that the country is able to affect world prices and its terms of trade). It is positive if the good is imported and negative if it is exported[19]. The second component of the tariff results from the existence of the foreign pollution externality. It is positive regardless of whether the good is imported or exported. Thus, it will raise the import tariff if the good is imported and lower the export tax if it is exported. Furthermore, Markusen shows that if 'home's' regulatory options are constrained to 'taxes only', its welfare will be lower than in the 'tax cum tariff' scenario.

Rauscher [1991b] replicates Markusen's result in a Ricardo-Viner model for the case of asymmetric environmental policies in two countries[20]. For the case of global pollution, he finds that if both countries regulate emissions by means of a pollution tax, a tightening of one country's environmental policy causes a rise in emissions in the other country. If pollution intensity varies across countries, this may lead to an overall decrease in environmental quality. However, if the tax can be complemented by an unilateral tariff the tariff-setting country can attain a second best optimum whereby the tariff serves to improve the terms of trade and to internalise the spill-over externality.

ECO-TARIFFS TO AVOID EMISSION LEAKAGE

Mæstad [1998] analyses global welfare implications of trade policy instruments to counteract global pollution in a two-country partial equilibrium model[21]. Mæstad shows that global efficiency is enhanced if a

structure consists of taxes on production, consumption and trade, and lump sum redistributions. The other country's ('foreign') government does not levy any taxes, nor does it retaliate to any tax implemented at 'home'. Markusen solves for necessary conditions which must be satisfied by the tax structure maximising social welfare at 'home'.

19 The effect of a tariff levied by a large country is to increase the domestic price of the import good; the price of this good in the rest of the world, however, is reduced. This improves the terms of trade of the tariff-setting country. Furthermore, the price reduction in the rest of the world reduces production of the good whose PPM pollutes the global environmental and therefore emissions.

20 Rauscher [1991b] considers two countries using two factors of production (capital and an environmental resource) for the production of two goods that are internationally traded. In both countries, one sector uses the environment as fixed input factor, thereby causing pollution.

21 It is assumed that only one country ('home') takes regulatory measures and 'foreign' does not retaliate to 'home's' policy.

domestic environmental tax at the Pigouvian rate is combined with an environmental tariff with which the global externality is internalised and no gains of trade maximisation is pursued. Also, if domestic environmental policy is partly offset by an increase in (environmentally harmful) production abroad, this so-called emission leakage should also be addressed by means of a tariff rather than by reducing domestic environmental control. Finally, he shows that trade provisions in the form of tariffs form part of an efficient unilateral environmental policy even if 'home' cannot influence world prices.

Hoel [1993] pursues the leakage problem. He uses a two-country many-good model, where one of the goods ('fossil fuel') causes a global externality ('global warming') when consumed or used as an input for production of other goods. One country ('home') implements measures to counteract global warming. 'Foreign' does not react to 'home's' policy. Hœl shows that 'home's' social optimum can be achieved by a (uniform) carbon tax combined with a trade tax[22] (tariff or export subsidy, including both the environmental and the optimal tariff component). Hoel further shows that 'home's' social optimum can no longer be achieved with a uniform carbon tax if the use of tariffs is ruled out. Under these circumstances, carbon taxes will be differentiated across sectors to counteract the leakage effect whereby sectors with relatively high carbon emissions will be charged with lower taxes.

STRATEGIC INTERACTION IN ECO-TARIFFS

Baumol & Oates [1988, ch.16] extend the graphical analysis developed by Baumol [1971] to analyse interaction between two countries both implementing environmental tariffs and effects of such a policy for global welfare. Countries are assumed to internalise the pollution externality by a combination of an optimal tax and an environmental tariff. If countries implement tariffs to internalise international pollution, but not to maximise their gains from trade, global welfare will increase relative to the zero tariff situation. Yet, if both countries charge both the environmental tariff and a tariff to maximise their gains from trade, the outcome will be globally inferior to a zero tariff situation.

Strategic interaction is also analysed by Ludema & Wooton [1994] in a two-country partial equilibrium model with the simplifying feature that an externality generated in 'foreign' only affects 'home'. It is shown that

22 This trade tax, levied on the good whose PPM pollutes the global environment has two parts: an optimal tariff part (see above) with which a large country uses its market power to change the price level to improve its terms of trade.

internalisation of the externality will reinforce the optimal tariff motive for 'home' if 'foreign' does not implement environmental regulation. Furthermore, Ludema & Wooton show that trade liberalisation, i.e. prohibition of tariffs, may no longer increase welfare in both countries. However, both in the case of trade liberalisation and when tariffs are allowed, 'foreign' will have an incentive to regulate the environmental externality although it does not suffer from it: either to improve its terms of trade or to reduce the tariff charged by 'home'.

The following conclusions emerge from the above summarised literature: Large countries have an incentive to levy eco-tariffs with the following objectives (i) improve their terms of trade, (ii) internalise spill-over pollution, and (iii) avoid leakage.

Such policy is welfare-enhancing for the country that introduces the eco-tariff if there is no retaliation from its trading partners. In that case, positive global welfare effects are possible. If, however, strategic interaction is taken into consideration, welfare implications of eco-tariffs are less rosy.

3. TRADE INSTRUMENTS TO ACHIEVE GLOBAL COOPERATION

We have already stated that international cooperation is crucial for an efficient protection of global environmental commons. However, it is highly uncertain that such cooperation does in fact emerge. Thus, it has been suggested that trade measures may provide an incentive for cooperation in international efforts to protect global environmental commons[23]. If relative pay-offs from cooperation and non-cooperation can be altered such that every country has an incentive to cooperate by complying with the provisions of an universal environmental agreement, a Pareto optimal solution can be achieved and sustained.

Trade sanctions against non-members and members that do not fulfil an agreement to protect the global commons serve as a negative incentive to join and obey a multilateral environmental agreement. However, there are a number of caveats against the use of trade sanctions to further international environmental cooperation.

- Mohr [1991] and Kirchgässner & Mohr [1995] draw attention to the history of the international debt crisis and conclude that trade sanctions have been poor instruments to instigate cooperation.
- A further argument against the use of trade sanctions is that if the threat is not sufficient to induce participation, it has to be carried out. If they

[23] See for example Baumol & Oates [1988], Subramanian [1992].

come to bear, however, trade sanctions not only reduce the welfare of the non-cooperating countries, but also efficiency of resource allocation and thus welfare of the cooperating countries, which of course puts into question the credibility of trade sanctions. Thus, other sanctions such as reduction in financial aid could be envisaged which would not lead to allocative distortions if they have to be carried out.[24]

- Moreover, it has been suggested that positive incentives to promote international cooperation such as compensation payments may be more promising than negative ones[25].

These arguments against the threat of trade sanctions to induce cooperation are to a certain extent shared even by their proponents[26]. Hence, the use of trade measures mentioned above is often confined to goods with negative environmental impact, such as goods whose PPM harms the global environment.

Applying trade restrictions on goods produced in or exported to countries that do not cooperate on global environmental issues then fulfils a double function in the sense that an incentive is created to implement appropriate environmental domestic measures and - if this does not work - at least production of the environmentally hazardous good is reduced. This two-fold purpose of eco-tariffs has been discussed by Barrett [1994a], Baumol & Oates [1988, ch.16], Bhagwati [1993b], Blackhurst & Subramanian [1992], Feketekuty [1993], and Subramanian [1992].

Barrett [1994a], discusses trade restrictions in the context of a global environmental problem (global warming). His results are that eco-tariffs can serve a double function, namely reducing emission leakage from countries who do not participate in international efforts to mitigate the global problem, and proving an incentive to actually implement environmental measures to address the problem[27].

24 See Subramanian [1992, 149]; also Barrett [1994a, 31].

25 Blackhurst & Subramanian [1992, 262] state:..."*most analysts with practical experience in promoting international cooperation have a clear preference for relying on positive incentives rather than sanctions whenever the necessary level of cooperation is not voluntarily forthcoming.*" Compare also Subramanian [1992, 139&146]. Advantages of positive sanctions are mostly psychological. However, they also have disadvantages, namely the problem that positive sanctions may induce opportunistic behaviour to obtain these sanctions.

26 For example, none of the existing multilateral environmental agreements contains provisions for trade sanctions, if sanctions are interpreted to apply to unrelated products (see Blackhurst & Subramanian [1992, 262]).

27 Barrett [1994b] formulates a partial equilibrium model to analyse trade restrictions in the sole function to bring about and sustain international cooperation to safeguard global environmental commons.

Baumol & Oates [1988, ch.16] consider eco-tariffs

> *"both in the role normally assigned to taxes in the externalities literature, and as part of a threat strategy designed to induce the generator of transnational pollution to modify his behavior."*

Owing to the fact that international environmental cooperation is difficult to attain, they consider such instruments necessary. They state that eco-tariffs should be widely used to become effective means to protect global environmental commons. Furthermore, an incidental and positive effect may also be that a wide use of (or threat to use) such eco-tariffs may facilitate cooperation[28]. Feketekuty [1993] takes a similar position[29].

Blackhurst & Subramanian [1992] discuss trade restrictions to promote multilateral efforts and cooperation for global environmental protection. They conclude that sanctions[30] are not a desirable or effective means to attain this objective. However, they view eco-tariffs on products causing the environmental problem somewhat more favourably. Such eco-tariffs provide an incentive to implement environmental measures and to prevent countries who do not take such measures from undermining efforts of others[31]. Similar arguments are advanced by Subramanian [1992] and Bhagwati [1993b][32].

[28] Baumol & Oates [1988, 277/8] state very clearly: "*Thus, the notion of transnational resources charges* [i.e. eco-tariffs] *may help in one of two ways: either as a threat that helps to stimulate effective cooperation, or by serving as an instrument of second resort in the event some countries, by refusing cooperation, continue to pose a threat to health and welfare in other nations.*"

[29] Feketekuty [1993, 194] finds that "*Trade measures are also sometimes used ...... to prevent the relocation of environmentally-damaging practices to non-signatory countries,...*" Feketekuty identifies an additional positive effect of trade measures, namely the solution of the free-rider problem by preventing non-cooperating countries from obtaining environmental benefits without contributing to emission reductions.

[30] Sanctions are not only seen as trade restrictions on all sorts of im- or exports but in a wider sense also as suspension of cooperation on other issues, or restrictions on financial transactions (Blackhurst & Subramanian [1992, 261]).

[31] Blackurst & Subramanian [1992, 262]: "*Generally speaking, the primary purpose of trade provisions is to prevent developments in the trade of* [non-cooperative countries] *from undermining the effectiveness of* [other countries' actions]. *But in most instances, the trade provisions have the incidental effect of treating participants more favourably than non-participants. ....., therefore, the trade provisions create a positive incentive to join the agreement...*".

[32] Bhagwati [1993b, 188]: "*I should imagine that the possibility of (second-best) remedial action* [i.e. eco-tariffs]..... *may even encourage the offending party to adopt appropriate (first-best) remedial action* [i.e. taxing pollution] *within its own jurisdiction to restrict the emission of cross-border pollution.*"

Conclusions from the literature summarised are that

- eco-tariffs applied against countries with no protective measures in place to safeguard the global environment are useful for two reasons, namely internalisation of spill-over externalities, and/or avoidance of leakage, and as incentive to introduce environmental policy; however,
- that such negative incentives may not be effective in changing behaviour because of their psychological effects.

4. DISCUSSION AND OPEN ISSUES

The literature presented above establishes that unilateral environmental trade measures are optimal policy instruments to internalise global externalities if international cooperation is not forthcoming. Trade instruments improve welfare in the country implementing the measure through pollution reduction and terms of trade improvement.

However, we find the theoretical contexts in which such results have been developed too restricted to support the conclusion that eco-tariffs should be implemented. In this context, we consider the absence of policy interaction between governments as the most important shortcoming of the modelling approaches[33].

To answer the question whether trade measures should be part of environmental policies for a country wishing to counteract global pollution thus requires a more realistic framework, in which the assumption of non-retaliation should be relaxed..

Furthermore, it has been suggested that the second best tariffs discussed above may have the incidental effect of serving as an incentive to implement control measures for pollution of the global environmental commons for countries at which such trade measures are addressed. A further investigation of this effect may add valuable insights to judge the suitability of pollution tariffs as environmental policy instruments.

33 The optimal tariff literature is a good example for the fact that relying on an analysis that excludes retaliation may well result in fallacious conclusions: A country large enough to improve its terms of trade by charging a tariff on imports (or levying a tax on exports) can maximise its welfare by charging optimal import tariffs and export taxes. Yet, the welfare improvement of the optimal unilateral trade policy vanishes as soon as the other country can respond to it. Krugman & Obstfeld [1997, 226] therefore conclude that the optimal tariff argument has little relevance for actual trade policy-making.

WELFARE EFFECTS OF ECO-TARIFFS WITH POLICY INTERACTION

If we relax the assumption of non-retaliation to eco-tariffs, further insight is gained into (global) welfare effects of such eco-tariffs. If the availability of the second policy instrument has positive welfare effects, eco-tariffs should be pursued when global cooperation for environmental protection is not forthcoming.

Inspection of the welfare-maximising tariff reveals that the tariff levied on the good that causes global pollution can be disentangled into an 'environmental' and an 'optimal tariff' component which serve different policy objectives:

- **environmental component**: part of environmental policy, corrects for allocative inefficiency caused by the environmental externality;
- **optimal tariff component**: part of trade policy, introduces allocative distortions to exploit a country's market power, improves terms of trade, and increases benefits from international trade.

If both countries implement tariffs, we expect two effects:

- global welfare **increases** as a result of the environmental component, yet
- global welfare effects resulting from the optimal tariff component are indeterminate since the tariff increases welfare for the country levying the tariff while its trading partners terms of trade decline[34].

In this study, we attempt an analysis of these eco-tariffs in our Heckscher-Ohlin-Samuelson framework which should indicate global welfare effects of eco-tariffs which will serve as an argument in favour (or against) recommending a change in multilateral trade rules to sanction tariffs[35].

[34] In an optimal tariff game, one country's optimal tariff negatively affects the terms of trade for its trading partner. The optimal tariff is thus an externality since its effect upon the other country's welfare is not taken into account. If both countries charge optimal tariffs, the reciprocal externalities cause a decrease in global welfare, although it is possible that one country still gains. The situation is similar to a Cournot duopoly where firms also cause each other negative externalities (Tirole [1988, 219]).

[35] We should note that positive global welfare consequences are a definite argument in favour of eco-tariffs. However, if the welfare effects are indeterminate, this should not lead to the conclusion that eco-tariffs are not to be recommended. The case one could make for them would only be weakened.

INCENTIVE EFFECT OF ENVIRONMENTAL TARIFFS

As mentioned above, a number of authors draw attention to the fact that eco-trade measures may have a positive side effect: if eco-tariffs are implemented to internalise cross-border externalities and to avoid leakage, they may also serve incidentally as incentives to implement environmental policies for countries whose products are subject to such tariffs. However, since the models analysing tariffs as second best instruments accompanying taxes focus on unilateral welfare maximisation, this issue has not received much attention so far[36].

The idea underlying the role of tariffs as incentive instruments runs as follows: if eco-tariffs are levied, countries subject to such duties find that implementing environmental policies serves to promote exports if the eco-tariff is conditional, i.e. if it is levied against imports from countries where no environmental policy measures are in place.

In this study, we attempt an analysis of incentive effects in our Heckscher-Ohlin-Samuelson framework[37]. Contributions regarding the incentive effects state beneficial effects of eco-tariffs only verbally. We consider it therefore worthwhile to undertake a more formal analysis.

If indeed such tariffs may be suitable to alter the pay-off of alternative policy options for countries that hitherto had no incentive to control spill-over emissions, the case for tariffs as second best environmental instruments would be reinforced.

5. SUMMARY AND CONCLUSIONS

Our discussion of the role of global cooperation showed that although global cooperation is necessary to reach a Pareto optimum in the presence of a global environmental externality, such cooperation is difficult to attain. As a consequence, unilateral environmental policy addressing a global

36 One exception are Baumol & Oates [1988, 276] who discuss "*tariffs both in the role normally assigned to taxes in the externality literature* [tariffs as cross-border Pigouvian taxes], *and as part of a threat strategy designed to induce the generator of trans-national pollution to modify its behaviour*". Furthermore, Ludema & Wooton's [1994] analysis shows that even in the absence of environmental benefits for the country taking the measure, strategic considerations serve as an incentive to control trans-border pollution.

37 Owing to the caveats against using unfocussed trade sanctions to discipline countries into obeyance of an international environmental agreement, we shall not address what has been termed 'issue linkage', i.e. the connection of general trade relations and environmental policy implementation. For a discussion of the potential of linking trade relations to policy measures addressing global environmental problems see Krumm [1996, ch. 8] and Bodecker [1997, ch. 5].

externality will be too lax because of free-riding, the neglect of welfare effects for the rest of the world, and leakage.

Our survey of the role of tariffs as second best instruments to internalise spill-over externalities and to avoid leakage showed that they are indeed optimal in the absence of international cooperation by preventing leakage.

Our survey of trade instruments used as sanctions showed that by altering the relative payoffs between cooperation and non-cooperation, trade restrictions serve to facilitate international cooperation to safeguard the global environmental commons. As a caveat, however, we found that historically, sanctions have performed rather poorly to pressurise countries into compliance with international rules[38].

Therefore, we find eco-tariffs considered in these contexts should not be implemented with a view to punish countries where no or little pollution control is in place. Rather, such tariffs are levied as an incentive to cooperate on global environmental issues and to complement domestic efforts to reduce emissions.

Our discussion of possible effects of the availability of eco-tariffs as policy instruments when pollution spills across borders and harms the global environmental commons shows that it is not clear whether such tariffs have indeed the intended effect. As regards the incentive effects of eco-tariffs, it still needs to be determined whether they bring about increased environmental protection. Furthermore, if governments pursue other than environmental goals, i.e. terms of trade improvement, or protection of a particular industry either for a strategic reasons or because they are subject to regulatory capture, such eco-tariffs may easily be abused. Hence, it should be determined whether welfare is indeed likely to rise if tariffs are levied not only for environmental reasons.

Finally, a formal analysis of incentive effects of eco-tariffs should be undertaken to determine whether indeed eco-tariffs or conditional eco-tariffs serve to alter incentives to internalise spill-over pollution such that former non-cooperating countries would take appropriate measures.

Chapters 9 and 10 take up these issues. Chapter 8 introduces modification of the Heckscher-Ohlin-Samuelson model from chapter 3 necessary to analyse aspects of international trade and global environmental pollution.

[38] However, a successful example exists with the Montreal Protocol which employs trade instruments with the twin aim of bringing countries to cooperate on global environmental issues while at the same time serving to avoid leakage of measures undertaken to reduce emissions.

Chapter 8

An International Trade Model with Spill-over Pollution

To lay the ground for our investigation of the role of tariffs in environmental protection when pollution caused by PPMs spills across borders, this chapter introduces a Heckscher-Ohlin-Samuelson model with which these issues can be addressed. Furthermore, we determine and compare nationally and globally optimal environmental policies.

1. SPILL-OVER POLLUTION

Virtually the complete set up laid out in chapter 3 valid with the exception of the definition of welfare within our economies.

Welfare, w, of society still consists of consumption utility, u, and pollution disutility, v, which are additively separable. However, emissions affecting welfare are now those generated abroad in addition to those generated domestically.

Assumptions regarding smoke generation do not change, i.e. domestic smoke is generated by capital employed in the x sector according to the linear relationship (3-5). Foreign smoke S is generated in the same way, i.e. by capital input in the x sector abroad. We assume now that smoke harms welfare everywhere, independently of the geographic location of the source of emissions. Hence, environmental externalities are global[1] and the welfare function (3-6) becomes

[1] Global environmental externalities are a special case of pollution that spills across borders. Often, the harm done to the global environmental commons is aggravated by local environmental harm or else not all pollution generated across the world equally harms a particular nation's population.

$$w = u(c^x, c^y) - v(s+S) \qquad (8\text{-}1)$$

Assumptions regarding u do not change; v is increasing in smoke (both domestic and foreign) and strictly convex. We assume that the externality is now global in nature, i.e. there is no difference between domestic and foreign smoke regarding its negative welfare effect:

$$v', v'' > 0,$$

Again we assume that the economy under consideration engages in international trade. With the relative price $p=p^y/p^x$, the welfare function (3-11) reads

$$w = u(f(k^x, l^x) + ph(k-k^x, l-l^x) - pc^y, c^y) - v(k^x+K^X) \qquad (8\text{-}2)$$

The FOCs resulting from profit-maximising producers and utility-maximising consumers in the absence of environmental regulation are still given by:

$$f_k - ph_k = 0 \qquad (3\text{-}12)$$

$$f_l - ph_l = 0 \qquad (3\text{-}13)$$

$$u_y - pu_x = 0 \qquad (3\text{-}14)$$

2. ENVIRONMENTAL POLICY IN THE PRESENCE OF SPILL-OVER POLLUTION

If environmental problems are no longer locally contained, environmental policy outside a country's borders directly affects welfare of domestic citizens. If countries follow a national environmental policy, they do not take into consideration effects of their actions accruing outside their borders by definition. We derive optimal environmental policies for non-cooperating, national welfare-maximising governments.

International cooperation with regard to environmental policies on the other hand is defined as a set of environmental taxes with which cooperating governments maximise global welfare. In that case, effects of policies for welfare abroad is taken into account.

In chapter 4 we have discussed how environmental policy in one country affects environmental policies elsewhere if pollution is locally contained. We elaborate how these effects change if pollution spills across borders.

Finally, we summarise reasons for underregulation of global environmental pollution.

OPTIMAL NATIONAL ENVIRONMENTAL POLICY

If a small country sets its environmental tax individually, the tax is derived by differentiating (8-2) w.r.t. g. This yields again the following FOC instead of (3-12):

$$f_k - (v'/u_x) - ph_k = 0 \tag{3-12'}$$

We observe that this result is formally identical to the optimal tax if environmental pollution is locally contained[2]; therefore, g is given by

$$g = v'/u_x \tag{3-16}$$

If a large country sets its environmental tax independently of others, the result is given by differentiating (8-2) w.r.t. g. The tax is found by solving

$$\frac{dw}{dg} = \left[u_x(f_k - ph_k) - v'\right]\frac{dk^x}{dg} + \left[u_x(h - c^y)\right]\frac{dp}{dg} + v'\frac{dK^X}{dg} \overset{!}{=} 0 \tag{8-3}$$

which yields

$$g = \frac{v'}{u_x} + \left(c^y - h\right)\frac{dp}{dg}\frac{dg}{dk^x} + \left(\frac{v'}{u_x}\right)\frac{dK^X}{dg}\frac{dg}{dk^x} \tag{8-4}$$

We observe that the tax for a large country when pollution harms the global environmental commons consists of three parts:

- which the domestically generated externality is internalised,
- $(c^y - h)(dp/dg)(dg/dk^x)$ with which the terms of trade effect is taken into account, and
- $(v'/u_x)\,(dK^X/dg)(dg/dk^x)$ with which the externality generated abroad is internalised.

[2] Compare chapter 3, equation (3-16). A discussion of differences between the optimality of $g = v'/u_x$ for domestic and spill-over pollution follows in below.

The first term in (8-4) is the domestic Pigouvian tax.

Terms of trade considerations are captured in the second term which is positive (negative) if x is imported (exported). Hence, these terms of trade considerations reduce the tax below the Pigouvian level if the good is imported. If the good is exported, terms of trade effects cause an increase of the tax.

Leakage effect: The effect of the trans-national pollution is captured in the third term, which is negative. Hence, the presence of spill-over pollution aggravates eco-dumping[3] if x is imported; it counteracts a NIMBY policy if x is exported. The tax reduction serves to internalise the cross-border externality. This works as follows: The tax implemented at home reduces production and therefore world-wide supply of x. As a result, its price increases and stimulates production and therefore harmful pollution abroad. This is the above-mentioned emission leakage: Emission reduction achieved in home by taxing capital input in the x sector is partly offset by production expansion elsewhere. A tax reduction has the opposite effect, i.e. it reduces the price of x to which the rest of the world reacts by curtailing supply and therefore harmful emissions.

We can further illustrate the leakage effect by scrutinising the environmental effect of the domestic tax:

$$\frac{dv}{dg} = v'\left[\left(\frac{dk^x}{dg}\right)+\left(\frac{dK^X}{dp}\right)\left(\frac{dp}{dg}\right)\right] \tag{8-5}$$

The first term in (8-5) is the direct effect of the tax on domestic emissions. Emission reduction alleviates environmental damage incurred by the population at home. However, the second term indicates that the indirect (price) effect of the tax reduces its environmental benefit by increasing emissions abroad. If production in the rest of the world generates much more emissions than the domestic PPM, the net effect of the tax may even be environmentally harmful. However, for the remainder of our arguments we shall generally assume that leakage - although positive - is below 100%.

[3] We still define eco-dumping as charging a tax below the domestic Pigouvian level v'/u_x.

GLOBALLY OPTIMAL ENVIRONMENTAL POLICY

As mentioned in chapter 7, internalisation of externalities polluting the global environmental commons requires cooperation between all countries who cause (and suffer from) such pollution[4].

Optimal environmental policy in the presence of spill-over pollution is determined by maximising a joint welfare function, denoted by w^J. We assume that cooperation is universal, i.e. that w^J comprises welfare of all countries. We furthermore assume that all these countries also partake in trade. In our notation, the entirety of the trading world is home and the rest of the world. w^J is hence given by

$$w^J = u(f(k^x,l^x)+ph(k-k^x,l-l^x)-pc^y,c^y) - v(k^x+K^X) +$$
$$U(F(K^X,L^X)+pH(K-K^X,L-L^X),pC^Y,C^Y) - V(k^x+K^X) \qquad (8\text{-}6)$$

w^J is maximised by the cooperative environmental tax g^J in home and the cooperative environmental taxes G^J in rest of the world by differentiating (8-6) w.r.t. g^J and G^J:

$$\frac{dw^J}{dg^J} = [u_x(f_k - ph_k) - v' - V']\frac{dk^x}{dg^J} + [u_x(h - c^y) + U_x(H - C^Y)]\frac{dp}{dg^J} +$$
$$[u_x(f_k - ph_k) - v' - V']\frac{dK^x}{dg^J} \stackrel{!}{=} 0 \qquad (8\text{-}7)$$

$$\frac{dw^J}{dG^J} = [u_x(f_k - ph_k) - v' - V']\frac{dk^x}{dG^J} + [u_x(h - c^y) + U_x(H - C^Y)]\frac{dp}{dG^J} +$$
$$[u_x(f_k - ph_k) - v' - V']\frac{dK^x}{dG^J} \stackrel{!}{=} 0 \qquad (8\text{-}8)[5]$$

If home and the countries making up the rest of the world are all small, (dp/dg^J), (dK^x/dg^J), (dp/dG^J), and (dk^x/dG^J) are all zero. Therefore, (8-7) and (8-8) simplify to

4 This becomes clear if we inspect the welfare function (8-2). Since welfare in home depends directly upon actions, i.e. capital allocation, in the rest of the world and therefore also upon their environmental policy, a globally optimal environmental policy in each country requires that welfare effects in all nations are taken into consideration when governments set their environmental policies.

5 In both (8-7) and (8-8) we neglected terms which become zero upon substituting FOCs.

$$\frac{dw^J}{dg^J} = \left[u_x(f_k - ph_k) - v' - V'\right]\frac{dk^x}{dg^J} \overset{!}{=} 0 \tag{8-7'}$$

$$\frac{dw^J}{dG^J} = \left[u_x(f_k - ph_k) - v' - V'\right]\frac{dK^x}{dG^J} \overset{!}{=} 0 \tag{8-8'}$$

The environmental taxes for small countries who cooperate to address global environmental problems are thus given by

$$g^J = \frac{v'}{u_x} + \frac{V'}{u_x} \tag{8-9a}$$

$$G^J = \frac{v'}{U_X} + \frac{V'}{U_X} \tag{8-9b}$$

We observe

- that g^J and G^J are higher than the nationally optimal taxes;
- if $v' = V'$ the taxes which maximise the joint welfare function (8-6) are exactly twice the value of the nationally optimal ones;
- assuming that u and U are similar - i.e. that home and the rest of the world value consumption equally, the relative values of (8-9a&b) depend on the relative wealth - or economic power - of home and the rest of the world. The wealthier a country, the lower the value of u_x and U_X. Therefore, if home is wealthier than the average of the countries making up the rest of the world, ($u_x < U_X$) and (8-9a) > (8-9b). If the rest of the world has on average more economic power than home, the opposite applies, i.e. (8-9a) < (8-9b).

If home is large and the rest of the world is made up by small countries[6], the environmental taxes in home and countries in the rest of the world are given by

[6] By definition, environmental policy choice in small countries does not affect the world price level.

$$g^J = \frac{v'}{u_x} + \frac{V'}{u_x} + \left[(c^y - h) + \frac{U_X}{u_x}(C^Y - H)\right] \frac{dp}{dg^J} \Big/ \frac{dk^x}{dg^J} \qquad \text{(8-9a')}$$

$$G^J = \frac{v'}{U_X} + \frac{V'}{U_X} \qquad \text{(8-9b)}$$

While the environmental tax G^J in the rest of the world is identical with the one given above when all countries are small, home's tax is augmented by the third term in (B.2-9a'). To determine the sign of the third term in (8-9a'), we note that $(dp/dg^J) < 0$, $(dk^x/dg^J) < 0$. Furthermore, the balanced trade condition

$$(c^y\text{-}h) + (C^Y\text{-}H) = 0 \qquad \text{(8-10)}$$

is satisfied since the entire trading world is comprised by home and the rest of the world. Therefore, the sign of the third term in (8-9a') is governed by the sign of (U_X/u_x) and the relative capital or labour abundance of home, and the rest of the world.

We find:

- The fact that home is large and faces small countries in the rest of the world augments home's tax if home is capital abundant and relatively wealthy; or labour abundant and relatively poor.
- Home's tax is reduced by its size if home is capital abundant and relatively poor; or labour abundant and relatively wealthy.

The tax increasing or reducing effect of the third term in (8-9a') is driven by the relative wealth of home and the rest of the world. If home is the relatively wealthy part of the world, it increases or reduces its tax to improve the rest of the world's terms of trade[7]. Otherwise, home increases or reduces its tax to improve its own terms of trade.

If home is large and the rest of the world consists of a single large country (foreign) the environmental taxes in home (g^J) and foreign (G^J) are given by

[7] We recall that the taxes are set to maximise global welfare.

$$g^J = \frac{v'}{u_x} + \frac{V'}{u_x} + \left[\left(h - c^y\right) + \frac{U_X}{u_x}(H - C^Y) \right] \frac{\left[\left(\dfrac{dp}{dG^J} \Big/ \dfrac{dK^X}{dG^J} \right) - \left(\dfrac{dp}{dg^J} \Big/ \dfrac{dK^X}{dg^J} \right) \right]}{\left[\left(\dfrac{dk^x}{dg^J} \Big/ \dfrac{dK^X}{dg^J} \right) - \left(\dfrac{dk^x}{dG^J} \Big/ \dfrac{dK^X}{dG^J} \right) \right]}$$

(8-9'')

$$G^J = \frac{v'}{U_x} + \frac{V'}{U_x} + \left[\frac{u_x}{U_X}\left(c^y - h\right) + (C^Y - H) \right] \frac{\left[\left(\dfrac{dp}{dG^J} \Big/ \dfrac{dk^X}{dG^J} \right) - \left(\dfrac{dp}{dg^J} \Big/ \dfrac{dk^X}{dg^J} \right) \right]}{\left[\left(\dfrac{dK^x}{dg^J} \Big/ \dfrac{dk^X}{dg^J} \right) - \left(\dfrac{dK^x}{dG^J} \Big/ \dfrac{dk^X}{dG^J} \right) \right]}$$

(8-9b')

The sign of the third terms in (8-9a''&9b') depends on two aspects

- the capital or labour abundance of home and foreign (governing (c^y-h) and (C^Y-H)); and
- the relative wealth of home and foreign, governing (u_x/U_X) and (U_X/u_x)).

The large country effect which comprises the terms of trade and leakage effect in the third terms in (8-9a'&9b') increases the tax g^J in home beyond (8-9a) if

- home is capital abundant and relatively rich; or
- home is labour abundant and relatively poor.

If these conditions apply, the tax in foreign G^J is reduced below the level of (8-9b) by the large country effects. For the other two constellations, i.e.

- home is capital abundant and relatively rich; or
- home is labour abundant and relatively poor

we observe that the effects driving the tax up or down if both home and the rest of the world large countries are the same as in the case when only home was large.

The reason for the tax-increasing or tax-reducing effect of the third terms in (8-9a'') and (8-9b') is the same we have given above for the tax-modifying effect of the tax, if a large home country faces small countries in the rest of the world.

In chapter 7 we developed that Pareto optimality in the presence of a global externality requires a uniform emission tax. However, inspecting (8-9a&b) and (8-9a''&b'), we observe that g^J and G^J are only uniform if

$$u_x = U_X \tag{8-11}$$

a condition which is satisfied with probability zero.

If (8-11) is not satisfied, maximisation of (8-6) with taxes as sole policy instruments is dominated by a combination of two instruments, namely taxes and a lump sum transfer which would yield the uniform taxes

$$g^J = G^J = \frac{v'}{u_x} + \frac{V'}{U_X} \tag{8-9c}$$

The lump sum transfer paid by the country (or countries) whose taxes were higher without the transfer results in a reduction of their taxes by increasing the marginal consumption utility. Taxes in the receiving part of the world are increases as marginal consumption utility declines with the transfer. We note that (8-9c) applies equally to small and large countries with the balanced trade condition (8-10). and the equalisation of the marginal consumption utility terms eliminates the third terms in (8-9a''&b'). Therefore, the transfer makes the condition (8-11) hold.

INTERDEPENDENCE OF ENVIRONMENTAL TAXES

Environmental policy in a large country affects environmental policy elsewhere through its effect on the price level. If pollution is domestically contained, such interdependence is driven by the terms of trade effect of environmental policy; if pollution crosses borders, the consequences of environmental policy for environmental pollution and for terms of trade play a role.

To compare the **interdependence of environmental taxes** internalising spill-over pollution with cross effects of environmental taxes for **local**

pollution, we first derive comparative statics for home's environmental tax g if the environmental policy in the rest of the world, i.e. G, changes. We find:

$$\frac{dg}{dG} \lesseqgtr 0 \tag{8-12}$$

A closer inspection of (8-12) shows the tax-increasing and tax-reducing effects

$$\frac{dg}{dG} = \frac{d(v'/u_x)}{dG} = \frac{(dv'/dG)u_x - (du_x/dG)v'}{u_x^2} = \left(v''u_x - u_{xx}gv'\right)\frac{dk^x}{dp}\frac{dp}{dG} +$$

$$u_{xx}v'(c^y - h)\frac{dp}{dG} - \left(u_{xy} - pu_{xx}\right)v'\frac{dc^y}{dp}\frac{dp}{dG} \tag{8-12'}$$

We observe that in (8-12') that

- the first term is positive
- the second term is positive if $(c^y - h) > 0$; i.e. home exports x and negative if $(c^y - h) < 0$; i.e. home imports x.
- the third term is negative

The following economic forces are at play:

- The first term picks up the fact that increased scarcity of x owing to the tax increase in the rest of the world drives up its relative price. This stimulates production of x and environmental pollution therewith. The latter drives the environmental tax g upwards.
- The second term picks up the terms of trade effect of g. It drives g up if home exports x; if x is imported, the terms of trade effect reduces the tax.
- The third term picks up the fact that the relative price increase for x stimulates consumption substitution towards y. This reduces the environmental tax g.

Therefore, the sign of (8-12) depends on the relative strength of the production and consumption substitution elasticity. If the rest of the world increases the environmental tax G, a similar reaction in home is more likely if home is capital abundant.

INTERDEPENDENCE OF ENVIRONMENTAL TAXES IF POLLUTION SPILLS ACROSS BORDERS

We now analyse interdependence of environmental taxes if pollution spills across borders. The effect for home's environmental tax if the rest of the world increases its efforts to curb globally harmful emissions is indetermined.

$$\frac{dg}{dG} \lessgtr 0 \tag{8-13}$$

A closer inspection of (8-13) reveals that spill-over pollution adds a fourth term:

$$\frac{dg}{dG} = \frac{d(v'/u_x)}{dG} = \frac{(dv'/dG)u_x - (du_x/dG)v'}{u_x^2} = \left(v''u_x - u_{xx}gv'\right)\frac{dk^x}{dp}\frac{dp}{dG} +$$
$$u_{xx}v'(c^y - h)\frac{dp}{dG} - \left(u_{xy} - pu_{xx}\right)v'\frac{dc^y}{dp}\frac{dp}{dG} + v''\left(\frac{dK^X}{dp}\frac{dp}{dG} + \frac{dK^X}{dG}\right) \tag{8-13'}$$

We observe that in (8-13')

- the first three terms are identical to those for local pollution in (8-12'); and
- the fourth term is negative.

The fourth term in (8-13') picks up the emission leakage effect. Emission increase in the rest of the world which follows from a tax increase in home drives *g* downwards.

Therefore, it is less likely that abatement efforts undertaken abroad trigger a similar reaction in home if emissions pollute the global environmental commons. Furthermore, if such measures are undertaken by countries who have little incentive to do so, i.e. countries importing *x* which have a terms of trade motive to actually reduce their tax, abatement efforts are more likely to be reinforced by their trading partners. If countries exporting *x* on the other hand increase their taxes, the effectiveness of the sought protection of the global environmental commons is reduced by two channels, namely

- the leakage effect discussed above, and
- the tax-reducing effect isolated in (8-13) above which is part of the 'free-riding' phenomenon.

Therefore, if some countries try to increase their (globally) suboptimal tax level towards the optimum (8-9c), the reaction of their trading partners is likely to be a downward move of their tax.

A problem often mentioned in the context of global environmental pollution is **free-riding**. Since protection of global environmental commons is a global public good from which all countries benefit, contributors to the problem have an incentive to rely on efforts of others to curb emissions. Just as free-riding is a source of underprovision of public goods, it causes suboptimal internalisation of a global externality.

We have already isolated two other sources of under-regulation, namely

- that countries do not take into account environmental benefit for other countries when they set individually optimal environmental policies, and
- that they reduce environmental regulation to avoid emission leakage

Furthermore, we found in the last section that free-riding causes emission abatement reduction if other countries increase their efforts to internalise the global externality.

Finally, we return to the tax formula to isolate a last source of too lax environmental policy in the presence of spill-over pollution. The tax for a small, national welfare-maximising country is given by ($g = v' / u_x$). We have already noted that it corresponds to the Pigouvian tax for local pollution given by (3-12). However, we have also noted that the global externality is caused by the sum of all capital used for the production of x .Therefore, a small country's abatement efforts will also not yield a noticeable benefit for the global environmental commons which may induce the government of a small country to neglect its part in alleviating the problem. In the extreme, small countries may therefore refrain altogether from internalising their part of globally harmful emissions.

We summarise our results with:

Proposition 8: *Spill-over pollution reduces the optimal national tax for large countries. If countries cooperate w.r.t. their environmental policies, they charge a tax higher than the Pigouvian level. However, if some countries increase their tax(es), their trading partners are likely to reduce theirs, thereby offsetting the beneficial effect for the global environmental commons from the higher taxes; reasons are the leakage effect and free-riding.*

(a) The tax for a small country when it maximises its social welfare-neglecting pollution effects in the rest of the world is the same regardless of the geographic dimension of pollution. In large countries, foreign pollution and terms of trade considerations cause the tax to be reduced below the Pigouvian level; if the good is exported, the effect of spill-over pollution counteracts the terms of trade effect.

(b) The globally optimal tax is above the domestic Pigouvian level regardless of a country's size.

(c) The interdependence between environmental taxes addressing global pollution in different countries for global pollution consists of two elements:

the terms of trade effect and the cross-border effect of pollution. The latter causes countries to free ride on abatement efforts of others.

3. CONCLUSIONS

The preceding sections showed that implications for optimal environmental policies from spill-over pollution are considerable. Since nationally rational policies no longer ensure optimal factor allocation, cooperation on environmental issues between countries becomes necessary, if protection of the global environmental commons is to be efficient. As pointed out in chapter 7, such cooperation is hard to achieve since countries try to free-ride on emission reduction efforts undertaken by others. The result is underregulation of the global environmental externality which is exacerbated by the leakage effect which reduces environmental taxes in large countries and by the fact that tax increases undertaken in large countries prompt tax reductions elsewhere.

If one or several large countries dominate the trading world, their trade policy decisions can affect resource allocation in two different ways. First, tariffs influence the pattern of excess demand and hence the relative price level, outputs and therefore emissions in the usual way. Second, tariff policy can serve as part of a strategy in which one country threatens to undertake price-influencing measures that would be damaging to other participants of the trading world in order to force the latter to modify his behaviour. The next two chapters consider trade instruments in both these roles, i.e. in the role normally assigned to taxes in the externalities literature, and as part of a threat strategy designed to induce countries generating spill-over pollution to modify their policy.

Chapter 9

Tariffs as Second Best Instruments to Internalise Spill-over Externalities

In his seminal paper, Markusen [1975] shows that PPM spill-over externalities add a further motive for a large country to levy a tariff if it imports the good whose PPM generates the spill-over pollution.[1]

In the remainder of this chapter we develop this result in our Heckscher-Ohlin-Samuelson model from chapters 3 and 8.

1. ECO-TARIFFS IN THE PRESENCE OF SPILL-OVER POLLUTION

If the option of trade policy exists in the form of an (implied) tariff τ countries maximise social welfare in the presence of spill-over pollution

$$w = u(f(k^x, l^x) + ph(k-k^x, l-l^x) - pc^y,\ c^y) - v(k^x+K^X) \qquad (8\text{-}2)$$

using the policy instruments environmental tax g and (implied) tariff τ.

If a country maximises (8-3), the optimal tax (implied) tariff combination is found by differentiating (8-2) w.r.t. g and τ. This yields:

[1] Similar results have been developed graphically by Baumol [1971] and Baumol & Oates [1988 ch.16], in a partial equilibrium model by Ludema & Wooton [1994] and Mæstad [1998] and in a general equilibrium Ricardo-Viner model by Rauscher [1991b].

$$\frac{dw}{dg} = [u_x(f_k - ph_k) - v']\frac{dk^x}{dg} + u_x(f_l - ph_l)\frac{dl^x}{dg} + (u_y - pu_x)\frac{dc^y}{dg} +$$
$$(h - c^y)\frac{dp}{dg} - v'\frac{dK^X}{dg} \overset{!}{=} 0 \qquad (9\text{-}1)$$

$$\frac{dw}{d\tau} = [u_x(f_k - ph_k) - v']\frac{dk^x}{d\tau} + u_x(f_l - ph_l)\frac{dl^x}{d\tau} + (u_y - pu_x)\frac{dc^y}{d\tau} +$$
$$(h - c^y)\frac{dp}{d\tau} - v'\frac{dK^X}{d\tau} \overset{!}{=} 0 \qquad (9\text{-}2)$$

For small countries, the last two terms in (9-1) and (9-2) are zero; in the first three terms we insert FOCs in the presence of a tariff given by (3-30), (3-31) and (3-32)

$$f_k - g - (p/\tau)h_k = 0 \qquad (3\text{-}30)$$

$$f_l - (p/\tau)h_l = 0 \qquad (3\text{-}31)$$

$$u_y - (p/\tau)u_x = 0 \qquad (3\text{-}32)$$

Inserting these FOCs in (9-1) and (9-2) and rearranging yields

$$\left(g - \frac{v'}{u_x}\right)\frac{dk^x}{dg} + p\left(\frac{1}{\tau} - 1\right)\left[h_k\frac{dk^x}{dg} + h_l\frac{dl^x}{dg} + \frac{dc^y}{dg}\right] = 0 \qquad (9\text{-}1')$$

$$\left(g - \frac{v'}{u_x}\right)\frac{dk^x}{d\tau} + p\left(\frac{1}{\tau} - 1\right)\left[h_k\frac{dk^x}{d\tau} + h_l\frac{dl^x}{d\tau} + \frac{dc^y}{d\tau}\right] = 0 \qquad (9\text{-}2')$$

Assuming that

$$g = \frac{v'}{u_x} \qquad (9\text{-}3a)$$

if follows from (9-1') that

$$\tau = 1 \tag{9-3b}$$

Dividing (9-1') by (9-2') under the assumption that ($g = (v'/u_x)$) yields

$$\frac{dk^x}{dg} \Big/ \frac{dk^x}{d\tau} = \frac{d(c^y - h)}{dg} \Big/ \frac{d(c^y - h)}{d\tau} \tag{9-4}$$

If (9-4) is fulfilled, (9-3a&b) yield an optimal tax (implied) tariff combination for a small country when pollution spills across borders.

We observe that (9-3a) is the optimal national environmental tax for a small country found in chapter 8 which is identical to the Pigouvian tax for a small country when pollution is local, given by (3-16). As regards (9-3b), the optimal (implied) tariff is identical to the optimal implied (tariff) for a small country when pollution is local given by (3-34) in chapter 3. Assuming that w is strictly concave in g and τ, (9-3a&b) is the only tax-(implied) tariff combination maximising (8-2) for a small country.

If the country is large, the last two terms in (9-1) and (9-2) are not zero; inserting the FOCs in the presence of a tariff and rearranging yields for a large country

$$\left(g - \frac{v'}{u_x}\right)\frac{dk^x}{dg} + p\left(\frac{1}{\tau} - 1\right)\left[h_k \frac{dk^x}{dg} + h_l \frac{dl^x}{dg} + \frac{dc^y}{dg}\right] +$$
$$(h - c^y)\frac{dp}{dg} - \left(\frac{v'}{u_x}\right)\frac{dK^X}{dg} = 0 \tag{9-1''}$$

$$\left(g - \frac{v'}{u_x}\right)\frac{dk^x}{d\tau} + p\left(\frac{1}{\tau} - 1\right)\left[h_k \frac{dk^x}{d\tau} + h_l \frac{dl^x}{d\tau} + \frac{dc^y}{d\tau}\right] +$$
$$(h - c^y)\frac{dp}{d\tau} - \left(\frac{v'}{u_x}\right)\frac{dK^X}{d\tau} = 0 \tag{9-2''}$$

Assuming that

$$g = \frac{v'}{u_x} \tag{9-3a'}$$

if follows from (9-1'')

$$\tau = \left[1 + \left(\frac{dp}{p}\right)\frac{(c^y - h)}{d(c^y - h)} + \left(\frac{v'}{p}\right)\frac{dK^X}{d(c^y - h)}\right]^{-1} \tag{9-3b'}$$

Dividing (9-1'') by (9-2'') yields under the assumption that $(g = v' / u_x)$

$$\frac{dk^x}{dg} \bigg/ \frac{dk^x}{d\tau} = \frac{d(h-c^y)}{dg} \bigg/ \frac{d(h-c^y)}{d\tau} - \frac{dp}{dg} \bigg/ \frac{dp}{d\tau} + \frac{dK^X}{dg} \bigg/ \frac{dK^X}{d\tau} \tag{9-4}$$

If (9-4) is fulfilled, (9-3a'&b') yield an optimal tax (implied) tariff combination for a large country when pollution spills across borders.

We observe that (9-3a') is identical to (9-3a), i.e. the Pigouvian tax for local environmental pollution. As regards the optimal (implied) tariff for spill-over pollution, we observe that it consists of two parts, namely

$$\left[1 + \left(\frac{dp}{p}\right)\frac{(c^y - h)}{d(c^y - h)}\right]^{-1}$$

which is similar to the optimal (implied) tariff for local pollution derived in chapter 4 and given by (4-30b), and

$$\left[\left(\frac{v'}{p}\right)\frac{dK^X}{d(c^y - h)}\right]^{-1}$$

by which the effect of the cross-border externality is taken into account.

We shall investigate the sign and effect of the spill-over pollution part of τ. Following the structure we have used so far, we shall first examine the case when home alone can affect the price level to improve the terms of trade and to internalise spill-over pollution while its trading partners cannot. Thereafter, we analyse interaction of two large countries.

HOME FACING ATOMISTIC COUNTRIES IN THE REST OF THE WORLD

We shall investigate for

$$\tau = \left[1 + \left(\frac{dp}{p}\right)\frac{(c^y - h)}{d(c^y - h)} + \left(\frac{v'}{p}\right)\frac{dK^X}{d(c^y - h)}\right]^{-1} \qquad (9\text{-}3b')$$

the sign of the tariff with its spill-over part, and rationale and effect for the spill-over part of the tariff.

Sign: in chapter 4 we found for an (implied) tariff consisting of the two first terms in (9-3b') that

- $\tau > 1$ if home is labour abundant, and
- $\tau < 1$ if home is capital abundant.

As regards the third term, we find that $(v'/p > 0)$ and $(dK^X / d(c^y - h) < 0)$. Therefore, the fact that pollution is global in nature increases τ.

Hence, in a labour-abundant country, the tariff charged on the good whose PPM pollutes the global environment is higher than the terms of trade improving tariff if pollution is only local. In a capital abundant country, the global nature of pollution causes home to reduce the export tax with which it improves terms of trade.

RATIONALE AND EFFECTS

The rationale for a large country to use trade policy is now two-fold as indicated by the last two terms of the trade policy instrument. This is explained by the fact that a tariff or an export tax not only affect the terms of trade but also emissions in the rest of the world.

An x-exporting country reduces its export supply and import demand to improve its terms of trade by increasing the relative price of its export good. However, since such appreciation of the relative price of x increases production of x and hence pollution in the rest of the world, home charges ceteris paribus a lower export tax if pollution in the rest of the world reduces welfare in home.

Effects of the export tax in the presence of spill-over pollution are similar to these derived for an export tax when pollution is local in chapter[2]:

$$\frac{dk^x}{d(-\tau)} < 0, \qquad \frac{dl^x}{d(-\tau)} < 0, \qquad \frac{dK^X}{d(-\tau)} > 0, \quad \text{and,} \quad \frac{dL^X}{d(-\tau)} > 0.$$

A labour-abundant x-importing country charges a tariff on its import good to improve its terms of trade by reducing the relative price of x. This reduction of the price for the good whose PPM pollutes the global environment improves home's welfare through a second channel, i.e. by reducing global pollution. Hence, the tariff is ceteris paribus higher if pollution spills across borders.

Effects of the eco-tariff in the presence of spill-over pollution are similar to those derived for a tariff when pollution is local in chapter 4. Excluding the Metzler Paradox, they are

$$\frac{dk^x}{d\tau} > 0, \qquad \frac{dl^x}{d\tau} > 0, \qquad \frac{dK^X}{d\tau} < 0, \quad \text{and,} \quad \frac{dL^X}{d\tau} < 0.$$

The tariff is tantamount to an excise tax on the part of the rest of the world's output which is exported. Therefore, it serves as a cross border Pigouvian tax by which the part of the externality associated with exports is internalised for home[3]. This is illustrated in Figure 9-1 where offer curves and trade indifference curves are depicted. Home's (the rest of the world's) export offer curve in the absence of trade policy is denoted by *eo* (*EO*); the corresponding welfare indifference curves by *wi* and *WI*; trade flows by x and y, and the resulting relative world price by p. If home charges a tariff to improve its terms of trade, its export offer curve is denoted by $eo(\tau(p))$; trade flows by $x(p(\tau(p)))$ and $y(p(\tau(p)))$. If the tariff is chosen to improve both home's terms of trade and to internalise spill-over pollution, home's export offer curve is denoted by $eo(\tau(p,S))$; trade flows by $x(p(\tau(p,S)))$ and $y(p(\tau(p,S)))$.

[2] We assume that the global nature of pollution does reduce the export tax but does not reverse its sign.

[3] Compare Baumol & Oates [1988, ch. 16].

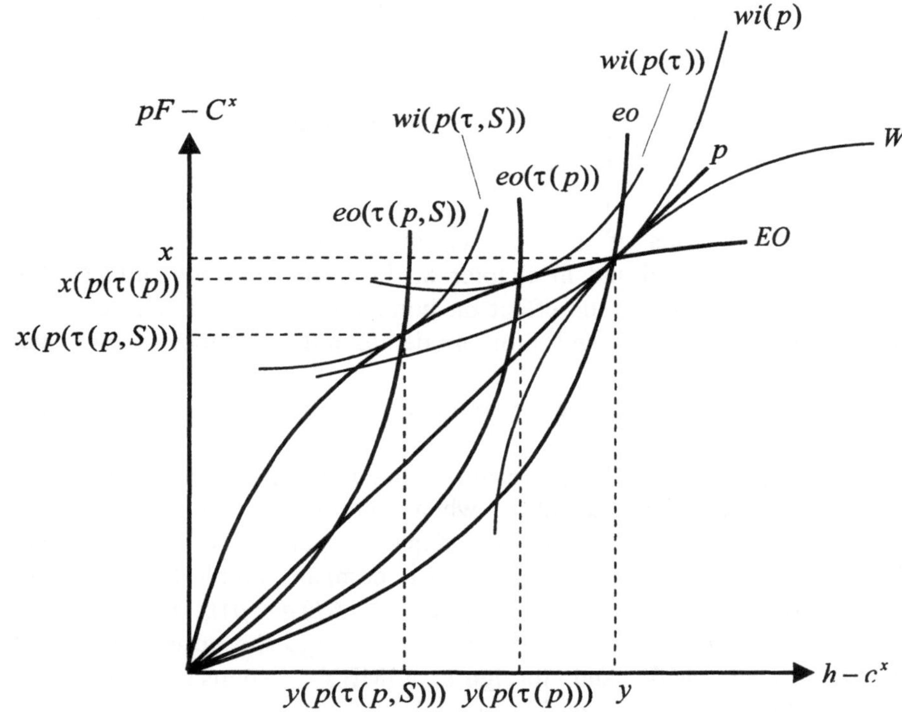

Figure 9-1. Effect of Spill-over Pollution on the Optimal Tariff

We observe:

- If home charges the tariff $\tau(p)$ solely to improve its terms of trade determined by the relative price p, trade flows are reduced from x and y to $x(p(\tau(p)))$ and $y(p(\tau(p)))$. If the tariff $\tau(p,S)$ also internalises the global externality caused by rest of the world's export of x, trade flows are further reduced to $x(p(\tau(p,S)))$ and $y(p(\tau(p,S)))$.
- The external cost associated with the rest of the world's production of x imported by home reduces the marginal social welfare home derives from it. Hence, home's welfare indifference curve $wi(p)$ when only terms of trade effects are considered is steeper at the point of intersection than $wi(p(\tau,S))$, the social welfare indifference curve if trans-border pollution S is taken into account.

HOME FACING A LARGE TRADING PARTNER

We now consider the case when both home and its large trading partner foreign can alter their terms of trade. Foreign cannot levy a tariff and hence charges the optimal tax for a large national welfare-maximising country exporting x given by (9-5)

$$G = \frac{V'}{U_X} + (C^Y - H)\frac{dp}{dG}\frac{dG}{dK^X} + \left(\frac{V'}{U_X}\right)\frac{dk^x}{dG}\frac{dG}{dK^X} \qquad (9\text{-}5)$$

To affect the terms of trade in its favour, foreign increases its tax. However, as we have found in chapter 8, the terms of trade induced tax increase is partly offset by its effect on home's emissions. Because of the leakage effect, the tax increase is more moderate in the presence of spill-over pollution.

The optimal tariff is increased by spill-over pollution effects as derived in (9-3b').

We assume that the Nash equilibrium in tax and tariff, which we derived in chapter 4 for two large countries when pollution is local, exists in the presence of global pollution too[4]. We depict the effects of the spill-over pollution in the tax-tax space in Figure 9-2 to compare the Nash equilibria in eco-tax/tariff for local and spill-over pollution. $NE(g(\tau(p)),G)$ is the Nash equilibrium in home's eco-tax g if home can charge the optimal terms of trade improving tariff, and foreign's NIMBY response to $g(\tau(p))$[5]. $NE(g(\tau(p,S)),G)$ is the Nash equilibrium in home's eco-tax g if home charges the optimal tariff to improve its terms of trade and internalises spill-over pollution S; and in foreign's NIMBY response to $g(\tau(p,S))$.

4 We assume that all conditions mentioned in chapter 4 hold.

5 It is given by the intersection of $R(g(\tau(p)))$ and $r^{\tau(p)}(G)$ - foreign's reaction curve which traces the tax foreign charges in response to home's tax-tariff combination, and home's reaction curve which traces the tax home charges in response to foreign's NIMBY policy if it can levy an eco-tariff.

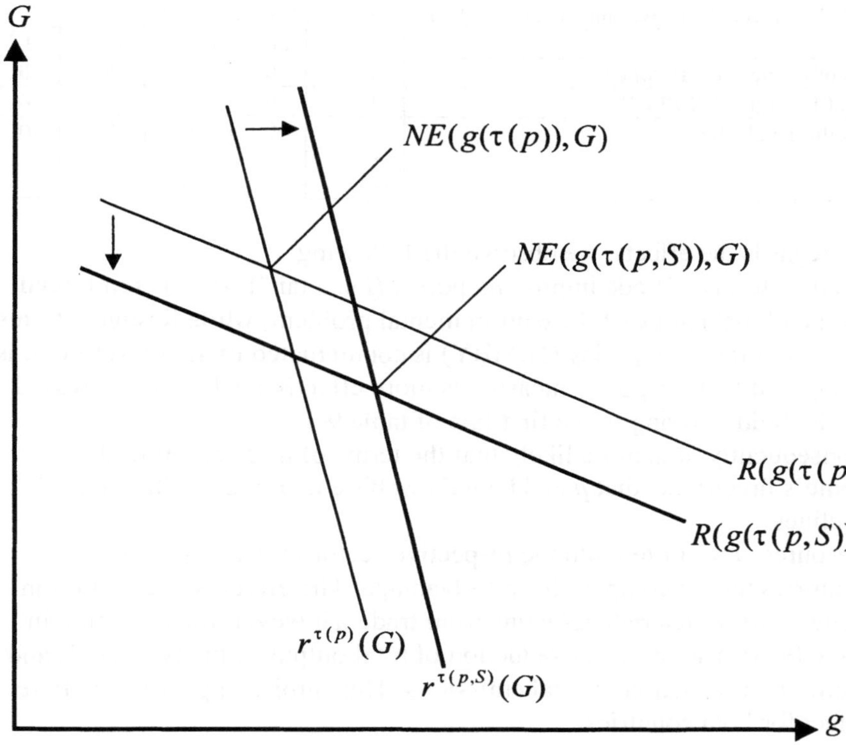

Figure 9-2. Outward Movement of Home's Reaction Function and Inward Movement of Foreign's Reaction Function if Pollution Spills Across Borders

We observe that

- home's internalisation of the spill-over pollution shifts its reaction function to the right from $r^{\tau(p)}(G)$ to $r^{\tau(p,S)}(G)$.
- foreign's reaction function moves downward from $R(g(\tau(p)))$ to $R(g(\tau(p,S)))$.
- the Nash equilibrium if pollution spills across borders $NE(g(\tau(p,S)),G)$ is characterised by lower tax in foreign and higher tariff in home compared with $NE(g(\tau(p)),G)$, the Nash equilibrium if pollution has only domestic environmental effects.

Effects of home's and foreign's respective optimal tax and tariff policies in the presence of spill-over pollution are summarised in the table below:

Table 9-1: Effects of an environmental tax and tariff war for spill-over pollution

	dp	dk^x	dK^X	dl^x	dL^X
Effects of Home's Tariff Policy	**>0**	**>0**	**<0**	**>0**	**<0**
Effect of Foreign's NIMBY Policy	<0	>0	<0	>0	<0
Sign of the Total Effect	< > (>)0	>0	<0	>0	<0

As regards the effects, we observe the following:

- Home's terms of trade improving policy (i.e. a tariff on x) is reinforced by the global nature of the environmental problem, while foreign's terms of trade improving policy (NIMBY) is counteracted by it. Therefore, it is likely that home's policy measure is more effective, which is expressed by the bold lettering in the first line of table 9-1.
- Consequently, it is more likely that the terms of trade are moved in home's favour, i.e. that p and home's welfare increase, while foreign's declines.
- Resources are shifted into the respective sector in which the two countries have a comparative disadvantage. The effect is a reduction in trade flows which reduces gains from trade. However, the reduction in trade flows also implies a reduction of total output of the two goods and therefore a reduction of total emissions. This implies a positive welfare effect for both countries.

We summarise with:

Proposition 9-1*: The welfare effect of an eco-tariff is negative for small countries in the presence of spill-over pollution. For a large country, a unilateral eco-tariff has positive welfare effects which are likely to be reduced yet not annihilated if there is retaliation.*

(a) A small country's eco-tariff cannot affect the price level and therefore neither its terms of trade nor pollution originating from abroad.

(b) A unilateral eco-tariff levied by a large country improves its terms of trade and reduces pollution in the rest of the world. It is therefore welfare-improving for home, and maybe globally welfare-enhancing.

(c) If there is retaliation, emissions in foreign are further reduced which has a positive welfare effect for home. Although foreign's NIMBY policy leads to a decline in home's terms of trade, the net welfare effect is still likely to be positive for home.

2. WELFARE EFFECTS OF ECO-TARIFFS FOR THE REST OF THE WORLD IN THE PRESENCE OF SPILL-OVER POLLUTION

From (9-3b'), we see that the optimal tariff in the presence of spill-over pollution consists of two parts of which the first serves to improve terms of trade while the second internalises the spill-over externality generated in the production of goods imported by home.

Clearly, both parts of the tariff serve to improve welfare in the home country, which levies the tariff. As regards the country exporting x, the case is less obvious. Since terms of trade mirror each other, the terms of trade effect which is positive for the tariff-levying country is negative for the country whose exports are charged with it. However, since the spill-over externality harms the population in both countries, the reduction in S benefits the exporting rest of the world as well. Therefore, the welfare effect of the tariff depends on world-wide emissions and on environmental regulation in home and the rest of the world.

Following a graphical analysis conducted by Baumol & Oates [1988, ch.16], this is illustrated as follows. We consider the case when - for whichever reason - the exporting rest of the world does not internalise the externality[6]. Its welfare indifference curves $WI^1(p)$, $WI^2(p)$ and $WI^3(p)$ thus do not take into account the environmental part $v(\bullet)$ of the welfare function. As regards home, we construct families of welfare indifference curves for both scenarios, namely when the environmental externality is taken into consideration in the formulation of the optimal tariff ($wi^1(p,S)$, $wi^2(p,S)$, $wi^3(p,S)$), and when it is not ($wi^1(p)$, $wi^2(p)$, $wi^3(p)$). Figure 8-3 illustrates alternative contract curves $c(p)$ and $c(p,S)$ in these two scenarios.

6 Reasons for failure to implement environmental policies may be manifold. It could be that the government does not maximise social welfare by refraining from taking environmental regulatory measures. Alternatively, it may be possible that although government is willing to implement such environmental measures, it is not possible because of pollution measurement problems, or the absence of a suitable tax collecting agency.

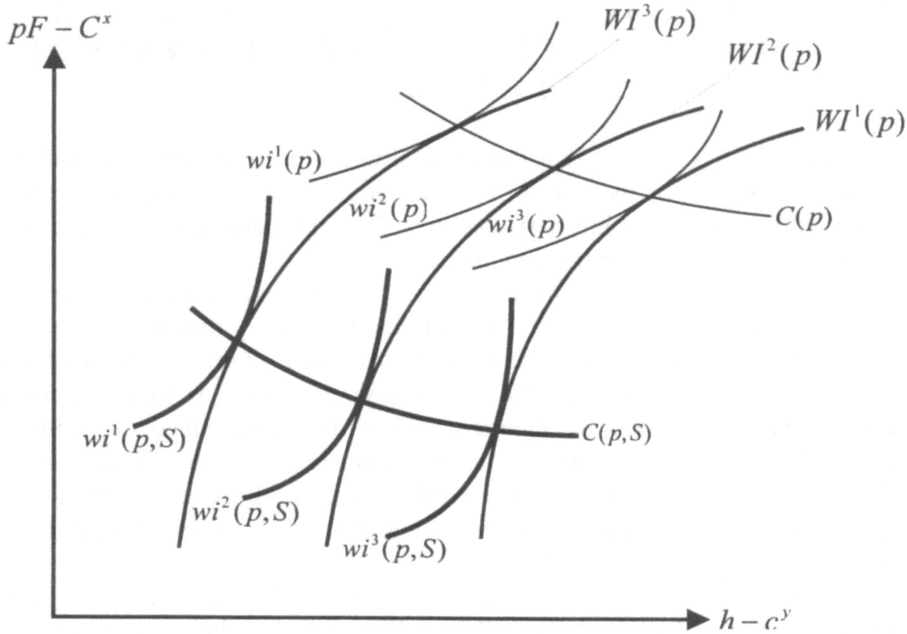

Figure 9-3. Trade Contract Curves Omitting and Considering Spill-over Pollution

We observe

- Since $wi^1(p)$, $wi^2(p)$, and $wi^3(p)$ are flatter than $wi^1(p,S)$, $wi^2(p,S)$, and $wi^3(p,S)$, the resulting contract curve $c(p)$ when spill-over pollution is neglected lies to the north-east of $c(p,S)$.
- Therefore, if environmental externality is taken into account a lower trade level results.

Contract curves c(p) and c(p,S) are inserted into Figure 9-1 above to depict welfare implications of an eco-tariff charged by home. Home's and the rest of the world's export offer curves are denoted by *eo* and *EO*; $wi(p(\tau))$ and $wi(p(\tau,S)$ are home's welfare indifference curves depending on whether effect of spill-over pollution is taken into consideration or not. $F(p)$ depicts the free market equilibrium which lies on the contract curve $c(p)$ and where *eo* intersects *EO*; it corresponds to trade flows $x(p)$ and $y(p)$. $F(p,S)$ is the Pareto optimum in the presence of spill-over pollution; it lies on $c(p,S)$ where $c(p,S)$ intersects EO and corresponds to trade flows $x(p,S)$ and $y(p,S)$.

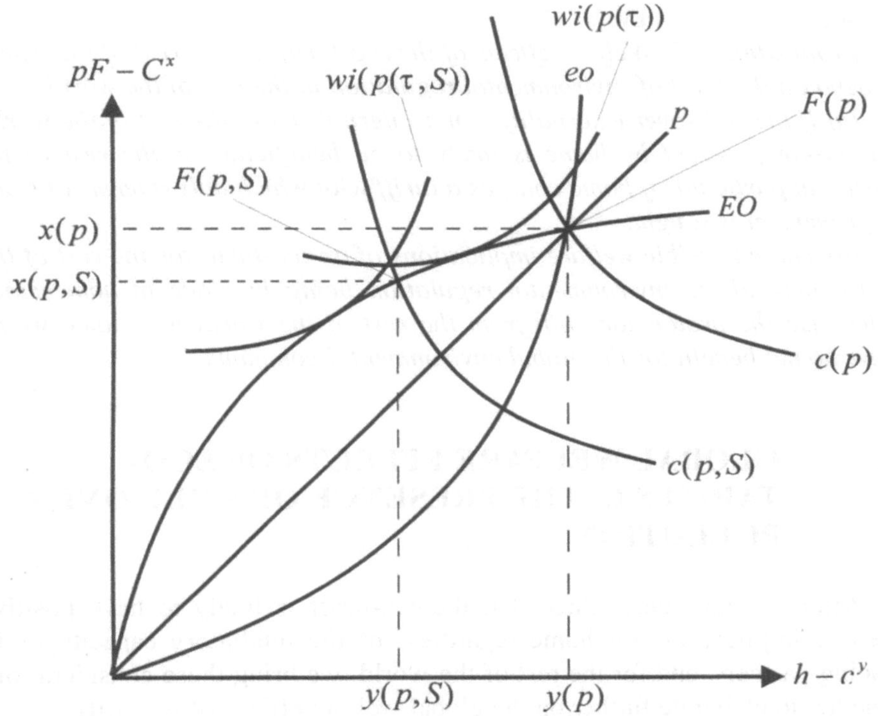

Figure 9-4. Export Offer Curves and Contract Curves Omitting and Considering Spill-over Pollution

We observe

- Since *F(p,S)* lies to the south-west of *F(p)*, the free trade equilibrium when the market participants do not internalise the spill-over externality implies too much trade.
- If home charges a tariff, the resulting reduction in trade flows increases home's welfare since terms of trade improve and spill-over pollution is reduced.
- As regards the rest of the world, the reduction of the trade flows achieved by home's tariff entails welfare gains because of the reduction in the externality and welfare losses because of the decline in its terms of trade associated with the tariff.
- If home charges the tariff associated with *wi(p,S)*, the resulting trade level is below the Pareto optimum *F(p,S)*; yet the welfare implication for the rest of the world of this trade level compared with the free trade situation *F(p)* or the allocation associated with *τ(p)* cannot be determined.

We summarise with:

***Proposition 9-2**: Welfare effects of the eco-tariff for the rest of the world depend on the level of environmental regulation in the rest of the world.*

(a) If the spill-over externality is not internalised in the rest of the world, an eco-tariff levied by home is likely to be beneficial for the rest of the world, in particular if home charges a tariff with which only a terms of trade improvement is sought.

(b) These possible welfare implications of an eco-tariff for the rest of the world depend on environmental regulation being in place in home since otherwise the production shift from the rest of the world into home would have no net benefit for the global environmental commons.

3. GLOBAL WELFARE EFFECTS OF ECO-TARIFFS IN THE PRESENCE OF SPILL-OVER POLLUTION

After we have determined that the eco-tariff is likely to have positive welfare implications for home regardless of the retaliatory capacity of its trading partners, and for the rest of the world, we bring these considerations together to elaborate further on the global welfare effects of the tariff.

We compare the non-cooperative tariff to the alternative, that countries recur to environmental taxes as the sole policy instrument. We undertake a welfare comparison for two scenarios, namely when home faces atomistic countries in the rest of the world and when it has a single, large trading partner.

If home faces **atomistic countries in the rest of the world** and it cannot charge an eco-tariff, it engages in eco-dumping, i.e. it charges a tax which is lower than the domestic Pigouvian level for reasons mentioned in chapter 7.

Such eco-dumping has the following welfare effects:

- it increases welfare in home by increasing its terms of trade, thereby increasing $u(c^x,c^y)$ which more than compensates for the increase in $v(k^x+K^X)$, and
- it reduces welfare in the countries in the rest of the world by hurting their terms of trade, thereby reducing $U(C^X,C^Y)$, and by increasing world-wide emissions which increases $V(k^x+K^X)$.

If home uses a tariff instead, welfare effects are qualitatively the same. However, since the tariff is a more effective means for home to improve its terms of trade, home's welfare will be increased by more if it can use a tariff compared with when it engages in eco-dumping to exploit its market power on the im- and export markets.

As regards the rest of the world, the additional decline in its terms of trade which it experiences if home uses a tariff should be offset by an emission reduction if home's tariff is accompanied by a higher tax. In that case, both home and the rest of the world are better off if home can use a tariff. This is all the more likely if the rest of the world does not internalise the environmental externality, i.e. if all countries try to free-ride and global emissions exceed the optimal level.

If home faces a **large trading partner** and cannot charge a tariff, home and foreign engage in a tax-tax war with home engaging in eco-dumping and foreign in a NIMBY policy.

A welfare comparison of these two Nash equilibria again reveals that home's welfare is higher when it can use two instruments while foreign suffers from a more pronounced terms of trade effect of home's tariff while it benefits from lower emissions if home internalises more of its externality. If the latter effect offsets the loss, again both home and its foreign trading partner are better off if home can use a tariff.

We can summarise with

***Proposition 9-3**: If home can charge an eco-tariff, the global welfare effects are likely to be positive.*

(a) Compared with the situation when home uses its environmental tax to manipulate its terms of trade, the tariff yields welfare improvements for home since a tariff is more suitable to affect the price level than a tax on capital.

(b) Since home charges a higher tax if it can levy a tariff, the rest of the world - or foreign - will benefit along with home from the higher environmental quality.

(c) If the emission reduction in home is large enough, allowing home to use a tariff is likely to yield a Pareto improvement. If the welfare loss in the rest of the world, or foreign, is not offset by the increase in environmental quality, it is still possible that the net effect, i.e. welfare effects in home together with welfare effects in the rest of the world, or foreign, is positive.

4. CONCLUSIONS

We have seen that an eco-tariff serves two objectives for the country levying it. Apart from terms of trade improvement, it also reduces emissions generated in the countries exporting the good whose PPM harms the global environmental commons. Moreover, if countries exporting x do not internalise the environmental externality, the tariff is the efficient means to internalise the global environmental externality.

Furthermore, if large x-importing countries use environmental policy to improve their terms of trade because multilateral trade rules prohibit tariffs, sanctioning such tariffs would very likely improve global welfare.

Yet, if an eco-tariff became sanctioned by the multilateral trade rules, it is by no means clear that the optimal level would be chosen. We could, however, at least ensure that it would only be levied in cases when free trade is clearly not optimal, i.e. when exporting countries do not internalise the environmental externality.

However, although we have established that an eco-tariff can play somewhat the same role for trans-border externalities that a Pigouvian tax performs for domestically generated emissions, the former will generally not be a perfect substitute for the latter for the following reasons:

– the price instrument does not affect directly the source of emissions K^X
– not all production in the rest of the world is exported and hence subject to the tariff.

Finally, we should keep in mind that a tariff is part of a non-cooperative environmental and trade policy. As we have seen in the preceding chapter, optimal environmental policy addressing spill-over pollution requires cooperation. The globally optimal taxes internalise all environmental externalities and will therefore not have to be accompanied by a tariff. Therefore, the global Pareto optimum will be characterised by zero tariffs in addition to higher environmental taxes than those chosen if countries individually set their policies.

Therefore, we shall in the next chapter address the question how tariffs affect the chances for a cooperative outcome.

Chapter 10

Incentive Effects of Eco-tariffs

Barrett [1994a], Baumol & Oates [1988, ch 16], Bhagwati [1993b], Blackhurst & Subramanian [1992] and Subramanian [1992] promote eco-tariffs in a double function. Eco-tariffs should provide an incentive for countries which do not internalise the global externality to do so. Furthermore, if international cooperation to safeguard the global environmental commons still cannot be achieved, eco-tariffs serve to avoid relocation of pollution intensive production from countries who do take protective measures into countries which do not.

We modify our Heckscher-Ohlin-Samuelson model to investigate whether eco-tariffs will be suitable for this double role.

1. ENVIRONMENTAL POLICY EFFECTS OF AN ECO-TARIFF

To contrast the effects of a conditional eco-tariff with the kind of eco-tariff we have considered so far, we shall first investigate the 'incentive effects' of an (unconditional) eco-tariff, i.e. we shall determine the changes in environmental policy measures in home and the rest of the world (made up by atomistic countries or a single large one) triggered by an eco-tariff in the (large) home country.

We assume that both home and its trading partner(s) behave non-cooperatively. Home hence charges the optimal environmental tax if it can also levy a tariff; its trading partners set the nationally optimal taxes.

EFFECTS IN HOME

If home charges the tax which is optimal if home can also levy a tariff given by

$$g = \frac{v'}{u_x} \tag{10-3a'}$$

we find the following tariff effect for g

$$\frac{dg}{d\tau} \lessgtr 0 \tag{10-1}$$

A close inspection of (10-1) shows tax-increasing and tax-reducing effects

$$\frac{dg}{d\tau} = \frac{d(v'/u_x)}{d\tau} = \frac{(dv'/d\tau)u_x - (du_x/d\tau)v'}{u_x^2} = (v''u_x - u_{xx}gv')\frac{dk^x}{d\tau} -$$

$$(u_{xy} - pu_{xx})\frac{dc^y}{d\tau} + u_{xx}v'(c^y - h)\frac{dp}{d\tau} + v''\left(\frac{dK^X}{dp}\frac{dp}{d\tau}\right) \tag{10-1'}$$

The first two terms in (10 -1') pick up tax increments following the tariff effect on the the domestic price level, while the last two terms are determined by tariff effects on the world price level.

Regarding the signs of the four terms in (10-1') we observe that

- the first term is positive,
- the second term is negative,
- the third term is positive, and
- the last term is negative.

The following economic forces are at play:

- The first term picks up the fact that the protective effect of the tariff stimulates production of x and hence environmental pollution in home. The latter drives the environmental tax upward.
- The second term picks up the fact that the relative price increase for x stimulates consumption substitution towards y and hence factor reallocation away from the x sector. This reduces g.
- The third term picks up the terms of trade effect of the tariff. The improvement in home's terms of trade increases society's desire for a cleaner environment and thus increases g.

- The fourth term picks up the leakage effect: The tariff increases the relative price of y abroad and hence stimulates production substitution away from x. The resulting lower level of global pollution reduces the necessity of environmental protection in home, triggering a reduction of g.

EFFECTS IN THE REST OF THE WORLD

If small countries in the rest of the world charge the nationally optimal tax given by

$$G = \frac{V'}{U_X} \tag{3-16}$$

we find the following effect of home's tariff for G

$$\frac{dG}{d\tau} \lesseqgtr 0 \tag{10-2}$$

Disentangling tax-increasing and tax-reducing effects of τ reveals

$$\frac{dG}{d\tau} = \frac{d(V'/U_X)}{d\tau} = \frac{(dV'/d\tau)U_X - (dU_X/d\tau)V'}{U_X^2} =$$

$$(V''U_X - U_{XX}GV')\frac{dK^X}{d\tau} - (U_{XY} - pU_{XX})\frac{dC^Y}{d\tau} + U_{XX}V'(C^Y - H)\frac{dp}{d\tau}$$

$$+ v''\left(\frac{dK^X}{dp}\frac{dp}{d\tau}\right) \tag{10-2'}$$

We find for (10-2') that

- the first and third term are negative, and
- the second and fourth term are positive.

The following economic effects can be isolated:

- The tariff-induced price reduction of x triggers a production substitution towards y which reduces environmental pollution in the rest of the world and G.
- Consumption substitution in the rest of the world towards x has the opposite effect of increasing G.
- Decline in the terms of trade in the rest of the world reduces G.

– Increase in world-wide pollution by home stimulates pollution control in the rest of the world.

EFFECTS IN A LARGE FOREIGN COUNTRY

If a large foreign country charges the nationally optimal tax given by

$$\mathrm{G} = \frac{V'}{U_X} + (C^Y - H)\frac{dp}{dG}\frac{dG}{dK^X} + \left(\frac{V'}{U_X}\right)\frac{dk^x}{dG}\frac{dG}{dK^X} \tag{10-4}$$

we find again an indeterminate effect of home's tariff on G

$$\frac{dG}{d\tau} \lesseqgtr 0 \tag{10-3}$$

The isolated tariff effect on the terms of (10-3) are

$$\frac{dG}{d\tau} = \frac{d(V'/U_X)}{d\tau} + \frac{d(C^Y - H)}{d\tau}\frac{dp}{dG}\frac{dG}{dK^X} + \frac{d(V'/U_X)}{d\tau}\frac{dk^x}{dG}\frac{dG}{dK^X} \tag{10-3'}$$

The first term of (10-3') is identical to (10-2'); the tax-increasing and tax-reducing effects isolated above for a small country thus apply to a large one as well. In addition, we have the following large-country effects:

$$\frac{d(C^Y - H)}{d\tau}\frac{dp}{dG}\frac{dG}{dK^X} < 0 \tag{10-3'a}$$

$$\frac{d(V'/U_X)}{d\tau}\frac{dk^x}{dG}\frac{dG}{dK^X} \lesseqgtr 0 \tag{10-3'b}$$

(10-3'a) picks up the terms of trade effect of the tax in foreign. It is negative since home's tariff reduces trade and therefore the leverage of G for foreign to affect its terms of trade. The importance of the positive part of G is thus reduced.

(10-3'b) picks up how home's tariff affects the leakage part in foreign's tax. Its sign depends on the effect of the tariff on home's tax. If home increases pollution control, the leakage effect is reduced for the determination of foreign's tax; otherwise, it is increased.

Therefore, effect of home's tariff is more likely to reduce the tax in a large country than in a small country, owing to the negative terms of trade effect. The reason is that the (negative) (10-3'a) captures a first order effect and the (indeterminate) (10-3'b) only a second order effect.

2. INCENTIVE EFFECTS OF A CONDITIONAL ECO-TARIFF

We now assume that home levies a conditional eco-tariff, i.e. that the tariff is removed if the rest of the world reacts to its implementation – or rather the threat of implementation – with an increase of its environmental tax G. We also assume that as a condition for home's ability to implement a conditional eco-tariff, it must internalise the global externality, i.e. its tax must be

$$g > 0 \tag{8-9}$$

Furthermore, we assume that prior to the threat of the conditional eco-tariff, no regulation of the global externality was in place in the rest of the world.

We shall investigate:

- incentive effects of a conditional eco-tariff for the rest of the world, whereby we distinguish as usual between a world in which home's trading partners are atomistic countries and one where it is a large foreign country, and
- how the conditional tariff affects environmental policy in home, depending on whether it *works*, i.e. the rest of the world increases its efforts to internalise the global externality and the tariff does not need to be implemented, or does *not work*, i.e. the rest of the world does not increase its efforts and the tariff is in fact implemented.

INCENTIVE EFFECT OF A CONDITIONAL ECO-TARIFF IN SMALL COUNTRIES

The conditional tariff will not increase the tax in the rest of the world if the rest of the world consists of small countries. We assumed in chapter 6 that the rest of the world does not coordinate its policies vis-à-vis home. Therefore, an individual small x-exporting country may reduce the tariff levied on its own exports, yet it does not change home's import demand nor, therefore, its terms of trade. As regards perceived potential environmental benefits of a small country's implementation of G, this will also be insignificant and hence not increase the benefits from raising the environmental tax in response to home's conditional eco-tariff.

INCENTIVE EFFECT OF A CONDITIONAL ECO-TARIFF IN HOME'S LARGE TRADING PARTNER

If we assume that the rest of the world consists of one large foreign country which exports x into home, the conditional eco-tariff is very likely to trigger an increase in foreign's tax. If home was to implement the eco-tariff, foreign's terms of trade would depreciate. Implementing an environmental tax G would serve foreign to increase its terms of trade, to reduce the global externality and to avoid the negative terms of trade effects from a tariff levied against its exports by home.

EFFECTS OF A CONDITIONAL ECO-TARIFF IN HOME

To determine the effect of the eco-tariff on home's environmental tax g, we now have to distinguish two cases, namely the environmental tax (taxes) in the rest of the world is (are) increased to avoid being subjected to the tariff and the tariff is hence removed, or the environmental tax (taxes) in the rest of the world is (are) not increased and the tariff stays in place.

If the **tariff is effective** in providing an incentive for the rest of the world to reduce their global pollutants by increasing G, the effect of the (threat of the) tariff for environmental policy in home given by

$$g = \frac{v'}{u_x} \tag{9-3a'}$$

is indeterminate

$$\frac{dg}{dG} \lesseqgtr 0 \tag{10-4}$$

This can be verified by inspecting (10-4)

$$\frac{dg}{dG} = \frac{d(v'/u_x)}{d\tau} = \frac{(dv'/dG)u_x - (du_x/dG)v'}{u_x^2} = (v''u_x - u_{xx}gv')\frac{dk^x}{dG} -$$

$$(u_{xy} - pu_{xx})\frac{dc^y}{dG} + u_{xx}v'(c^y - h)\frac{dp}{dG} + v''\left(\frac{dK^X}{dG}\right) \qquad (10\text{-}4')$$

For the signs of the four terms in (10-4') we find the

- first term positive,
- the second and last term negative, and
- the third term determined by the sign of $(h\text{-}c^y)$; if home imports x $(h\text{-}c^y) > 0$ and the third term is negative.

The following effects are captured in those four terms:

- The first term picks up the fact that a tax increase in the rest of the world increases the scarcity and the price of x which stimulates production and pollution in home. This has a tax-increasing effect.
- The second term captures the consumption substitution effect. As the price increases, consumption of x is reduced and therewith production and pollution. This drives the tax downward.
- The third term picks up the terms of trade effect of the tax increase in the rest of the world. Such a tax increase worsens home's terms of trade and thereby reduces home's desire for a cleaner environment. This reduces g.
- The last term stems from the global nature of pollution: the pollution reduction achieved by the increased protection in the rest of the world reduces the necessity of such efforts in home. Consequently, g decreases.

We can conclude that although the effect of an increase in G on g is not definite, it is most likely that the negative effects dominate.

If the **tariff is not effective** in providing an incentive for the rest of the world to increase their tax (taxes), the effect of the tariff for environmental policy in home is given by (10-1); it is therefore indeterminate.

We can summarise with

Proposition 10:

(a) If home levies an (unconditional) tariff, the effect for its environmental tax is indeterminate. The same is true for home's trading partners: both tax increasing and tax reducing forces are present. However, since in large countries terms of trade considerations enter the tax determination and home's tariff reduces the terms of trade leverage of the tax in large countries, it is more likely that home's tariff reduces the tax than it is in small countries.

(b) If home's trading partners are small countries, a conditional eco-tariff fails to provide an incentive for the implementation of environmental regulation. If home trades with a large country, we shall observe the opposite effect.

(c) If the conditional eco-tariff is successful in increasing G in the rest of the world, home will reduce its environmental tax as a result. If the eco-tariff fails to trigger a change in the rest of the world's environmental policy, home's environmental policy reaction is indeterminate.

3. DISCUSSION AND EXTENSION

We shall first discuss conditional eco-tariffs in more detail by elaborating on efficiency implications of conditional eco-tariffs. Furthermore, we discuss the plausibility of the application of the conditional eco-tariff concept. Finally, we sketch problems arising for the role of conditional eco-tariffs in international environmental cooperation.

EFFICIENCY IMPLICATIONS OF CONDITIONAL ECO-TARIFFS

In the context of eco-tariffs in countries where a domestic environmental externality is present and which are subject to regulatory capture, we introduced the concept of contingent protection in II.A.5.3.2. This concept was applied to the case of a global environmental externality above. In both contexts, we focused on effects of the conditional eco-tariff for environmental protection in countries against whose exports the tariff was applied. We did not, however, discuss the analytical justification, i.e. efficiency implications, of such conditional eco-tariffs[1].

If low (or no) environmental taxes in exporting countries are instances of eco-dumping, a tariff can offset this (implicit) subsidy to producers of x. As a result, the domestic price level in the tariff-setting country is at the efficient level. The distortion caused by too low environmental taxes in exporting nations vanishes. The terms of trade effect stemming from the tariff does not impair global efficiency since it represents a mere transfer of income from exporting to importing countries.

Hence, there is an analytical justification for the introduction of conditional eco-tariffs which can restore a globally efficient allocation of resources. If the conditional eco-tariff deters eco-dumping, i.e. when (large)

1 For the following exposition we draw on Markusen et al. [1995, 359/360].

countries raise their tax to the optimal level in response to the (threat of the) eco-tariff, global optimality of resource allocation is also ensured since neither eco-dumping nor trade restrictions would prevail in this case.

Notwithstanding the efficiency enhancing effect of conditional eco-tariffs, an incentive problem arises for their application.

PLAUSIBILITY OF THE APPLICATION OF A CONDITIONAL ECO-TARIFF

While charging an unconditional eco-tariff has two positive effects for an importing country, namely an increase of its terms of trade and a reduction in global emissions, the (threat) of a conditional eco-tariff may reduce its terms of trade if it is successful. Therefore, it may not be rational for an importing country to ever consider the application of a conditional eco-tariff.

By the same token, it is highly unlikely that a large exporting country would not have internalised (at least part) of the global externality even in the absence of the threat of a tariff since the tax on capital in the x sector has two positive effects, namely an increase in its terms of trade and a reduction in the externality. Therefore, the assumption that the exporting country had no environmental policy directed at the global externality in place prior to home's threat of the conditional eco-tariff is on weak grounds.

Despite these plausibility considerations, conditional eco-tariffs have been discussed in the context of a regime to protect the global environmental commons. However, a number of problems arise for rules according to which a large importing country might apply a conditional eco-tariff.

RULES FOR ENVIRONMENTAL COOPERATION AND CONDITIONAL ECO-TARIFFS

Above, we stated that an importing country may only levy a conditional eco-tariff if home itself internalises the environmental externality. However, we did not specify to which degree. Yet, this may be a crucial question if the rules of the multilateral trading regime were to be changed to allow eco-tariffs. Leaving measurement problems aside for a moment, we would have several levels of home's tax rate which would need to be in place to qualify a large importing country for implementation of an eco-tariff, namely:

- the optimal tax for a large x-importing country, i.e. the Pigouvian tax less the terms of trade element and the leakage correction element, as specified in chapter 8, or
- the domestic Pigouvian tax, or

- the globally optimal tax, determined in chapter 8

If a large importing country's motive for charging a (conditional) eco-tariff is to coax the rest of the world into cooperation on global environmental matters, it seems reasonable to require it to charge the globally optimal tax. However, this might be a considerable burden since charging such a high tax would harm its terms of trade apart from putting the burden of 'cleaning up for the planet' entirely on one country's economy.

These problems to determine what level of environmental regulation is needed for a country to legitimately employ eco-tariffs is exacerbated by measurement problems.

Therefore, it seems that a plethora of practical problems would be associated with the sanctioning of conditional eco-tariffs.

4. CONCLUSIONS

We have seen that a conditional eco-tariff is a more suitable instrument to induce countries to internalise the global environmental externality than an unconditional one. If levied against small countries, its effect is identical with an unconditional eco-tariff; if levied against a large country, however, a conditional eco-tariff triggers an increase in the environmental tax while an unconditional eco-tariff would make foreign reduce its tax.

These welfare-enhancing incentive effects of a conditional eco-tariff are corroborated by the fact that conditional eco-tariffs can restore global efficiency even if they do not deter eco-dumping and free-riding.

However, we have also identified two main problems which would arise if a conditional eco-tariff was sanctioned by the GATT/WTO regime:

- The first one is the determination of the level of internalisation of the global environmental externality a country would need to achieve to charge others with a conditional eco-tariff.
- Furthermore, a large country might not have an incentive to implement a policy whose result is an enhancement of global environmental quality at the expense of its terms of trade.

Hence, although a change of GATT rules to sanction a conditional eco-tariff might be a useful step towards solving global environmental problems, it is not sure whether this step would actually be taken.

To complete the theoretical investigation of the role eco-tariffs may play in environmental protection if countries are linked through trade we shall now summarise the results we derived in our modified Heckscher-Ohlin-Samuelson trade model.

5. ARE ECO-TARIFFS WELFARE-ENHANCING MEASURES TO AVOID ECO-DUMPING OR TO PROTECT THE GLOBAL ENVIRONMENTAL COMMONS?

ECO-TARIFFS TO AVOID ECO-DUMPING AND ERTB?

The first part of our analysis concerned itself with the question whether eco-tariffs increase environmental quality if trade relations cause governments to set suboptimal environmental taxes to internalise a domestic externality. Particular attention was given to the query whether eco-tariffs can prevent eco-dumping and environmental races towards the bottom in case they occur. Furthermore, if eco-tariffs seem warranted from an ecological point of view, we attempted to assess whether their availability would result in welfare enhancement.

Before we summarise our conclusions to evaluate whether a change of current GATT/WTO rules might be indicated by our theoretical results, we assess the relevance of the three scenarios which we have shown result in eco-dumping for trade reasons.

Regarding the theoretical explanations for eco-dumping, Rauscher [1994] concludes that regulatory capture by import-competing or export industries is the most likely explanation for eco-dumping[2]. The reason is that large rents accrue to producers whose interests are served while the costs are widely dispersed across society[3]. This view is shared by Shrybman [1992][4]. As regards welfare maximisation through terms of trade, Rauscher [1997]

[2] Rauscher [1993, 12]: "... *hidden subsidisation* [in the form of low pollution requirements is the] *in my view preferable approach to explaining environmental dumping and low levels of environmental regulation.*". And Rauscher [1994, 838]: "*Applied to the real world, the interest group approach is the most promising among different candidates for an explanation of ecological dumping.*"

[3] See Rauscher [1993a] referring to Hillman [1989].

[4] Shrybman [1992, 101]: "*Governments ... have a strong inclination to accommodate corporate interests before the point of confrontation is reached. In many cases, governments will anticipate and avoid confrontation by choosing not to put forward initiatives that are likely to provoke a negative response from powerful corporations or business associations.*"

concludes that the relevance of terms of trade improvements by means of environmental policy is negligible since the impact of environmental regulation on total cost is very small and consequently their impact on prices insignificant. Hence governments will have little incentive to manipulate environmental policy in order to achieve a terms of trade improvement[5]. The potential for environmental policy to be used as strategic trade policy is similarly minuscule. Empirical studies investigating the effects of strategic trade policy by means of direct subsidies all conclude that the welfare effects are marginally positive at best[6]. Rauscher [1995a] therefore concludes that strategic environmental policy which introduces an additional distortion would most likely have negative welfare effects.

Hence, we should keep in mind that eco-dumping for terms of trade reasons and strategic environmental policy does not seem to be a serious threat to the environment.

In chapter 4 we found that large countries' terms of trade improve if they curtail import demand and export supply to change the relative price level in their favour. Hence, a country importing the good whose PPM pollutes the environment engages in eco-dumping, while an exporting nation's government follows a NIMBY policy. Therefore, no environmental race towards the bottom occurs.

Since a tariff is a better instrument than an input tax to affect relative world prices, importing countries substitute the eco-tariff for eco-dumping if it is available. This substitution yields environmental and terms of trade benefits for the importing country. However, its trading partners' welfare declines.

In chapter 5, we have shown that strategic use of environmental policy in form of eco-dumping yields benefits for countries hosting a duopolist since eco-dumping increases duopoly and consumer rents. Since both countries hosting such a duopolist follow the same strategy, an environmental race towards the bottom results. Therefore, rents from eco-dumping are partly dissipated as duopoly rents plunge, while environmental quality is suboptimal yet consumer rents increase.

5 See Rauscher [1997, 277].

6 Furthermore, according to Stevens [1995, 178] there seems to be very little evidence that governments engage in strategic environmental policy to influence the trade performance of domestic industries. However Trebilcock & Howse [1995, 364] assess that it is nevertheless likely that governments should selectively and strategically alter environmental regulations in order to help domestic firms prevail in global competition if the industries are characterised by intense and imperfect competition and environmental costs represent a substantial part of doing business.

Availability of a trade policy instrument may relieve the pressure on governments to engage in eco-dumping, yet terms of trade effects offset this effect. Welfare implications of eco-tariffs remain inconclusive.

We now come to the most relevant case, namely eco-dumping if governments are subject to regulatory capture which was analysed in chapter 6. If governments are subject to regulatory capture, they engage in eco-dumping to afford producers of the good whose PPM pollutes the environment an output expansion. All countries whose governments are subject to regulatory capture engage in eco-dumping with the result of an environmental race towards the bottom. While this does not change market share for their producers, the positive output effect prevails, i.e. the race does not lead to a dissipation of rents accruing to governments.

If eco-tariffs are available, they are substituted for eco-dumping in importing countries since the tariff is the better instrument to increase output of the good whose PPM pollutes the environment. However, since both ex- and importers engage in eco-dumping, the environmental race towards the bottom is not completely prevented.

Since international differences in environmental regulation fuel eco-dumping if governments are subject to regulatory capture, we also investigated eco-tariffs conditional upon implementation of (stricter) environmental regulation in exporting countries. Such conditional eco-tariffs cannot avoid an environmental race towards the bottom either.

Welfare effects of eco-tariffs if there is regulatory capture are mixed: if implemented by small countries to cater to the interests of import-competing industries, environmental quality appreciates yet gains from trade are diminished. If implemented by a large country, the tariff has positive welfare effects since both environmental quality and terms of trade improve. However, the large country's trading partners lose.

Finally, we may thus state that there is no theoretical indication that a change of current GATT/WTO rules would bring more than minute environmental benefits. Availability of an eco-tariff would only alleviate protection of ailing industries and possibly terms of trade exploitation.

ECO-TARIFFS TO PROTECT THE GLOBAL ENVIRONMENTAL COMMONS?

The second part of our theoretical investigation dealt with the role of eco-tariffs in the protection of global environmental commons. If pollution damages the global environment, countries do not fully internalise the externality because of free-riding, non-cooperation, and possibly terms of trade reasons. In view of the potentially very dire consequences of neglecting the global environmental commons, their insufficient protection is particularly alarming. Thereforé, we focused our analysis on two issues, namely whether eco-tariffs serve to internalise the global externality if such internalisation is not pursued; and secondly, whether eco-tariffs could increase the world wide level of internalisation.

In chapter 99, we have seen that eco-tariffs can serve protection of the global environmental commons by reducing world-wide production of the good whose PPM pollutes the global environment. Furthermore, global welfare effects of such eco-tariffs are likely to be positive, in particular if exporting countries have little or no environmental measures in place.

In chapter 10, we investigated whether conditional eco-tariffs might enhance incentives for environmental protection. Although this would be the case, we find it unlikely that such eco-tariffs would be implemented because of the negative terms of trade effect of a conditional eco-tariff for countries importing the good whose PPM pollutes the global environment. If they were realised, however, they would most likely raise global welfare.

Regarding a change of current GATT/WTO regulation, our theoretical results indicate that such a change should be considered, albeit that practical problems are likely to abound. However, alarming projections of the future of global environmental commons and the world community's reluctance to protect them should be reason to allow all instruments in the arsenal to counteract global environmental problems.

Chapter 11

Policy Debate: Introductory Remarks

Trade restrictions in the form of eco-tariffs addressing PPM pollution of imports have been considered by policy-makers, both in the context of domestic and global pollution. However, so far such eco-tariffs have not become part of environmental or trade policy. One reason for this is that they are not sanctioned by the multilateral trade regime, codified in the GATT/WTO. At the conclusion of the Uruguay Round[1], a Committee on Trade and Environment (CTE) was established to assess whether a change of the regulations to further environmental protection and sustainable development may be warranted.

The policy debate surrounding eco-tariffs is subject of chapters 12 and 13; the remainder of this chapter gives a brief summary of current GATT/WTO rules affecting trade and environmental protection, tensions arising from them, and the mandate of the CTE.

BACKGROUND: GATT RULES, ENVIRONMENTAL PROTECTION AND THE CTE

The GATT is a multilateral treaty which lays down a set of rules that contracting parties of the GATT have to follow in their trade relations with each other[2]. Although the GATT rules are complex, they are based on a

[1] The Uruguay Round lasted from 1986-1993; it was the last one of eight trade rounds between the Contracting Parties of the GATT; see next section.

[2] GATT, which came into being in 1947, is charged with overseeing international trade in goods and, in particular, the liberalisation of trade by means of negotiated reduction in tariff barriers. Trade negotiations have taken place through a succession of 'Rounds' of which the last ('Uruguay Round') resulted in the integration of the GATT into the WTO in 1995. The WTO encompasses administration of a liberal, open system of trade in goods,

limited number of basic principles. These are non-discrimination between products imported from different sources (Article I, the most favoured nation clause)[3] - and between imported and domestically produced goods (Article III, the national treatment rule).

The GATT does not contain any direct references to the environment or environmental protection. Yet existing rules put only few constraints on countries' ability to pursue policies to protect the environment. Countries can take any environmental measure against imported products, provided that equivalent measures are in place for domestically produced goods and that the measure does not discriminate between products from different importing countries[4]. Similarly, export restrictions can be maintained if there are equivalent restrictions on the domestic sale of the same good. Furthermore, GATT Article XX contains exceptional circumstances under which countries are allowed to take measures otherwise inconsistent with GATT strictures, provided such measures are taken pursuant to goals specified in Article XX. As regards environmental protection, such measures are usually subsumed under policies to protect human, animal or plant life and health, or policies relating to the conservation of natural resources[5].

Nevertheless, tensions have arisen between environmental protection policies and the free trade regime. These tensions work both ways[6]: environmental policy may be formulated in such a way as to hinder trade flows, and trade rules may prevent adequate environmental protection.

Environmental policy measures suspected to hamper free trade are product standards. GATT's National Treatment Rule ensures that domestically produced goods and imports are to be treated equally, i.e. subjected to the same standards and regulations. Nevertheless, exporters - in

---

services and trade related-intellectual property rights. The WTO's larger scope of responsibilities and its status as an international organisation corresponds to the intent of the 1944 Bretton Woods Agreement to set up an International Trade Organisation (ITO) to administer a multilateral trade regime. The ITO was to cooperate with two other international organisations whose establishment was decided in Bretton Woods: the International Monetary Fund with the mandate to monitor exchange rate stability, and the International Bank for Reconstruction and Development with the task to provide developing countries with capital to build up their economic capacity. However, only the latter two organisations were created. Instead of the ITO, GATT was negotiated, originally as a provisional agreement (compare Trebilcock & Howse [1995, 20/21]).

3 For the relevant paragraphs from GATT Articles see Appendix.

4 This includes environmental product taxes which can be adjusted at the border to prevent imported products from undermining the environmentally beneficial effect of domestic taxes and regulations (compare Eglin [1995, 772]).

5 See Appendix.

6 We give here only a brief overview of these controversial issues; they are taken up in detail in chapters 12 and 13.

particular in developing countries - fear that their products are put at a disadvantage by the growing number of product standards[7].

Environmental criticism of trade rules is two-fold:

- GATT rules prevent contracting parties from making access to their market conditional upon environmental policies adressing PPM standards in exporting countries[8]. Consequently, GATT rules cannot be invoked by countries which want to restrict market access in order to alleviate competitive pressure on their domestic environmental PPM standards. The wording of GATT rules induces governments to use design rather than PPM performance standards to regulate imports and domestically produced goods alike. However, depending on the environmental problem at hand, such policy measures may be inadequate[9].
- The second criticism addresses the fact that GATT does not make a distinction between purely domestic and global environmental problems in its prohibition of trade instruments based on PPM regulation in exporting countries[10]. Hence, trade restrictions as part of multilateral environmental agreements addressing global environmental problems would not be exempted from GATT strictures and could thus be challenged at the WTO[11].

The establishment of the WTO 1995 in Marrakesh marks a cornerstone for the future of the relationship between trade and environmental protection. In contrast to the GATT texts, the preamble to the Agreement Establishing

7 See OECD [1995b, 7; 30] and Sorsa [1995, 1/2; 7]. GATT conformity of product standards is achieved by the Technical Barriers of Trade (TBT) and Sanitary and Phytosanitary Standards (SPSS) Codes which are designed to prevent countries from using product-related standards and technical as well as sanitary and phytosanitary regulations to create unnecessary obstacles to trade. Furthermore, TBT and SPSS codes develop rules and disciplines to prevent implicit discrimination against imports through the use of product standards. (See Hauser & Schanz [1995, 113-116] for more details on the TBT Code and Hauser & Schanz [1995, 184-186] for more details on the SPSS Code). Apart from binding standards, there are also voluntary ones - so called eco-labels - which can be potent barriers to entry into markets of environmentally sensitive goods (Bhagwati [1993a, 46]). Owing to their voluntary nature, eco-labels are not subject to GATT regulations and often influenced by domestic producer lobbies to discriminate against foreign importers (Gornig & Silagi [1992, 757], Sorsa [1995, 4/5]). Similarly, specifications of packaging requirements or recycling content are often set in a discriminatory fashion (Sorsa [1995, 5]).

8 A distinction or discrimination of a product at the border is only possible if the criterion upon which such discrimination takes place is incorporated in the product (Mikesell [1993, 15], Thomas & Tereposky [1993b, 26]).

9 See Feketekuty [1993, 184] and Sorsa [1995, 7].

10 See French [1993b, 14] and Mikesell [1993, 17].

11 See Sorsa [1995, 9 & 1992, 128].

the WTO mentions environmental issues in its objectives[12]. Furthermore, at their meeting in Marrakesh, WTO member states also decided to initiate a comprehensive work programme on trade and environment. The objective of this initiative was to relieve the tensions between environmental protection and the multilateral trade rules, and to further coordination between trade and environmental policies. The Ministerial Decision on Trade and Environment established the Committee on Trade and Environment (CTE) with the following analytical and prescriptive mandate[13]: to identify the relationship between trade and environmental policy, and to advance recommendations for necessary modifications of the GATT/WTO regime to make international trade and environmental policies mutually supportive[14].

The CTE's work is guided by two parameters, namely as a WTO Committee, its competence is limited to trade policy and such aspects of environmental policy which may result in significant trade effects for its Members; and if problems of trade and environmental policy coordination are identified, steps proposed by the CTE to resolve them have to be consistent with the principles of the multilateral trading system.

According to its mandate, the CTE's work evolved around 10 subjects of which the relationship between the provisions of the multilateral trading system and trade measures for environmental purposes, including those pursuant to multilateral environmental agreements; and the relationship between the provisions of the multilateral trading system and charges and taxes for environmental purposesare of relevance for the issues addressed in our study[15]. Results of the discussions in the CTE were summarised in the CTE's first Report[16] which was submitted to the first WTO Ministerial Conference in Singapore[17].

[12] See Appendix.

[13] See Appendix for extracts from the mandate of the CTE. The CTE is not the first body dealing with these issues. Its work builds upon the foundations laid by the former GATT Working Group on Environmental Measures and International Trade which met from 1991 - 1993 and the Sub-Committee of the Preparatory Committee of the WTO which met though 1994 (OECD [1995b, 15/16]).

[14] This mandate is based on Principle 12 of the Rio Declaration which states that "*states should cooperate to promote a supportive and open international economic system that would lead to economic growth and sustainable development in all countries to better address the problems of environmental degradation*", and on Agenda 21, Section I, Chapter 2 where §21 states as an objective: "*to make international trade and environmental policies mutually supportive in favour of sustainable development.*" (Sand et al. [1994]).

[15] For the remaining items which are discussed in the CTE see Appendix.

[16] WTO [1996a].

[17] The conference took place December 1996; for a summary of the conference's results see IMF [1997, 6].

Chapter 12

Eco-tariffs and Domestic Environmental Policy

Trade restrictions in form of eco-tariffs have so far not become part of environmental or trade policy. However, they have been deliberated by policy makers in the context of domestic pollution[1]: Policy proposals have been formulated to introduce tariffs to offset international differences in environmental policy stringency. Yet, current GATT/WTO rules do not sanction such eco-tariffs; neither does the work of the CTE indicate changes which would make eco-tariffs in the context of domestic environmental problems consistent with multilateral trade rules. However, if environmental policy is pursued by means of taxes, border tax adjustments might become possible for both product and PPM taxes.

The reason why differences in domestic environmental policies should be counterbalanced by trade measures is the presumption that differences in stringency of environmental regulation are instances of eco-dumping and unfair trade. To avoid environmental deterioration and loss of competitiveness, policies to introduce eco-tariffs to 'level the playing field' have been proposed. Such eco-tariffs can be analysed in the light of the theoretical evidence gathered in chapters 4,5 and 6.

Eco-tariffs and other trade measures to 'level the playing field' are banned by the current reading of GATT/WTO rules, and deliberations in the CTE do not indicate but minor departures from this stance. Again, these rules can be analysed in the light of the theoretical evidence gathered in chapters 4, 5 and 6.[2].

1 Compare Bhagwati [1996, 5].

2 As an alternative to trade measures to adjust internationally differing environmental standards, some environmentalists and agencies propose and pursue harmonisation. This is not the focus of our study, yet we provide a brief summary and discussion at the end of this chapter.

1. ISSUE, POLICY INITIATIVES AND PROPONENTS

We shall first introduce the issue - namely competitiveness consequences of internationally differing environmental standards - which has prompted the demand for eco-tariffs to offset these differences. Furthermore, we shall present these policy proposals which up to date remained initiatives since none of them has ever been put into legislation. Finally, we shall present the main proponents of eco-tariffs in their role as countervailing measures against less stringent environmental policy.

COMPETITIVENESS AND INTERNATIONAL DIFFERENCES IN ENVIRONMENTAL POLICY

North American economies, many western European countries and Japan have increased stringency in environmental regulation over the past decades[3]. However, central and east European countries, most developing nations and also the boosting Asian economies have not implemented comparable environmental policy measures[4].

These international differences in environmental regulation change comparative advantages. Producers in high regulation countries complain that they operate in an unfair global trade environment or that imports are more favourably treated by laxer environmental policies[5]. Therefore, cost differences stemming from internationally differing environmental standards and ensuing competitiveness issues have gained increasing importance in the political debate[6].

Such political pressures result in demands for trade instruments. Justification is sought on grounds of 'unfair trade' with the objective to offset competitiveness effects of internationally differing environmental regulation, and to grant domestic producers protection because of the

[3] See Sorsa [1994].

[4] See Levin [1992, 231pp], Repetto [1993,4], OECD [1994], and OECD [1995a].

[5] "*Producers within high-standard countries have long complained that they operate in a relatively unfair trade environment, since their costs are significantly higher than those of comparable producers in neighbouring countries.*" (Whalley [1991, 188]; see also Anderson [1995, 2] and Shrybman [1992, 100/101]).

[6] An example is the heated debate in the U. S. on 'pollution heavens' in Mexico prior to signing the North American Free Trade Agreement (NAFTA), and the fear that American health and environmental standards may be undermined. (see Esty [1994, 35] and Feketekuty [1993, 187pp]).

'unlevelled' playing field[7]. These demands are supported by environmental pressure groups. They argue that trade instruments support environmental protection by reducing the pressure on governments from producer lobbies to level the playing field by lowering environmental standards[8].

POLICY PROPOSALS IN THE UNITED STATES

To avoid international differences in environmental regulation, harmonisation of standards has been proposed. However, since so far no agreement upon any (minimum) standards has been reached[9], politicians - mainly in the U. S. - have advanced a legislative process to sanction trade measures contingent upon environmental stringency abroad[10].

In the last decade, the U. S. has increased its efforts to reduce environmental degradation. Thereby, substantial costs have arisen[11]. Other countries' failure to address their industries' impact on the environment and the perceived trade advantage this creates has led members of the U.S. Congress to call for inclusion of environmental issues in national trade policy and the international trade regime[12].

One of the tacks pursued is to condition trade on environmental protection, similar to Congress' treatment of labour rights and conditionality in the 1980s[13]. If passed, such legislation would have introduced

[7] Compare Whalley [1991, 186] who states: "*An element of the emerging interface between environmental and trade policies ... is the pressures on trade policies created by differing environmental standards.*" See also Bhagwati [1993, 44] or French [1993b, 18].

[8] "*Environmental groups perceive trade policy as a means .... of raising national environmental standards at home and abroad.*" (Anderson [1995, 4]; see also Esty [1994, 162]).

[9] See Levinson [1996, 431].

[10] See Levin [1992, 232] and Stevens [1995, 178].

[11] Cost for environmental protection in the U. S. was 1,4% of GDP in 1980 and 1,6% in 1990 according to Sorsa [1994, 14].

[12] See Levin [1992, 232].

[13] In the U. S. Omnibus Trade and Competitiveness Act of 1988, the U. S. Congress made clear that the failure to provide certain worker rights could be considered an 'unreasonable' trade practice against which the U. S. Trade Representative might retaliate under Section 301 of the 1974 Trade Act (compare Charnovitz [1992, 341]). Section 301 and Super 301 provisions of U. S. trage legistlation as updated in the 1988 Act demand negotiations from specific countries on 'priority' practices that the U. S. find unacceptable, regardless of whether they are procribed by the GATT or another treaty. Furthermore, under Section 301, the U. S. might seek abolition of such practices on a time schedule set by the U. S. using tariff retaliation if deemed necessary (see Bhagwati [1992b, 449/50]). Similar to the arguments of labour regulations, concern for internationally differing environmental protection efforts is mainly rooted in the fear that they negatively affect competitiveness of U. S. industries. In addition, concern for environmental quality or

environmental conditionality by forcing trading partners of the U. S. to comply with minimum environmental standards, or risk trade sanctions[14]. However, so far Congress has not yet enacted an environmental protection provision analogous to the one for labour rights[15].

Another initiative taken by Congress was to impose countervailing duties against countries whose environmental protection efforts do not match the level required in the U. S.[16].

The first example is a proposed amendment to the Clean Air Act[17]. If it had been passed, this amendment would have enabled the Secretary of Commerce to levy a fee upon any imported good for which PPM regulations would have been found in breach with the Clean Air Act. This fee would hence be tantamount to a countervailing (eco)duty[18].

Legislation which has a similar thrust yet broader scope is the Boren bill[19] which proposes a duty that would have amounted to the

> *"...cost which would have to be incurred by the manufacturer or producer of the foreign articles of merchandise to comply with environmental standards imposed on U.S. producers of the same class or kind of merchandise."*[20]

If passed, this bill would have imposed countervailing eco-duties on imports produced under environmental standards violating any U.S. environmental regulations.

So far, all of these proposals have been - even if sometimes narrowly[21] - defeated. However, a sequel of attempts to pass a 'Green 301'[22] provision

---

workers' rights outside the U. S. play a role which is likely to increase with the severity of the environmental problem (compare Levin [1992, 250] and Whalley [1991, 187]).

14 If applied to environmental policy, the relevant provisions of the Omnibus Trade and Competitiveness Act of 1988 would characterise lax environmental policy as an unfair trade practice under Section 301 of the Trade Act of 1974. If applicable, Section 301 grants the President of the U. S. discretion to retaliate against products originating from countries violating U.S. environmental standards (see Levin [1992, 252]).

15 See Levin [1992, 250].

16 Article VI of the GATT specifies that countervailing duties can be levied by contracting parties on imports that are causing harm to domestic industries because they are subsidised by a foreign government (see Appendix and Trebilcock & Howse [1995, 125]).

17 Amendment 1321 to the 1967 Clean Air Act (also called Gorden amendment) was defeated in 1990 (see Levin [1992, 254] and Esty [1994, 163/164]).

18 See Levin [1992, 254].

19 See Levin [1992, 254].

20 Levin [1992, 254/255]; hence, this duty would not be just tantamount to a countervailing eco-duty but defined as such since the Boren bill identifies "*the failures of a government to impose effective environmental controls on production and manufacturing within its borders as a significant and unfair subsidy*". (Levin [1992, 254]).

21 The Gorden Amendment was defeated 52:47 (see Esty [1994, 163/164]).

22 Compare footnote 13.

may be expected if international differences in environmental regulation stirs protest of American producers again[23].

PROPONENTS

Eco-tariffs as countervailing eco-duties are supported by politicians concerned with competitiveness of U. S. industry, and by environmentalists who fear that competitive pressure might lead to a world-wide ERTB. Furthermore, they are supported by producers' interest groups, i.e. by lobbyists who hope to gain protection against competing imports.

We have already stated that - at least some - U.S. **politicians** support eco-tariffs to offset competitiveness effects of internationally differing environmental standards. Vice President Al Gore also voiced such an opinion, blaming lax environmental standards as unfair trading practices[24]. A similar position has been taken by the parliament of the European Union[25].

Producers who are subject to environmental regulation driving up their cost of production object to such a burden on competitiveness grounds; their position either on the domestic or on foreign markets is undermined if other countries' governments have weak environmental standards, or ineffectually enforce existing pollution control measures. If opposition against stringent domestic environmental policy fails, producer lobbies support trade measures to offset competitive advantage of foreign producers. Import restrictions on products from low standards countries " .... *reduce opposition by local firms to higher standards at home* ..."[26]

[23] See Esty [1994, 155] who mentions House of Representatives' Majority Leader Gephardt's intent to do so.

[24] See Esty [1994, 164].

[25] Non-uniform environmental regulation is a "....*disincentive to the adoption of progressive environmental laws - as in the recent case of the European Community's reluctance to adopt a proposed tax on CO2 emissions in the absence of a similar commitment by its industrial competitors Japan and the U. S.*" (French [1993a, 29]; see also Esty [1994, 164]).

[26] Anderson [1995, 2]. Shrybman [1992, 100/101] gives a concrete example: "*The Canadian Chemical Producers Association, for instance, warned several years ago that 'if unnecessary or excessive costs are introduced unilaterally by any country, innovation and development will simply cease or be transferred to jurisdictions with a more favourable business climate*'." See also Cairncross [1993, 317].

In the U. S. in particular, passage of legislation in the labour rights field has encouraged producers to lobby for trade conditioning environmental bills and resolutions.[27]

Environmentalists promote stringent environmental protection, possibly around the world. Therefore, they prefer harmonisation of international environmental standards at the highest possible level[28]. However, for fear of successful opposition of industry lobby groups[29], potentially resulting in an ERTB, environmentalists support policies catering to the interests of those opposed to stringent environmental regulation[30], namely

> *"sweeping programs of [eco]-duties to be imposed on imports from countries they deem to have weak environmental programs."*[31]

2. ECO-TARIFFS AND OTHER TRADE RESTRICTIONS TO OFFSET COMPETITIVE EFFECTS OF ENVIRONMENTAL REGULATION: POLICY ANALYSIS

We shall first map the issues and policy proposals relating to eco-tariffs against the theoretical evidence we gathered in chapters 3, 4 and 5. As we find that the contexts in which eco-tariffs have been demanded do not convincingly fit the stylised facts of avoidance of eco-dumping either for terms of trade or for strategic environmental policy, we advance the

27 See Levin [1992, 250].

28 See Levin [1992, 234].

29 The "*environmental camp has articulated* [the] *concern ... that trade liberalisation may degrade the environment by putting competitive pressure on environmental standards....*" (Charnovitz [1995, 6]).

30 "*... producer interest groups and some environmental groups are nevertheless finding it advantageous to use environmental arguments in support of their claims for unilateral import restrictions, particularly following the costly imposition of stricter environmental standards on domestic producers.*" (Anderson [1995, 10]; see also Beghin et al. [1994a] and Levin [1992, 234] on coalitions between environmental and producer interest groups).

31 Arden-Clarke [1993]. Arden-Clarke writes for the World Wide Fund for Nature (WWF) and promotes tariffs to reduce short-term economic cost of introducing environmental regulation (see also Arden-Clarke [1991&1992]). Furthermore, GATT [1992, 28] states: "*When it comes to the impact of environmental policies on production costs, demands by domestic producers for a 'level playing field' often find support among environmental groups. One reason is that they fear that if 'low' standards abroad regarding industrial pollution are perceived at home to be detrimental to competitiveness, they could give rise to political pressures to lower the standards at home.*"

alternative explanation for the surge of eco-tariffs: their intent is primarily protectionism behind which regulatory capture is looming large.

ECO-TARIFFS TO AVOID ECO-DUMPING?

The issue at the heart of the debate is the fact that internationally differing environmental standards affect competitiveness. Lower standards are interpreted as an instance of eco-dumping, and trade instruments are demanded to offset such an unfair advantage for exports or import-competing products. Furthermore, we note that the unfairness of lower standards elsewhere is stressed most forcefully along with the pressure this exerts on domestic standards[32].

These observations are not consistent with stylised facts of eco-tariffs to avoid eco-dumping for terms of trade reasons. If terms of trade improvement was the motive for introducing eco-tariffs, the reason for the demand for eco-tariffs would predominantly be the protection of the domestic environment through the relief of downward pressure on domestic standards. Furthermore, the attempt to blame other countries for implementing too lax environmental regulation is also inconsistent with our theoretical results: both small and large countries have no incentive to downgrade environmental protection measures for terms of trade reasons[33].

Regarding trade instruments to avoid eco-dumping for strategic reasons, we find the emphasis on competitiveness effects of lower environmental standards abroad consistent with the stylised facts. However, the fact that almost exclusively foreign nations hosting firms exporting into the domestic market are blamed for eco-dumping is not. Furthermore, if strategic environmental policy was the issue, again the downward pressure on environmental standards should be stressed as the main reason to introduce trade measures in response to eco-dumping elsewhere. Finally, a more diverse set of measures should be demanded, i.e. the possibility to subsidise domestic firms subject to environmental regulation, or the possibility to rebate environmental charges in excess of the level predominant for competitors at the border.[34]

Policy proposals trying to offset lax environmental standards in exporting countries are consistent with the circumstances which arise if governments are subject to regulatory capture[35]. However, avoidance of eco-dumping and

[32] Whalley [1991, 188] mentions unfairness of lower environmental standards as the central argument advanced in this context.

[33] Compare chapter 4.

[34] Compare chapter 5.

[35] Compare chapter 6.

hence improvement of environmental quality is not the main concern; more important is safeguarding competitiveness.

Therefore, we conclude that although eco-tariffs in the form of countervailing eco-duties are demanded, it does not seem that this request has an environmental intent. Safeguarding high environmental standards or the avoidance of an ERTB is not the driving force behind the call for eco-tariffs. Instead, the most prominent argument is countervailance of unfairly low standards which are seen to afford indirect subsidies to imports[36].

TARIFFS TO AFFORD PROTECTION?

If eco-tariffs in response to internationally differing environmental standards have the predominant objective to protect industries subject to environmental regulation, regulatory capture is looming large as the explanation. This ties in with results in chapter 10 where we concluded that the most likely reason for eco-dumping is in fact regulatory capture.

The view of differing - in particular lower - environmental standards as an incidence of unfairness which could legitimise countervailing trade measures is flawed: environmental conditions differ internationally and such differences constitute competitive advantages or disadvantages which are the very engine of trade[37]. The legitimacy of internationally differing environmental standards has been accepted as a guiding principle of international environmental policy-making[38].

Therefore, if countervailing eco-duties supposedly aimed at domestic environmental protection are supported by politicians and environmental pressure groups, we might suspect the following:

– an instance of constraint regulatory capture where producers of goods whose PPM pollutes the environment may influence trade policy yet not

[36] Proponents of eco-tariffs "*.... have justified using countervailing duties on imports produced under low environmental standards on the grounds that not requiring producers to internalise their pollution subsidises these products.*" (Mikesell [1993, 16]). A good example is the following quote from the former German secretary of agriculture Kiechle (cited in Meinheit [1996, 1/2]): "*Denn auf die Dauer wäre es doch paradox, wenn wir in der EG mit großem finanziellen Aufwand die landwirtschaftlichen Produkte immer umweltverträglicher gestalten, gleichzeitig aber immer mehr Agrarprodukte in die EG hineinlassen müssen, die anderswo auf der Welt ohne Rücksicht auf die Umwelt billig produziert worden sind.*"

[37] Compare chapter 2; also Esty [1994, 164].

[38] The Rio Declaration Principle 11 states: "*Standards applied by some countries may be inappropriate and of unwarranted economic and social cost to other countries....*" Furthermore, Agenda 12, Section I, Chapter 2 elaborates in §20: "*...account should be taken of the fact that environmental standards valid for developed countries may have unwarranted social and economic cost in developing countries.*" (Sands et al. [1994]).

environmental policy. Rather than downward pressure on domestic standards, they hence put upward pressure on trade protection; or
- environmental pressure groups caring for environmental quality abroad who support eco-tariffs with the objective of avoiding eco-dumping in foreign countries[39].

VanGrasstek [1992] finds empirical support for the former hypothesis: politicians and policy-makers with a protectionist agenda invoke environmental protection and seek the support of environmentalists to disguise their protectionist intent[40]. VanGrasstek's data offer partial confirmation for the hypothesis that environmental claims do in fact work to the benefit of trade protection[41].

With regard to the latter hypothesis, our results from chapter 6 are relevant: we have shown that conditional eco-tariffs are not promising environmental policy instruments to improve environmental conditions abroad. Hence, the policy analysis seems to support the alternative that environmentalists arguing for green protection[42] join forces with industrialists arguing for trade protection rather than for the protection of the environment[43].

3. GATT/WTO RULES: CURRENT INTERPRETATION, POSSIBLE CHANGES AND EVALUATION

We have stated above that GATT puts virtually no constraints on countries' ability to protect the environment. With respect to product-related externalities, this is true for the domestic and global environment: as long as national treatment and the most favoured nations clause are observed, policies do not collide with GATT strictures. However, as far as the externalities addressed in this study, i.e. PPM-related externalities, are concerned, the above statement has to be modified: GATT/WTO puts no constraint on countries' ability to **directly** protect their domestic

39 They have been coined 'supergreens' (compare Hillman & Ursprung [1992&1993] and Rauscher [1995b]).

40 VanGrasstek [1992] empirically addresses the question whether the U. S. Senate's voting record on selected issues involving trade and environmental issues between 1980 and 1990 supports the claim that protection is more attractive to legislators when it is presented in environmental guise.

41 See VanGrasstek [1992, 239].

42 See Pearce [1993, 8].

43 See Mikesell [1993, 16].

environment. Indirect protection, i.e. using trade policy to countervail lower environmental standards abroad to equalise differences – be it to maintain high domestic standards or for other reasons – are not consistent with the current interpretation of GATT/WTO rules[44]. The result of the CTE's deliberations regarding trade measures and domestic environmental problems confirm this position, with the exception of border tax adjustment for which a change of rules might be considered.

RELEVANT GATT/WTO RULES AND THEIR INTERPRETATION

ARTICLE XX AND THE ISSUE OF EXTRAJURISDICTION

Under certain exceptions specified in Article XX (b) and (g), contracting parties of the GATT can take trade measures otherwise inconsistent with their GATT obligations to protect the environment[45].

According to the interpretation of the GATT, however, trade policy instruments cannot be levied against products on account of differences in PPMs. The reason is that this would amount to an extrajurisdictional application of domestic laws and regulations which is inconsistent with the multilateral and consensus-based nature of the GATT/WTO[46].

The Dispute Settlement Panel on United States - Restrictions on the Imports of Tuna states[47]:

> " ... *the consensus of the drafters of Article XX (b) focused on the use of sanitary measures to safeguard life or health of humans, animals or plants within the jurisdiction of the importing country.* "

The same applies also to Article XX (g). Therefore, the GATT exceptions clause does not enable contracting parties to apply trade measures

44 Protection of the global environment by trade policy instruments addressing PPM externalities is also not consistent with GATT/WTO rules or their interpretation. This is addressed in the next chapter.

45 Or rather to protect human, animal or plant health, or to conserve natural resources (see chapter 12).

46 GATT [1992, 23] states explicitly: "*In principle, it is not possible under GATT's rules to make access to one's own market dependent on the domestic environmental policies or practices of the exporting country.* " The reason given is that "[This requirement] *exists ... to protect each member of GATT from the unilateral imposition of domestic standards or policies by importing countries through the threat of market access restrictions.*" (GATT [1992, 23/24]).

47 Cited after Mattoo & Mavroidis [1996, 64]. It should be noted that the Tuna Panel has never been adapted, and is hence not an official GATT/WTO document.

against imports, if the PPMs of such imports are suspected or found to harm environmental conditions outside the jurisdiction of the importing country.

ARTICLE III AND THE INTERPRETATION OF THE 'LIKE PRODUCT' TERM

Article III states that laws and regulations - inter alia those to protect the environment - can be applied to imported products under the condition that similar laws and regulations are in place for domestically produced goods.

According to the interpretation by GATT Dispute Settlement Panels, however, environmental laws and regulations cannot be applied against imports on the basis that their PPMs pollute the environment, unless such environmentally polluting PPMs can be traced in the physical characteristics of a product.

> *"GATT Dispute Panels have found ... that GATT Article III applies only to regulations aimed at risks or attributes of a' product as such', and not to those aimed at environmental harmful activities involved in the PPM of a Product. "*[48]

The argument boils down to the fact that policies may not differentiate between 'like products'[49].

The 'like product'-term, however, is nowhere defined in GATT/WTO. The GATT Working Group on Border Tax Adjustment which had been established to examine taxes and related provisions of the GATT makes the following comment on this issue:

> *"With regard to the interpretation of the term .....'like or similar products' ... which occurs some sixteen times throughout the General Agreement, it was recalled that considerable discussion has taken place ..... but that no further improvement of the term had been achieved. The Working Party concluded that problems arising from the interpretation of the term should be examined on a case-by-case basis. "*[50]

Hence, since the case-by-case decisions imply that differences in environmental PPM regulations do not make a product 'unlike' in the eyes of the GATT/WTO, one has to conclude that laws and regulations addressing PPMs cannot be applied to imported products, unless these PPMs are discernible in the characteristics of the final product.

[48] Lallas et al. [1992, 277].

[49] This is stated in Article III.4: "*The products of the territory of any contracting party imported into the territory of any other contracting party shall be accorded treatment no less favourable than that accorded to like products of national origin in respect of all laws, regulations and requirements affecting their internal sale, offering for sale, purchase, transportation, distribution or use....*" (GATT [1994]).

[50] GATT [1970, § 16] cited after Helm [1995, 101].

However, ruling and argument by another Dispute Settlement Panel (United States Measures Affecting Alcoholic and Malt Beverages) indicates that this interpretation may not be carved in stone[51]:

> "... *the findings of the* [United States Measures Affecting Alcoholic and Malt Beverages] *Panel appear to loosen the strict 'physical characteristics' criteria to include policy objectives ... for which the measure was designed to achieve.* "

GATT/WTO SUBSIDIES AGREEMENT

Under Article VI of the GATT, countervailing duties can be levied by contracting parties on imports if such imports are subsidised by the exporting country's government and cause harm to domestic industries.

According to the definition of subsidies under the Uruguay Round Subsidies Agreement, however, no or lax environmental policy measures cannot be interpreted as an indirect, countervailable subsidy[52]. Subsidies are:

- financial contribution by the government or any public body, involving a direct monetary transfer; or
- a direct transfer of liabilities; or
- foregone government revenue which would otherwise have been due; or
- any of the above carried out by a private body but initiated and financed by the government or any public body.

This definition clarifies that the absence of environmental policy measures would not be considered under GATT/WTO regulations as a subsidy to domestic producers[53]. The absence of adequate environmental policy measures is neither a direct transfer of funds or liabilities nor foregone government revenue. The latter would only apply if governments would afford a break of taxes or charges to specific industries or firms.

RULES FOR BORDER TAX AND REGULATION ADJUSTMENT

The GATT allows its contracting parties in general to adjust taxes at the border, i.e. to tax imported products provided that similar taxes are levied domestically, or to rebate taxes upon exportation.

This rule, however, cannot be applied to environmental taxes addressing PPM externalities since a GATT Working Party on Border Tax Adjustment specified in its final report the following conditions regarding the eligibility for border tax adjustment:

51 Cited after Chakarian [1994, 119].

52 See Trebilcock & Howse [1995, 131].

53 The same accounts for suboptimally low environmental policy measures.

> *"The Working Party concluded that there was convergence of views to the effect that taxes directly levied on products were eligible for tax adjustment....Furthermore, the Working Party concluded that ... certain taxes that were not directly levied on products were not eligible for tax adjustment."*[54]

This interpretation was reinforced by a GATT Dispute Settlement Panel which followed the interpretation set forth by the Working Party on Border Tax Adjustment. The Dispute Settlement Panel on United States - Taxes on Petroleum and Certain Imported Substances stressed that eligibility for border tax adjustment is guided by the question whether the tax is levied on the **product**, while the policy purpose of the tax is irrelevant in this context[55].

A further GATT Panel adjudicated that the rule that only taxes directly levied upon a product can be adjusted at the border also applies to (environmental) regulations[56].

We can hence conclude that the current interpretation of GATT rules on border tax adjustment and border regulation adjustment clearly prohibits any measures to offset international differences in environmental PPM taxes or regulations.

CTE'S DELIBERATIONS AND RECOMMENDATIONS

The CTE submitted a Report on its recommendations and ongoing deliberations to the WTO Ministerial Conference in Singapore in 1996[57]. Regarding trade restrictions as environmental policy instruments, the CTE prefers national environmental policy addressing the problem at its source. Trade instruments addressing PPM externalities were specifically referred to: such

[54] GATT [1970, § 14] cited after Chakarian [1994, 116]. Examples of direct taxes are specific excise duties, sales taxes and value-added taxes; example for an indirect tax is a social security charge.

[55] See Chakarian [1994, 116/117].

[56] Such has been the interpretation by the GATT Panel on restrictions which were applied by the U. S. against tuna imports from Mexico because of harvesting methods used by Mexican fishermen (GATT [1991]; we address the Tuna Case in more detail in the next chapter).

[57] WTO [1996a].

"measures should not be applied in such a way as to differentiate 'like products' at the border."[58]

This is stated even more explicitly in an earlier publication where it was found

"that unilateral trade measures aimed at achieving environmental objectives which lie outside the jurisdiction of the country imposing them or ... must be avoided."[59]

The CTE's negative stance vis-à-vis trade measures to offset competitiveness effects of internationally differing environmental standards is stated forcefully in the Report:

"WTO Member governments are committed not to introduce WTO-inconsistent or protectionist trade restrictions or countervailing measures in an attempt to offset any real or perceived adverse domestic economic or competitiveness effects of applying environmental policies; not only would this undermine the open, equitable and non-discriminatory nature of the multilateral trading system, it would also prove counterproductive to meeting environmental objectives and promoting sustainable development."[60]

As regards border tax adjustments on the other hand, the CTE had not come to conclusions which could have been put to the Ministerial Conference as a recommendation. The CTE agreed that it was unclear whether taxes on inputs incorporated but not exhausted in PPMs could be adjusted. However, while some Members suggested that environmental taxes should qualify for a different treatment than other fiscal measures, others supported the view that non-product-related PPMs should not be made eligible for border tax adjustment[61]. Hence the Report concluded that "*further work on this Item is needed.*"[62]

Further work on this issue by the CTE identified advantages - such as efficiency gains - as well as drawbacks of extending the scope of border tax adjustment to include PPM taxes[63]. To better judge positive and negative effects, the CTE suggested

58 WTO [1996a, § 101].
59 WTO [1995].
60 WTO [1996a, § 168].
61 See WTO [1996a, § 51].
62 WTO [1996a, § 181].
63 Difficulties were expected to arise in administering border tax adjustment for PPM taxes; the danger of protectionist abuse was discerned, and a possible reduction of the

"to conduct an analysis of the feasibility, environmental benefits and potential disguised protectionism associated with adjusting taxes at the border based on the way in which goods were produced or processed."[64]

EVALUATION

The central conclusion from the GATT/WTO rules and their interpretation regarding indirect environmental protection is that measures applied to imported products cannot be taken on the basis of such products' PPMs.

Although the Dispute Settlement Panels are not taking a unanimous and definite view on trade measures addressing PPM externalities, the CTE's stance on the issue indicates that the WTO does not envisage to sanction trade measures addressing environmental externalities caused by non-product-related PPMs.

GATT/WTO's main arguments against trade measures addressing PPM externalities are that

- they may lead the trading system down a 'slippery slope'[65] of protectionism as PPM-based border measures could easily be used for protectionist purposes, and
- the use of trade measures to enforce PPM standards abroad would be tantamount to an extrajurisdictional imposition of standards on an importing country's trading partners.

While the former would jeopardise the functioning of the international division of labour and hence the positive welfare effects associated with it, the latter would run counter to the fundamental principles underlying the international trading system.

Our theoretical investigation in II.A has shown that although there are some instances when eco-tariffs or other trade instruments addressing PPM externalities may be environmentally beneficial, these instances are rare. Furthermore, even in the cases in which eco-tariffs have been found to possibly improve environmental quality, they are not necessarily welfare-enhancing.

---

effectiveness of eco-taxes in achieving their environmental goals was noted (WTO [1997, 4]).

64 WTO [1997, 4].

65 GATT [1992, 22] on this issue: "*If the door were opened to use trade policies unilaterally to offset the competitiveness of differing environmental standards, or to attempt to force other countries to adopt domestically-favoured practices and policies, the trading system would start down a very slippery slope.*"

Therefore, our results do not refute or even challenge the unwavering position of the GATT/WTO to ban eco-tariffs and other environmentally motivated trade measures to avoid a reduction in trade flows and to maintain an open, equitable and non-discriminatory trading system. As our investigation has shown that sanctioning eco-tariffs would most likely lead to a deterioration of both environmental quality and social welfare, our results support the GATT/WTO's position.

As far as border tax adjustments are concerned, the CTE's view is less strict; a change in the current rules to allow border tax adjustments not exclusively on direct, product-related taxes is deliberated. Efficiency arguments in favour of such a change have been made: the current ban on border tax adjustments for indirect taxes give governments concerned about the competitiveness implications of environmental policy an incentive to apply product taxes, even if the character of the environmental externality would call for a PPM tax[66]. If border tax adjustments for the latter would be sanctioned, optimality of environmental regulation might thus be restored[67].

4. CONCLUSIONS

The central focus of the debate is the legitimacy and desirability of trade-restricting measures as a response to other countries' environmental policy level in the context of national environmental pollution.

In general, one can distinguish two different motivations for justification of environmentally related trade measures:

– they are demanded for their direct environmental effect, or

[66] The European Commission states in its Communication to the Council: "... *it seems possible that present GATT rules on border tax adjustment might create an inefficient choice of environmental tax instruments. Current rules on border tax adjustments seem to be biased against environmentally and economically efficient production taxes, as supposed to product taxes. ... One general effect of the present unbalance is that countries might tend to adopt product taxes for environmental purposes rather than production taxes, thus creating distortions in environmental policy making.*" (Commission of the European Communities [1995, 15]; see also Sorsa [1995, 7]).

[67] Opening up the border tax adjustment mechanism to cover production process charges "... *would minimize the unfairness of border tax adjustment and create an incentive for governments to shift environmental regulation toward the use of pollution charges to internalize costs. This would at the same time move environmental regulation toward more efficient and less trade-restrictive market mechanisms.*" (Esty [1994, 169]; see also Feketekuty [1993, 184] and Pearce [1993, 24].). Sorsa [1995, 7] adds that change of GATT/WTO's provisions regarding border tax adjustment could induce a shift away from command and control measures which cannot be rebated at the border. One should, however, keep in mind that border tax adjustment might also undermine the very objective which environmental taxes were designed to address (compare Sorsa [1995, 6/7]).

- their seeming objective is an indirect environmental benefit through an environmental policy effect.

The policy proposals we have summarised in this chapter centre around trade measures addressing the latter, i.e. trade measures as a response to the risk of an ERTB, or simply addressing alleged unfairness of lower environmental standards abroad. Our policy analysis clarified that claims for trade measures focus only superficially on the harm to the environment and its prevention. Their main thrust is on harm to domestic producers resulting from the supposed competitive disadvantage in having to comply with more stringent environmental standards than foreign competitors. Trade measures are sought for trade protection, i.e. to equalise any competitive disadvantage that domestic producers may suffer if competitors are subject to lower environmental standards.

Since the generally accepted notion is that environmental endowments differ and that an exploitation of such differences enhances welfare gains from trade, efficiency considerations do not support trade instruments addressing differences in environmental regulation.

As shown above, the stance taken by the GATT/WTO so far has been negative with regard to eco-tariffs, countervailing eco-duties and other trade measures addressing PPM requirements. Our evaluation showed that there is little ground to challenge GATT/WTO's position. The only issue for which the CTE's work indicates the possibility of changing current rules and interpretations is the issue of border tax adjustment. Since in some instances the current GATT/WTO rules on border tax adjustment may give rise to inefficient environmental policies, such a change may yield more efficient environmental policies, and therefore be beneficial for the environment.

Apart from such efficiency driven arguments, the main argument advanced by the GATT/WTO in support of its rules and interpretations is that sanctioning trade instruments addressing PPM requirements outside a country's jurisdiction would interfere with the principles of international law which protect the sovereign right of countries to formulate policies pursuant to domestic environmental goals[68]. If a change in environmental policies outside a country's jurisdiction is sought, the predominant opinion is that this should be done by international cooperation to harmonise environmental policies[69].

[68] Compare Chakarian [1994, 119].

[69] The European Commission considers international harmonisation of environmental policies an effective way to address competitiveness concerns (EU [1995, 6]); so does Esty [1994, 172]. The OECD (OECD [1994, 10/11]) considers harmonisation of environmental standards beneficial for trade and the environment. However, harmonisation is judged more desirable if the environmental problem is global.

Since harmonisation of environmental policies falls somewhat outside the scope of our investigation, we have so far not addressed such proposals. We shall, however, devote the last section of this chapter to the issue of harmonisation as an alternative to trade instruments addressing internationally differing environmental standards.

HARMONISATION

So far, we have considered trade instruments as a possible reaction to individual countries' low standards in exporting countries. An alternative to trade instruments would be a world-wide harmonisation of standards[70], i.e. a coordination of environmental policy actions and measures in order to reduce international differences of such policies[71]. It is not clear, however, whether environmental policy in particular environmental policy addressing domestic PPM externalities is a policy area suitable for world-wide harmonisation[72].

Johnson [1971] states that international policy harmonisation should be pursued in cases when there is a potential for increased efficiency through international policy coordination by eliminating policy induced distortions of production and trade[73]. International differences in pollution control clearly affect the international distribution of comparative advantage. However, these competitiveness effects of different standards in general do not reduce efficiency of international resource allocation. On the opposite, they usually reflect differences in endowments which are driving gains from trade. Differences in environmental policies, however, can also result from international differences in policy formation. If environmental regulation is set at a suboptimal level, the actual international distribution of comparative advantage is created rather than natural, and may differ from the actual

70 Some go as far as demanding that trade liberalisation should not proceed unless and until appropriate environmental policies are in place to avoid that environmental problems are aggravated by trade liberalisation (see Eglin [1995, 771] for examples).

71 This definition follows Hansson [1990, 1] and Robertson [1992, 310].

72 As far as consumption externalities, i.e. product-related externalities are concerned, the question whether relevant standards should be internationally harmonised is already answered in the affirmative: The conclusion of the Tokyo Trade Round in 1979 marks the adoption of the TBT Code as an attempt to harmonise technical laws and standards to reduce the likelihood that technical rules and standards are used as disguised barriers to international trade (the SPSS Code which was adopted at the conclusion of the Uruguay Round does the same with reference to technical barriers to trade in agriculture). In addition, harmonisation of product standards is expected to alleviate trade by reducing the need to meet multiple standards (see Lallas et al. [1992, 316]).

73 See Hansson [1990, 8].

distribution. If this is the case, harmonisation may correct artificially induced comparative advantages and therewith increase efficiency of resource allocation.

Hence, whether or not harmonisation of environmental policies addressing PPM externalities would be welfare-enhancing by correcting artificial manipulation of comparative advantages, remains a question of assessment and judgement; no universal argument in favour of or against harmonisation can be distilled.

The fact that there are no obvious standards to point to as a focal point would be in the way of successful harmonisation[74]; if policy implementation is made conditional upon agreement on internationally harmonised standards, implementation might even be unduly postponed[75]. A further drawback of harmonisation at a high level as demanded by environmentalists[76], is the potential discrimination of countries whose environment is particularly absorptive, i.e. often developing nations[77]. Also, in many instances proposals for harmonisation are made by environmental and industry lobbies - the same coalition which favours trade instruments to level differences - with a hidden agenda of protectionism[78]. Finally, the loss of policy independence and resulting economic costs arising from harmonisation is neglected by proponents of international harmonisation[79].

This in mind, we are inclined to agree with Hansson [1990, 116] that in the case of domestic pollution international harmonisation of environmental policies would not be desirable from a global economic efficiency point of view[80].

[74] See French [1993a, 35].

[75] Compare Robertson [1992, 312].

[76] See Robertson [1992, 312 & 1994, 25].

[77] See Robertson [1994, 20].

[78] See Robertson [1992, 312].

[79] Compare Robertson [1992, 321].

[80] This negative assessment is confined to harmonisation in the context of environmental policies addressing domestic externalities. In the context of global environmental externalities, we consider international policies harmonisation a more promising approach; see next chapter.

Chapter 13

Eco-tariffs and Global Environmental Policy

Trade restrictions in the form of eco-tariffs have so far not become policy instruments for the protection of global environmental commons. However, other trade instruments addressing PPMs have been introduced in the context of the protection of the ozone layer, codified in the Montreal Protocol on Substances that Deplete the Ozone Layer. Furthermore, they figure in policy proposals addressing global warming.

To date, it is not clear whether GATT/WTO would sanction eco-tariffs or other trade measures taken pursuant to global environmental protection regardless of whether such measures were taken unilaterally or as part of a multilateral environmental agreement. Some of the arguments found to violate GATT rules if trade measures were taken in the context of domestic externalities also apply to global environmental pollution. Therefore, concern has been expressed that current GATT/WTO rules might limit or even prevent efficient and effective policies to protect the global environmental commons. The discussions in the CTE show that a change or amendment of current GATT/WTO rules to explicitly sanction trade measures taken pursuant to global environmental protection is envisaged by WTO Members, although there is still a dispute over form and scope of such a change or amendment.

We present two global environmental problems in whose context eco-tariffs or other trade measures addressing PPM pollution have been proposed, namely ozone layer depletion and global warming. Furthermore, we outline the trade measures taken in the Montreal Protocol pursuant to the protection of the stratospheric ozone layer and those proposed to combat global warming. These policies and policy proposals as well as GATT/WTO provisions can be analysed in the light of theoretic evidence gathered in chapters 8, 9 and 10.

1. ISSUES AND POLICY INITIATIVES

We shall introduce two of the major environmental issues with a global dimension, namely the destruction of the stratospheric ozone layer and global warming[1]. Furthermore, we shall present the trade provisions in the Montreal Protocol and trade measures proposed to combat global warming.

OZONE LAYER DEPLETION AND GLOBAL WARMING

OZONE LAYER DEPLETION

In 1974, two American scientists[2] advanced a theory linking two man-made chemical compounds - chlorofluorocarbons (CFCs) and halons - to the destruction of the stratospheric ozone layer[3]. The depletion of the ozone layer reduces its ability to absorb ultraviolet-B (UV-B) radiation before it reaches the earth's surface. Increased amounts of UV-B reaching the earth's surface pose a threat to human, animal and plant health[4]. After a period of scientific dispute, the Antarctic ozone hole discovered in the mid-80s gave conclusive evidence for the theory presented 10 years before.

International reaction to the discovery of the ozone hole was the adoption of the Vienna Convention for the Protection of the Ozone Layer in 1985 (in force since 1988). Parties agreed to cooperate in areas such as research, implementation of measures to reduce emissions of ozone-depleting substances, exchange of information, and development and transfer of substitute technologies. Two years after the adoption of the Convention, growing scientific evidence for a serious threat to the ozone layer prompted the signatories of the Convention to negotiate a Protocol to the convention.

1 A third environmental problem with the global dimension is the reduction of biodiversity. However, since the protection of biodiversity calls for trade measures which mainly address trade in the products, i.e. rare organisms, rather than PPMs, protection of biodiversity is not considered here. For a survey of the problem and international action taken pursuant to its solution see Boyle [1994] and Brown et al. [1993]. For trade policy in the context of biodiversity see Burgess [1994].

2 See Molina & Rowland [1974].

3 When such ozone-depleting substances are released into the atmosphere, they slowly migrate up until they reach the ozone rich stratosphere. In this altitude (10 to 50 km above sea level) solar radiation is sufficiently powerful to break up the otherwise stable CFC or halon compounds. The chlorine or bromine atoms thus released trigger a chain reaction that leads to the destruction of ozone molecules. For a detailed discussion of ozone chemistry see Parson [1993].

4 It induces for example skin cancer, cataracts and a suppression of the human immune system. In addition, both the aquatic food chain and crop yields may be seriously harmed by higher than normal levels of UV-B radiation. For further details see UNEP [1989] and World Bank [1992].

Thus, the Montreal Protocol on Substances that Deplete the Ozone Layer was signed in 1987; it entered into force in 1989. The Montreal Protocol regulates which chemicals are to be controlled, whether controls should be imposed on their production or consumption, the timing and size of cutbacks, measures to restrict trade with non-parties, and the treatment of developing countries with low levels of production and consumption of ozone-depleting substances[5]. Furthermore, Parties to the Protocol have the obligation to regularly submit data on production and trade of controlled substances, and to cooperate in areas of research and development, public awareness, and exchange of information[6]. To date, 169 nations have ratified the protocol and production and consumption of ozone-depleting substances in developed countries has been reduced to a negligible amount[7].

GLOBAL WARMING

Global Warming is caused by the so-called greenhouse effect. Within the earth's atmosphere, some gases allow solar radiation to reach the earth's surface but trap infrared radiation on its way back into space. Thus energy with warming potential remains within the atmosphere. This accounts for surface heating of some 33°C in excess of the direct radiation of the sun[8]. The natural trapping of heat is similar to the way a greenhouse functions - hence the trace gases that cause this effect[9] are called 'greenhouse gases' (GHG). Man made emissions of GHGs will over the next century enhance this natural greenhouse effect[10]. The most important andropogenic GHG is CO_2, of which roughly 3% of the annual intake by the atmosphere is due to human activities[11]. Manmade CO_2 is mainly caused by fossil fuel combustion and deforestation. From the scientific point of view, there is still a high level of uncertainty concerning the exact effects and the magnitude of the climatic changes as well as the timing[12]. Nevertheless, it is beyond doubt

5 For developing countries which are Parties to the Protocol, the Parties established a Multilateral Fund in 1990 to provide financial and technical assistance for the elimination of production and consumption of ozone-depleting substances (see Twum-Barima & Campbell [1994, 43]).

6 For the full text of the Montreal Protocol see Ozone Secretariat [1993].

7 See www.unep.ch/ozone.

8 See Cline [1991] and Solow [1991].

9 The most important natural GHGs are water vapour (H_2O), carbon dioxide (CO_2), methane (CH_4) and nitrous oxide (N_2O).

10 See Houghton et al [1990].

11 The rest is due to natural exchange with the oceans, soils and plants.

12 In order to summarise the results of world-wide research and to agree upon a working hypothesis on the magnitude of the threat, an Intergovernmental Panel on Climate Change (IPPC) was established in 1988. IPPC's mean prediction for the increase of the average temperature on the earth's surface due to emissions of GHGs is 0.3°C per decade over the next century. The mean predicted sea level rise is 6 cm per decade. Land surfaces will

that an increase in the mean temperature will change our eco-system. Likely effects of such a change - an increased number of hurricanes, tidal waves and other natural disasters - will reduce human welfare[13]. Furthermore, if this trend were to continue over several centuries, the effects, especially those stemming from a rise in the sea level, might well become catastrophic[14]. Therefore, curbing GHG emissions seems imperative, in particular since the change in atmospheric GHG concentration is essentially irreversible over centuries[15].

International reaction to the discovery of the greenhouse effect prompted the Rio Conference in 1992 where the United Nations Framework Convention on Climate Change and the Rio Declaration were adopted. The aim to bring states together to discuss the challenge of global warming has been successful: as of 1998, 176 states have become Parties to the Framework Convention[16]. The Framework Convention which entered into force in 1994 stipulates that its Parties provide information regarding national emissions of GHG and measures taken to mitigate them, cooperate in research, and development and transfer of GHG reducing technologies, and promote precautionary measures. Furthermore, Parties have the obligation to adopt national policies to mitigate climate change with the objective to return to earlier levels of GHG emission by the year 2000. Finally, they shall provide financial resources and technology transfer to developing nations who are Parties to the Convention[17]. In terms of stabilisation or reduction of GHG emission, or a deadline for doing so, and establishing a financial mechanism to support developing nations to reduce their emissions, the Convention did not achieve firm commitments from its Parties. In 1997, a follow up conference on climate change adopted the Kyoto Protocol which is more specific: Parties agreed to return to no more

---

warm more rapidly than the seas, and there will certainly be regional differences in climate change. For example, it is expected that Southern Europe and North Africa will warm more rapidly than average. However, all mean predictions from individual global climate models have a substantial variance and the range of predictions from different models also varies widely (see Houghton et al. [1990]).

13 Most studies focus primarily on the increase in mean global temperature but there is reason to believe that the temperature rise is not the most threatening issue. Change in the distribution of rainfall and an increase in droughts or freezes as well as climatic catastrophes which are expected to result from global warming are likely to be much more important (see Pulvenis [1994, 74]). We should thus interpret the estimates of mean temperature rise as an index for the climate changes associated with other important variables.

14 See Cline [1991].

15 See Pulvenis [1994, 75].

16 See www.cop4.org; for the full text of the Framework Convention see Sands et al. [1994, 249-270].

17 See www.cop4.org.

than 5% in excess of their 1990 GHG emissions between 2008 and 2012; a 'clean development mechanism' was defined to assist developing countries to achieve sustainable development and to facilitate compliance of developed countries with their obligations under the Protocol[18]. The Kyoto Protocol has not yet entered into force, but Parties have agreed on a deadline for finalising outstanding details on the Protocol in a follow-up meeting in Buenos Aires 1998[19].

Apart from the uncertainties regarding effects of climate change[20], the main reason for the slow progress of efforts to curtail GHGs is that any commitment to control in particular CO_2 emissions is estimated to be very expensive. Both the rise in energy prices and the loss in international competitiveness, if measures were taken unilaterally, would be considerable for countries committed to internalising this global environmental externality[21].

TRADE MEASURES TO PROTECT THE OZONE LAYER AND TO COMBAT GLOBAL WARMING

TRADE MEASURES TO PROTECT THE OZONE LAYER

Article 4 of the Montreal Protocol specifies trade restrictions between Parties and non-parties of the Protocol. These measures are designed to enable the Parties to manage trade in

- Ozone-depleting chemicals controlled under the Protocol[22],
- products containing ozone-depleting chemicals[23],
- products manufactured with, but not containing ozone-depleting substances[24], and

[18] See UN Framework Convention on Climate Change [1997].

[19] A further highlight of the meeting in Buenos Aires was the signing of the Kyoto Protocol by the U. S. which previously had taken a very low profile in the combat of climate change (see www.cop4.org).

[20] Scientific results regarding the magnitude of climate change effects are still vague (see Boisson de Chazournes [1995, 2]).

[21] See Boisson de Chazournes [1995, 5]. It is not entirely clear whether energy prices would rise as a result of measures to counteract global warming: while prices – including taxes – will most likely rise in countries where environmental control measures such as carbon taxes would be introduced, the world market price is likely to decline as a result of the demand reduction. It is thus possible – yet somewhat unlikely – that energy prices may in fact not rise.

[22] Trade in these substances is banned between Parties and non-parties (see Ozone Secretariat [1993]).

[23] Trade restrictions apply to certain products containing controlled ozone-depleting substances; they are obligatory against non-parties if Parties agree to a list specifying these products (see Ozone Secretariat [1993]).

– technologies for producing or utilising controlled substances[25].

Parties of the Protocol hence considered it necessary for an effective protection of the ozone layer to control not only trade in ozone-depleting substances and products containing them, but also in goods whose PPMs involve ozone-depleting chemicals[26]. The third item on the above list constitutes a trade restriction on the basis of PPMs, albeit it is not an eco-tariff as considered in our study, but a quantitative restriction[27].

These PPM-based trade measures are one component of an incentive package that ensured the success of the Montreal Protocol in controlling ozone-depleting substances.

In the negotiation process of the Montreal Protocol, concern of the largest producers and consumers of ozone-depleting substances (the U. S. and Europe[28]) centred around two issues:

– their relative competitive position in the market for ozone-depleting substances, and
– the potential of production shifting to non-parties[29].

If the countries remaining non-parties account for a substantive share of the market, the Parties have to bear the cost of the loss of the market, while their environmental objective is jeopardised.

The trade measures in the Montreal Protocol address these issues: By denying access to their market to non-parties, the Parties significantly reduce the incentive to remain a non-party since the countries committed to control ozone-depleting substances - the U. S. and Europe - accounted for the lion's

---

24 The Protocol provides that Parties should determine the feasibility of restricting or banning imports from non-parties of goods produced with ozone-depleting substances; see footnote 25 below.

25 Export to non-parties of products, equipment or technology that would facilitate the production of ozone-depleting substances is discouraged (see Ozone Secretariat [1993]).

26 The text of the Montreal Protocol Art. 4.4 reads: "*Within five years of the date of entry into force of this Protocol, the Parties shall determine the feasibility of banning or restricting, from States not party to this Protocol, the import of products produced with, but not containing, controlled substances. If determined feasible, the Parties shall .... elaborate in an annex a list of such products. Parties that have not objected to it ... shall ban or restrict, within one year of the annex having become effective, the import of those products from any State not party to this Protocol.*" (Ozone Secretariat [1993]).

27 The fact that a quantitative restriction rather than a tariff has been chosen is related to the domestic control scheme of ozone-depleting substances by means of quantitative ceilings rather than taxes for production and consumption (see Enders & Porges [1992, 134] and Twum-Barima & Campbell [1994, 68/69] on the discussion of taxes vs. quantitative restrictions for ozone-depleting substances).

28 Each of these accounted for 30% of consumption of ozone-depleting substances at the time according to Enders & Porges [1992, 132].

29 See Slooten [1994, 88].

share of this market[30]. Thereby Parties hoped to achieve widespread participation in the Montreal Protocol[31]. At the same time, the trade provisions were designed to prevent an undermining of the environmental objective of the Montreal Protocol, in case the negative and positive incentives to join the Montreal Protocol were to fail[32].

The effect of the incentive package has been successful; the participation of 169 nations is nearly universal[33]. Clearly, the contribution of the PPM-related trade measure to this success cannot be assessed, in particular since there was in fact no need to ever implement it[34]. Its role was hence a credible threat rather than one which could actually be measured by foregone trade flows[35]. Slooten [1994, 89], however, assesses that "*... there is evidence to suggest that the Parties regard it* [the PPM-based trade provision] *as an important contributor to the effectiveness of the Montreal Protocol.*"

TRADE MEASURES TO COMBAT GLOBAL WARMING

Unlike the Montreal Protocol, the Framework Convention does not contain provisions for trade measures pursuant to its environmental objective. On the contrary, Article 3.5 of the Framework Convention discourages trade measures, in particular unilateral ones.

> *"The Parties should cooperate to promote a supportive and open international economic system that would lead to sustainable economic growth and development in all Parties, particularly developing country Parties, thus enabling them better to address the problems of climate change. Measures taken to combat climate change including unilateral ones, should not constitute a means of arbitrary or unjustifiable discrimination or a disguised restriction on international trade."*[36]

[30] This was accompanied by a positive incentive to join the Montreal Protocol, particularly for developing countries, in form of the Multilateral Fund (see footnote 5 above).

[31] See Benedick [1991, 91] and Twum-Barima & Campbell [1994, 51/2].

[32] See Lang [1993, 365] and Slooten [1994, 88].

[33] Other factors like scientific assessment stressing the urgency of measures to halt the depletion of the ozone layer, and rapid technical progress with substitutes for ozone-depleting substances also contributed to the widespread participation (Slooten [1994, 88/89] and Twum-Barima & Campbell [1994, 100]).

[34] The PPM-based trade restrictions in the Montreal Protocol are thus ex-ante restrictions - as supposed to ex-post sanctions - in the terminology of Kirchgässner & Mohr [1995, 7] since they were only provided but not exercised.

[35] The threat was only too credible since it was actually hammered out in the Protocol. The extent of the threat has been considered significant by Enders & Porges [1992, 138]: "*... judging by current trade statistics, a possible ban on imports of products produced with but not containing CFCs would have a much broader impact on exports of non-parties to Parties....*".

[36] Sands et al. [1994].

Refraining from trade measures to address climate change is also stipulated by the Rio Declaration on Environmental and Development[37] drafted simultaneously with the Framework Convention. Principle 12 of the Rio Declaration reads:

> *"Unilateral actions to deal with environmental challenges outside the jurisdiction of the importing country should be avoided. Environmental measures addressing transboundary or global environmental problems should, as far as possible, be based on international consensus."*[38]

The main reason for the fact that the Framework Convention does not envisage the use of trade measures in the fashion of the Montreal Protocol are concerns voiced especially by developing countries that they might become targets of "*abusive unilateral sanctions, notably exercised against so-called environmentally unfriendly production methods.*"[39]

However, as it stands, the above cited provisions do not preclude the use of trade measures. Trade provisions based on international consensus which were found neither to discriminate arbitrarily or unjustifiably nor to constitute a disguised trade restriction would be fully compatible with both the Framework Convention and the Rio Declaration[40].

However, so far no multilateral attempt has been made for the use of trade restrictions pursuant to the combat of global warming: The Kyoto Protocol does not contain any reference to trade provision between Parties or between Parties and non-parties.

Apart from multilateral efforts addressing climate change, a unilateral route has been explored by the European Community and the U.S. in proposing CO_2 taxes in 1991. Although both proposals were not turned into actual legislation, their features are relevant in the present context.

In 1991, the European Community proposed to levy a tax on CO_2 emissions and energy content of products such as coal, natural gas, mineral oil and certain kinds of electricity[41]. The tax was devised as a consumption tax on energy with rising duties. An additional feature of the tax was the

[37] For the full text of the Rio Declaration see Sands et al. [1994, 189-228].

[38] Sands et al. [1994].

[39] Boisson de Chazournes [1995, 11].

[40] See Boisson de Chazournes [1995, 12/13]; Bhagwati [1993a, 49] states for example that "*... trade sanctions would seem to be acceptable as an option against non-signatories to a multilateral agreement [to combat climate change], provided that this agreement was successfully argued to be both efficient and equitable*". Similarly Barrett [1994a, 1] who argues that trade restrictions should be part of an (enhanced) climate change agreement to avoid leakage and induce participation in the agreement if certain rules are drawn to preclude that such trade measures serve protectionist intents.

[41] The proposal also included a tax on nuclear energy to avoid favouring nuclear energy over fossil fuel combustion in energy generation (see Barrett [1994a, 13]).

exemption for six particularly energy-intensive sectors competing on global markets[42]. Apart from protecting competitiveness of these sectors, this feature was also devised to prevent European efforts to reduce CO_2 emissions from being undermined by stimulating production and thus emissions in countries where no efforts to control CO_2 would be made. The same intent was followed by making the introduction of the tax conditional upon other member states of the OECD also implementing comparable measures[43].

The BTU (British Thermal Unit) tax proposal advanced in the U.S. in 1991 provided for the imposition of a specific excise tax on refined petroleum products, natural gas, coal, electricity, and other fossil fuels. Apart from various exemptions of energy-intensive industries, products manufactured for export were not to be levied with the tax[44]. Furthermore, the proposal contains (GATT/WTO consistent) provisions for border tax adjustment of the BTU tax for imports[45].

Exemptions of energy-intensive industries from the taxes in Europe and the U. S. is somewhat counterintuitive[46]. By exempting the largest emitters, the tax has to be relatively higher for the remaining subjects to achieve a given reduction objective. Furthermore, exempting the most polluting industries will result in a resource reallocation within economies that runs counter the intent of a CO_2 regulation[47].

In that context, Hoel [1993] showed that tariffs rather than a sectorally differentiated tax should be employed to avoid leakage[48]. Therefore, Pearson & Smith [1991] suggested that carbon reduction might be more effective if the tax were charged on all sectors and accompanied by trade measures:

> *"One possible course of action would be ... to impose import duties on the products from ... competitor*[s]*, at a level reflecting the cost involved in carbon control."*[49]

[42] Reason for these provisions was to safeguard competitiveness of Community economies and to avoid pronounced economic losses for specific sectors (steel, chemicals, non-ferrous metals, cement, glass and pulp and paper); see Barrett [1994a, 13].

[43] See Barrett [1994a, 14] and Pearson & Smith [1991, 22].

[44] See Stewardson [1994, 94] and Esty [1994, 161].

[45] See Stewardson [1994, 97].

[46] Nevertheless, most countries that have already imposed carbon taxes provide tax exemptions or reductions for energy-intensive industries (e.g. Denmark, Finland, Norway, Sweden; see Barrett [1994a, 14]).

[47] See Barker [1993, 251].

[48] See chapter 7.

[49] Pearson & Smith [1991, 25]; similar suggestion has been made by Düerkop [1994, 831]. These proposals are supported by results found by Hœl [1993].

Stewardson [1994, 95] advances border tax adjustment with a similar intent for the BTU tax in the U. S.:

> *"An alternative approach to granting exemptions to categories of industry is to remit the tax on exported products and to impose it on imported products. The exported products thus remain on a competitive footing on overseas markets, while the domestically manufactured .... bear the same tax costs as imported like products. While some domestic products are thereby exempted from the tax (those exported), the exemption is not as categorical and incoherent as granting a block exemption for energy-intensive producers."*

2. ECO-TARIFFS AND GLOBAL ENVIRONMENTAL PROBLEMS: POLICY ANALYSIS

Mapping trade provisions of the Montreal Protocol and proposals in the context of climate change against theoretic evidence in chapters 8, 9 and 10, we find that trade instruments have been introduced and proposed in the double function we elaborated in chapter 7, namely to ensure widespread participation in a multilateral environmental agreement and to avoid leakage. However, there is also evidence that regulatory capture was an important motor for introduction and proposals of trade measures to offset competitiveness effects of global pollution control.

TRADE MEASURES TO FURTHER INTERNATIONAL ENVIRONMENTAL COOPERATION?

It has been argued that the foremost objective of the trade restrictions in the Montreal Protocol was the achievement of international cooperation[50]. This is corroborated by reasons for the U. S.' reluctance to increase control of ozone-depleting substances prior to negotiation and signing of the

[50] Benedick [1991, 91] for example states. "*At the first session in Geneva 1986, the United States offered specific proposals to restrict trade in controlled substances with non-parties. The objective of such restrictions was to stimulate as many nations as possible to participate in the protocol, by preventing non-participating countries from enjoying competitive advantages and by discouraging the movement of CFC production facilities to such countries. These provisions were critical, since they constituted the only enforcement mechanisms in the protocol.*"

Montreal Protocol[51]. The fact that the PPM based trade restrictions in the Montreal Protocol were in fact never implemented ties with our results from II.B.4 where we found that such conditional trade instruments will not be implemented if it is welfare enhancing for exporting countries to adopt environmental regulation rather than subject their exports to a tariff.

In chapter 7 we found that negative incentives in the form of trade instruments should be accompanied by positive ones to ensure widespread participation in a multilateral environmental agreement. The Montreal Protocol provides such positive incentives in the form of the Multilateral Fund.

The Framework Convention does not contain negative incentives in the form of trade restrictions applied against non-signatories. The reason given by Boisson de Chazournes [1995, 10/11] is that

> "*some countries, especially developing countries, expressed concerns about the risk that trade barriers would be erected for climate protection reasons*"

during the negotiations in Rio[52]. As regards positive incentives, only vaguely phrased commitment to support developing countries financially and with technology transfer was taken. The Kyoto Protocol marks an improvement in this respect by establishing the 'clean development mechanism'[53]. However, it remains to be seen whether the positive incentive scheme established so far will suffice to ensure widespread participation and success in combating global warming since - compared to the safeguarding of the ozone layer - the financial transfers needed in the case of global warming are much higher[54].

[51] Barrett [1994a, 4] cites the United States Environmental Protection Agency in this context: "*In 1978 the United States restricted the use of CFCs in aerosols. While several nations adopted similar restrictions ... and others cut back their use ... there was no widespread movement to follow the United States' lead. Concerns existed then that other nations had failed to act because the United States ... were making the reductions thought necessary to protect the ozone layer.*"

[52] It was feared in particular that a multilateral non-compliance scheme with trade measures based on PPMs would be established (see Boisson de Chazournes [1995, 11]).

[53] The 'clean development mechanism' facilitates emission abatement for countries that agreed to reduce GHGs (all OECD countries and most of the Economies in Transition). Within the framework of the 'clean development mechanism' emission trading schemes will be established to increase the efficiency of world-wide reduction of GHGs (

[54] Compare Markandya [1991, 72].

TRADE MEASURES TO ADDRESS LEAKAGE?

Another function of the trade restrictions in the Montreal Protocol is avoidance of leakage[55]. We showed in chapter 10 that in the absence of cooperation, tariffs are effective instruments to avoid leakage, and in fact the efficient course of action for countries employing them. Since widespread participation in the Montreal Protocol was achieved, the trade measures were in fact not needed to avoid leakage.

As far as proposals to combat climate change are concerned, we have to recur to the motives for tax exemptions in the European and U. S. tax proposals to isolate the leakage avoidance factor. Barrett [1994a, 14] states that avoidance of leakage has been the driving force of tax exemption in the European tax proposal.

If in the future, effective control of GHGs is not achieved by the Framework Convention and the Kyoto Protocol, those countries committed to combating climate change may have to revert to a unilateral regime of GHG control. To avoid emission leakage, trade measures should be considered since they are the most efficient policy measures to internalise emissions generated in countries not controlling global pollution.

TRADE MEASURES TO AFFORD PROTECTION?

Apart from the roles of the trade provisions of the Montreal Protocol elaborated above, it was also found that regulatory capture by affected industries shaped the trade measures to offset negative competitiveness effects of global pollution control[56].

[55] Commentators disagree about which of the two functions was predominant; Twum-Bamima & Campbell [1994, 51/52] consider the avoidance of leakage the most important: *"The primary impetus behind negotiating a multilateral agreement to protect the ozone layer was the recognition that if individual countries or even regional or economic groups took action rather than reaching global agreement, an increase in the production of ozone-depleting chemicals in non-participating countries could negate the environmental benefits of actions by a limited number of countries."*

[56] GATT [1992, 25]: *"... the Parties to the Montreal Protocol .... could have structured the Protocol in such a way that it reduced consumption of CFCs in the participating countries by the target amount, without the necessity of including provisions for special restrictions on trade with non-parties. Since, however, the drafters had other goals as well, including that of providing compensation to CFC producers in the participating countries (by allowing them to receive extra profits from selling the diminishing quantity of CFCs), trade provisions which discriminate against non-participants were included in the Protocol."* Also Benedick [1991, 91]: *"The objective of such* [trade] *restrictions was to stimulate as many nations as possible to participate in the protocol, by preventing non-participating countries from enjoying competitive advantages..."* See also Oberthür

As far as policies addressing climate change are concerned, core provisions in the European and U. S. tax proposals are also driven by protectionist motives.

Barker [1993, 251] thinks that the European Carbon tax exemptions were given primarily because of the feared competitiveness effect[57]. Barrett [1994a] argues that apart from the tax exemptions, other features of the European tax proposal were routed in competitiveness concerns[58].

In the U. S., the motive for tax exemptions from the proposed BTU tax was also driven by competitiveness concerns and achieved by lobbies of affected industries:

"To accommodate competitiveness concerns raised by industries with powerful sponsors in the Congress, Clinton's administration created exemptions to BTU tax proposals for certain industries and fuels.'[59]

Both in the European Community and in the U.S. lobby groups were in the end powerful enough to force administrations to abandon their proposals for energy and specifically BTU taxes[60]. This indicates that these lobby groups would favour trade measures accompanying a renewed tax proposal if the implementation of the tax itself cannot be prevented.

3. GATT/WTO RULES: CURRENT INTERPRETATION, POSSIBLE CHANGES AND EVALUATION

We shall analyse how GATT/WTO rules are currently and in the future interpreted with respect to the GATT/WTO compatibility of trade measures introduced and proposed to safeguard the global environmental commons.

[1992a] who analyses the role of producer interest in shaping other provisions of the Montreal Protocol.

57 Stewardson [1994, 93] attributes these exemptions to the working of lobby groups.

58 The reason for the fact that the tax is not only levied on CO_2 but also on nuclear energy is not to confer competitive advantages to those members of the EU who rely more heavily on nuclear energy (see Commission of the European Communities [1991, 8/9] cited in Barrett [1994a, 12]. Furthermore, the conditionality of the tax on other OECD countries undertaking similar measures was also driven by competitiveness considerations: "*Whereas, in order to safeguard the competitiveness of Community industry, the tax arrangement cannot be applied in the Member States until such time as other member countries of the OECD have brought in a similar tax or measures having an equivalent fiscal impact.*" (Commission of the European Communities [1991, 8], cited in Barrett [1994a, 13]).

59 This view is shared by Stewardson [1994, 93].

60 See Esty [1994, 161] and Stewardson [1994, 93].

In the last chapter, we summarised GATT/WTO's negative position vis-à-vis trade measures addressing PPM externalities abroad if trade measures are legitimised as an indirect protection of the domestic environment, i.e. maintenance of stringent environmental standards. Some of these rules and interpretations also apply to direct or indirect protection of the global environment. Two further issues arise in the context of GATT/WTO regulations and global environmental protection, namely the question whether trade measures to protect the global environment are covered by Article XX, and whether trade measures taken pursuant to multilateral environmental agreements violate GATT/WTO strictures. Since none of the existing Dispute Settlement Panels addressed the question of trade measures for global environmental protection, uncertainty as to GATT/WTO compatibility of such instruments reigns[61]. Therefore, a clarification of GATT/WTO's position is indicated. Such a clarification is attempted by the CTE.

RELEVANT GATT/WTO RULES AND THEIR INTERPRETATION

Regarding Article III and the 'like product' term, subsidies and border tax adjustment, reasons given in the last chapter why these provisions preclude trade measures to indirectly protect the domestic environment, also apply to the protection of the global environment by trade measures addressing PPM pollution[62].

That leaves us with an outline of the discussion of

- scope of Article XX, and
- Article I in relation to trade measures in multilateral environmental agreements.

SCOPE OF ARTICLE XX

Article XX does not make explicit reference to the territorial location of humans, animals or plants whose health is to be protected. However, the Dispute Settlement Panel on United States - Restrictions on the Imports of

[61] See WTO [1996b, §8].

[62] Some argue for a different concept with regard to PPMs that pollute the global environmental commons. Pearce [1993, 24] proposes to define products as 'unlike' if they have different pollution impacts. Arden-Clarke [1993, 76] also argues that discrimination between products on the basis of PPM pollution should be allowed to further protection of the global commons.

Tuna[63] concluded that the U. S.' ban on Mexican tuna could not be justified under GATT Article XX. The Panel's interpretation was that Article XX applies only to measures safeguarding life or health of humans, animals or plants within the jurisdiction of the country taking the measure[64]. This conclusion by the Panel has been interpreted to imply that trade measures taken to protect the global environmental commons would violate GATT/WTO rules[65].

One should note, however, that the Tuna Panels have not interpreted the incidental killing of dolphins by Mexican fishermen (at which the U.S. trade measures were addressed) as a degradation of a global environmental common[66].

Furthermore, the above interpretation of the Tuna Panel findings seem to contradict the UNCED resolution that:

> "*States have the responsibility to ensure that activities within their jurisdiction or control do not cause damage to the environment of other states or of areas beyond the limits of national jurisdiction*" and that it is recognised "*that...domestic measures targeted to achieve certain*

[63] The following provides a brief background on the Tuna Panel Rulings: The U.S. Marine Mammal Protection Act requires the U.S. government to take steps to curtail the incidental killing of marine mammals by commercial fishermen (the Marine Mammal Protection Act instructs the secretary of commerce to prohibit the importation of tuna products from countries whose dolphin kill ratio, i.e. dolphin death per net dropped, exceeds that of U.S. fishermen beyond a certain margin; see Esty [1994, 268]). In 1988, an environmental group went to court to enforce the congressional mandate on the basis that dolphins in the Eastern Tropical Pacific Ocean were being killed by foreign fishermen in violation of the law. A federal judge agreed that the government was failing to uphold the law and ordered Mexican tuna imports to be banned from the United States. Mexico saw its right to sell tuna in the United States violated and asked for a GATT dispute settlement Panel to adjudicate the matter (see Esty [1994, 268]).

[64] Compare last chapter; these Panel findings (for a summary see Esty [1994, 268/269]), however, have not been adopted by the GATT Council. Since Mexico did not pursue its GATT victory in the first tuna case to ratification by the GATT Council, the European Community brought its own complaint against the U.S. Marine Mammal Protection Act before GATT in 1992. The second case raised similar questions as the first about the right of a nation to impose environmental trade measures unilaterally and extrajurisdictionally. The second Dispute Settlement Panel Report came to essentially the same conclusion as the first (for a summary see Petersmann [1995, 122/123]). It has not yet been adopted by the GATT Council either.

[65] See for example Trebilcock & Howse [1995, 347pp] and French [1993b, 14]. Yet it should be kept in mind that the Panel was never adopted.

[66] See Düerkop [1994, 838].

environmental objectives may need trade measure to render them effective".[67]

It therefore seems that, legally, trade measures taken pursuant to the protection of the global commons might be GATT conform. Yet, GATT has repeatedly voiced opposition against trade measures addressing environmental degradation taking place outside a country's jurisdiction on the grounds that trade measures addressing other countries' environmental policies have primarily the function to enforce environmental priorities upon others[68]. Furthermore, allowing trade measures taken in reaction to such environmental policies in other countries would lead to a degeneration of the multilateral trading system[69].

ARTICLE I AND MULTILATERAL ENVIRONMENTAL AGREEMENTS

Article I (the most favoured nations clause) precludes differential treatment of contracting parties. Therefore, compliance with trade provisions against non-parties in multilateral environmental agreements would be at odds with current GATT/WTO rules if such non-parties to a multilateral environmental agreement would be contracting parties of the GATT, or Members of the WTO.

CTE'S DELIBERATIONS AND RECOMMENDATIONS

In its report to the WTO Ministerial Conference, the CTE devoted large sections to the clarification of the seeming conflict between current GATT/WTO rules, or rather their interpretation and protection of the global environmental commons.

As regards sanctioning trade measures taken to protect global environmental commons not part of a multilateral environmental agreement, the CTE's stance was negative. Regarding the seeming contradiction between Article XX and other principles of environmental protection and trade relations outlined above, the CTE aimed at sending a "*...political signal*

[67] Extracts from Principle 2 of the Rio Declaration (cited after Petersmann [1993a, 46]) and Chapter 17 of Agenda 21 (cited after Petersmann [1993a, 50]); compare also Düerkop [1994, 838] who argues that "*categories of 'extrajurisdiction' do not apply in limiting protective trade measures* [adressing global pollution], *bearing in mind the results of investigations into global interactions between different environmental factors in the last decade.*"

[68] See Sorsa [1992, 123].

[69] The argument is often advanced; see for example Eglin [1993] and GATT [1992].

... to discourage the use of ... trade disruptive and less environmentally efficient unilateral [trade measures]"[70]. Furthermore,

> *"Concern was expressed over any possible extension of or derogation from WTO rules for measures which are not specifically prescribed or authorised in multilateral environmental agreements, since this could permit justification for unilateral measures disguised as multilateralism and open the door for protectionist measures."*[71]

As indicated by the last quote, there was convergence in the CTE that the WTO should be supportive of trade provision in multilateral environmental agreements. The view was developed that

> *"... subject to specific conditions being met, certain trade measures taken pursuant to multilateral environmental agreements should benefit from special treatment under WTO provisions."*[72]

As regards the modalities for a change of WTO rules to accommodate trade restrictions, however, the CTE had not yet come to a conclusion. While some Members think that a temporary or permanent waiver should be sought for multilateral environmental agreements according to GATT Article IX[73], others think that the GATT/WTO rules should be amended to achieve consistency between multilateral environmental agreements and the multilateral trading system by amending Article XX[74].

EVALUATION

The fact that the CTE has achieved a clarification of GATT/WTO rules regarding trade measures addressing global environmental pollution is very welcome as the uncertainty regarding GATT/WTO's position vis-à-vis trade measures taken pursuant to multilateral environmental agreements in particular has stirred much opposition against the GATT.

[70] WTO [1996a, § 17].

[71] WTO [1996a, § 25]; in this context, the CTE also made a reference to Principle 12 of the Rio Conference (see above) which discourages unilateral trade measures pursuant to the protection of global environmental commons.

[72] WTO [1996a, § 15]; this approach has been described as creating an environmental window in the WTO. If such a tack were pursued, GATT/WTO would follow the example of the NAFTA Side Agreement on Environmental Cooperation; see Thomas & Tereposky [1993a] and Schulz [1994].

[73] WTO [1996a, § 12]; since the GATT-waiver is limited in its time scope, the CTE also considered amending Article IX to provide a multi-year waiver for multilateral environmental agreements (WTO [1996a, § 13]).

[74] WTO [1996a, § 15].

The CTE's position that trade provisions in multilateral environmental agreements should not collide with GATT rules is supported by our results in chapter 10 where we found that they are a valuable means both to ensure widespread cooperation for global environmental issues and to avoid leakage if multilateral environmental agreements are not universal.

The CTE's firm rejection of unilateral, or rather non-multilateral, use of trade measures to safeguard the global environmental commons, however, is not fully supported by our results. While our analysis of trade measures taken to counteract global environmental degradation showed that protectionist abuse of such trade measures is a very real possibility, our theoretical results in chapter 10 have shown that trade measures may be environmentally beneficial and global welfare enhancing, regardless of whether they are sanctioned by a multilateral environmental agreement.

The track record of the combat of climate change in particular showed that multilateral efforts are still quite far from a solution. Although recent steps toward such a solution seem encouraging, it remains unclear whether the decisive steps needed to curtail GHG emissions can really be achieved without a subset of the world's governments charging ahead with unilateral measures. If such were the case, trade measures seem necessary to accompany domestic measures as indicated by the failure of the two past attempts to introduce carbon taxes by the European Communities and the U. S..

Therefore, in our opinion, the CTE's refusal to consider a more differentiated view regarding unilateral trade measures is tantamount to an environmental failure of the committee. It may be possible - or at least worth-while - to attempt drafting rules which would not jeopardise the functioning of the multilateral trading system while still sanctioning unilateral or non-multilateral trade instruments to protect global environmental commons.

4. CONCLUSIONS

The focus of the debate is again legitimacy and desirability of trade measures. However, while in the context of the last chapter, the objective of these measures is an indirect protection of the environment, this chapter presented trade measures taken both for indirect and direct protection of the (global) environment.

We identified policy measures and proposals in the context of ozone layer protection and climate change combat whose objective is to ensure that environmental policy is introduced to protect global environmental commons, or to avoid emission leakage from countries reluctant to introduce control measures.

Our policy analysis showed that it is not possible to disentangle whether trade measures were proposed to ensure wide-spread participation in a multilateral environmental agreement, or to avoid emission leakage from countries not willing to join in such multilateral efforts to safeguard the global environmental commons. Furthermore, there is also evidence that the primary motive for such trade measures was protection of industries whose competitiveness was threatened by environmental policies addressing global pollution.

Our results from the theoretical analysis support that trade measures may be part of an efficient regime addressing trans-border spill-overs. Furthermore, our results from chapter 6 indicate that availability of trade measures may increase environmental protection, although they are likely to reduce social welfare in the country employing them. Therefore, our conclusion is that trade measures seem warranted for the sake of safeguarding global environmental resources.

Current GATT/WTO rules are unclear regarding trade measures taken to protect the global environment since the territorial and jurisdictional scope of Article XX is not defined. Furthermore, trade measures taken pursuant to a multilateral environmental agreement are clearly at odds with GATT Article I if they differentiate between contracting parties on the participation in a multilateral environmental agreement. The CTE's results indicate a change of rules to sanction trade measures supported by multilateral consensus, although the modality of the change is still debated. The CTE's stance is equally clear - yet negative - when it comes to non-multilateral trade measures: such restrictions are not covered by Article XX.

The main argument advanced by the GATT/WTO is that trade measures may be employed by powerful countries to coerce others into following a policy they would otherwise not pursue. Furthermore, it is feared that opening the door for trade measures based on PPMs would weaken the trade system.

With the changes of GATT/WTO rules envisaged by the CTE, the Montreal Protocol will be not only a successful solution for a pressing global environmental problem, but also consistent with GATT/WTO rules. It may hence serve as a role model to combat climate change. Yet, initiatives to curtail GHGs have still a number of problems to solve before a similarly effective regime with wide-spread international support will emerge. Therefore, non-multilateral complements to the Kyoto Protocol might have to be explored to prevent a potentially disastrous increase of GHG emissions.

The opposition of many countries to unilateral and multilateral trade measures has prompted support for international harmonisation of environmental policies addressing global problems, in particular if such problems stem from PPM related externalities[75]. Robertson [1992, 309] draws attention to the fact that harmonisation serves one of the objectives of trade restrictions, namely to induce cooperation for global environmental cooperation. Furthermore, as harmonisation does not entail the aspect of sanctions, he considers it the "*benign approach to global or trans-frontier problems*."[76] Finally, regarding Johnson's [1971] analysis that harmonisation should only be pursued in cases when such harmonisation has the potential to increase effectiveness of economic relations, we refer to our results in II.B.2.2: internalisation of trans-border pollution would indeed require harmonisation of environmental standards if pursued in a first best cooperative manner. This corroborates Hansson's result that:

> "*... in the case of true trans-national pollution, can international ... harmonisation of pollution control be motivated from the point of view of global economic efficiency.*"[77]

Therefore, we consider it worthwhile to exploit the tack of international harmonisation of environmental policies for protection of the global environmental commons. However, owing to the lack of scientific certainty and the high costs involved, difficulties arising for harmonisation of global environmental policies at a high level are identical to those faced by proponents of a multilateral environmental agreement. While neither of those are forthcoming in the case of global warming, efficient non-multilateral efforts to address climate change will have to rely on trade measures, both to increase support for control measures and to prevent an undermining of the effectiveness of non-universal measures. Furthermore, since the majority of GHGs arise during the production process of goods, efficient trade measures would be inconsistent with GATT/WTO regulations, even if they would be qualified as suggested above. However, if trade restrictions taken pursuant to global environmental protection would meet these qualifications, the GATT/WTO concerns outlined above should be contained, although a residual risk to the trading system would remain.

According to our opinion, the seriousness of global environmental problems, in particular those associated with climate change, indicates that

[75] This claim has been made inter alia by the OECD: "*Harmonisation of on-product related PPM requirements ..... may be necessary and desirable to address transboundary and global environmental concerns.*" (OECD [1995b, 30]; see also Boisson de Chazournes [1995, 15] and French [1993a, 36]).

[76] Robertson [1992, 310]; see also chapter 7 where we drew attention to the fact that negative incentives such as sanctions may be poor instruments to induce voluntary cooperation.

[77] Hansson [1990, 116].

the residual risk to the open, equitable and non-discriminatory trading system would be worth taking. Especially if trade measures were accompanied by simultaneous efforts to achieve harmonisation of global environmental policies and to bring about an effective multilateral agreement.

Chapter 14

Concluding Remarks

The present study has undertaken an investigation of suitability and relevance of import tariffs to support environmental policy instruments. We have analysed theoretical claims for the suitability of eco-tariffs to improve environmental quality and to enhance welfare in a unified framework of an international trade model, enriched by an environmental externality. Furthermore, we have applied our theoretical results to a policy analysis of eco-tariffs and other trade instruments proposed in the context of domestic and global environmental protection to assess the relevance of eco-tariffs in environmental and trade policy making. Finally, we presented GATT/WTO rules and regulations which to date ban use of eco-tariffs for environmental objectives. Results from our theoretical investigation enabled us to propose some changes not yet on the WTO agenda.

The first part of our theoretical analysis (chapters 2 – 6) concerned itself with the question whether eco-tariffs increase environmental quality if trade relations cause governments to engage in eco-dumping. Particular attention was given to the query whether eco-tariffs can prevent eco-dumping if it results in ERTB. Furthermore, if eco-tariffs seem warranted from an ecological point of view, we attempted to assess whether their availability would confer a welfare improvement.

In all three contexts where we could show that governments have an incentive to engage in eco-dumping - terms of trade improvement, strategic environmental policy and regulatory capture - we found that the pressure on environmental policy would be relieved if governments were to command a trade policy instrument. However, we also found that the trade instrument suitable to reduce eco-dumping may not always be an eco-tariff and that, furthermore, welfare implications of the availability of the trade policy instrument in addition to an environmental tax are ambiguous.

The second part of our theoretical investigation (chapters 7 – 10) dealt with the role of eco-tariffs in the protection of global environmental commons. We focused our analysis on two issues, namely whether eco-tariffs serve to internalise the global externality from sources in countries where domestic internalisation is not pursued; and secondly, whether eco-tariffs could increase the world-wide level of internalisation.

We found that eco-tariffs can serve in the protection of the global environmental commons by reducing environmentally harmful production in countries that do not undertake sufficient efforts to protect the global environment. Global welfare effects of such eco-tariffs are likely to be positive, depending on the degree of pollution control in countries on whose products the tariff is levied.

As regards the role of eco-tariffs to further world-wide environmental cooperation, we found that (conditional) eco-tariffs are suitable incentives for environmental protection. Unfortunately, their implementation is hampered by the fact that the conditionality feature entails negative terms of trade effects for the tariff setting country. If they are realised, however, they are likely to raise global welfare.

The first part of our policy analysis (chapter 12) addressed trade measures in the context of domestic environmental problems. We found that the legitimisation of trade measures in this context is rarely danger of eco-dumping or ERTB. Claims for trade measures do not focus on the harm to the environment and its prevention, but on harm to domestic producers, resulting from the competitive disadvantage in having to comply with more stringent environmental standards. Trade measures are thus sought for trade protection, i.e. to equalise any competitive disadvantage that domestic producers may suffer, if competitors are subject to lower environmental standards, rather than to support environmental policy instruments undermined by trade relations.

Since the generally accepted notion is that environmental endowments differ and that an exploitation of such differences enhances welfare gains from trade, efficiency considerations do not support trade instruments addressing differences in environmental regulation. The stance taken by the GATT/WTO regarding the trade measures sought in the context of domestic environmental policy has been negative. Our assessment showed that there is little ground to challenge this position.

The second part of our policy analysis (chapter 13) presented trade measures taken and proposed for the protection of the global environment. We identified that policy measures and proposals have the objective to ensure a wide participation in international efforts to control global externalities in the form of a multilateral environmental agreement, and to contain such pollution if cooperation is not universal. However, we also found evidence for protectionist intent behind the trade policy measures sought to complement environmental policy instruments.

The current GATT/WTO position vis-à-vis trade measures to safeguard the global environmental commons is mixed. Although current GATT/WTO rules may be in the way of eco-tariffs regardless of whether they are sanctioned by a multilateral environmental agreement or not, a reform to sanction trade measures taken pursuant to a multilateral environmental regime is envisaged. However, the deliberations of the CTE clearly indicate that non-multilateral trade restrictions for environmental protection will not meet with WTO approval. This decision by the WTO Members is based on the assessment that eco-tariffs not sanctioned by a multilateral environmental agreement would present a grave danger to the international trade regime, and that potential environmental benefits would not outweigh potential cost to the global community. In view of the seriousness of global environmental problems - those discovered so far, and those that may still be unknown - our assessment differs from that of the CTE: the negative welfare implications of uninternalised global environmental problems may well be worse than those associated with the mere risk of environmentally motivated trade restrictions upsetting the open, equitable and non-discriminatory trade regime.

In conclusion, we may thus state that our study has shown that trade measures may sometimes be found to improve environmental quality and welfare, yet these instances are rare. Consequently, their policy relevance should be restricted to very specific areas of global environmental protection. In most circumstances, environmental protection and free trade complement each other to achieve a global, social welfare optimum. With trade liberalisation as the general recommendation, the challenge remains for researchers and policy makers alike to isolate specific instances where trade restrictions are warranted, and to consult and act accordingly. For this, our study is a contribution.

References

ANDERSON, K.(1995), The Entwining of Trade Policy with Environmental & Labour Standards, Nota di Lavoro 39.95, Milan: Fondazione Enrico Eni Mattei.

ANDERSON, K. & BLACKHURST, R. (1992), Trade, the Environment and Public Policy, in: ANDERSON, K. & BLACKHURST, R. (eds), The Greening of World Trade Issues, 3-22, New York: Harvester Wheatsheaf.

ARDEN-CLARKE, C. (1991), The General Agreement on Tariffs and Trade, Environmental Protection and Sustainable Development, Gland: World Wide Fund for Nature.

ARDEN-CLARKE, C. (1992), South-North Terms of Trade, Environmental Protection and Sustainable Development, Gland: World Wide Fund for Nature.

ARDEN-CLARKE, C. (1993), An Action Agenda for Trade Policy Reform to Support Sustainable Development: A United Nation Conference on Environment and Development Follow-up, in: ZAELKE, D., ORBUCH, P. & HOUSMAN, R. (eds.), Trade and the Environment, Law, Economics and Policy, 71-81, Washington, D.C: Island Press.

BARKER, T. (1993), The Carbon Tax: Economic and Policy Issues, in CARRARO, C. & SINISCALCO, D. (eds.), The European Carbon Tax: An Economic Assessment, 239-254, Dordrecht: Kluwer Academic Publishers.

BARKER, T. & JOHNSTONE, N. (1998), International Competitiveness and Carbon Taxation, in: International Competitiveness and Environmental Policies, BARKER, T. & KÖHLER, J. (eds.) International Studies in Environmental Policy Making, 71-139, Cheltenham: Edward Elgar Publishing Ltd..

BARKER, T. & KÖHLER, J. (1998), Introduction, in: International Competitiveness and Environmental Policies, BARKER, T. & KÖHLER, J. (eds.) International Studies in Environmental Policy Making, 1-10, Cheltenham: Edward Elgar Publishing Ltd..

BARRETT, S. (1994a), Climate Change Policy and International Trade, CSERGE Working Paper, 94-12, London.

BARRETT, S. (1994b), Trade Restrictions in International Environmental Agreements, CSERGE Working Paper, 94-13, London.

BARRETT, S. (1994c), Strategic Environmental Policy and International Trade, in: Journal of Public Economics, Vol. 54, 325-338.

BAUMOL, W. (1971), Environmental Protection, International Spillovers and Trade, Stockholm: Almquist Wiksell.

BAUMOL, W. & OATES, W. (1988), The Theory of Environmental Policy, 2nd Edition, Cambridge: Cambridge University Press.

BEERS, C. VAN & BERGH, C. VAN DEN (1996), An Overvierw of Methodological Approaches in the Analysis of Trade and Environment, in: Journal of World Trade, Vol. 30, 143-167.

BEGHIN, J., DESSUS, S., ROLAND-HOLST, D. & MENSBRUGGHE, D. VAN DER (1994), A Survey of the Trade and Environment Nexus: Global Dimensions, in: OECD Economic Studies No. 23, 167-192.

BENEDICK, R. (1991), Ozone Diplomacy, Cambridge: Harvard University Press.

BHAGWATI, J. (1987), The Generalized Theory of Distortions and Welfare (orginally published 1971), in: BHAGWATI, J. (ed.), International Trade: Selected Readings, 265-286, Cambridge: MIT Press.

BHAGWATI, J. (1992a), Aggressive Unilateralism, in: GIERSCH, H. (ed), Money, Trade and Competition. Essays in Honour of E. Sohmen, 201-231, Berlin: Springer.

BHAGWATI, J. (1992b), The Threats to the World Trading System, in: The World Economy, Vol. 15, 443-456.

BHAGWATI, J. (1993a), Trade and Environment, in: The American Enterprise, May/June, 43-49.

BHAGWATI, J. (1993b), Trade and Environment: The False Conflict, in: ZAELKE, D., ORBUCH, P. & HOUSMAN, R. (eds.), Trade and the Environment Law, Economics and Policy, 159-190, Washington, D.C.: Island Press.

BHAGWATI, J. (1996), Introduction, in: BHAGWATI, J. & HUDEC, R. (eds.), Fair Trade and Harmonization, 1-6, Cambridge: MIT Press.

BHAGWATI, J. & SRINIVASAN, T. (1971). The Theory of Wage-Differentials: Production Response and Factor Price Equalisation, in: Journal of International Economics, Vol. 1, 19-35.

BHAGWATI, J. & SRINIVASAN, T. (1996), Trade and the Environment: Does Environmental Diversity Detract from the Case for Free Trade?, in: BHAGWATI, J. & HUDEC, R. (eds.), Fair Trade and Harmonization, Vol. 1: Economic Analysis, 159-223, Cambridge: MIT Press.

BLACKHURST, R. & SUBRAMANIAN, A. (1992), Promoting Multilateral Cooperation on the Environment, in: ANDERSON, K. & BLACKHURST, R. (eds.), The Greening of World Trade Issues, 247-268.

BLAZEJCAK, J. et al. (1993), Umweltschutz und Standortqualität in der Bundesrepublik Deutschland, in: DIW Wochenberichte, Vol. 60, 199-206.

BODECKER, M. (1997), Internationale Umweltprobleme - Ökonomische Auswirkungen und Lösungsansätze, Frankfurt: Peter Lang.

BOHM, P. & RUSSEL, C. (1985), Comparative Analysis of Alternative Policy Instruments, in: KNEESE, A. & SWEENEY, J. (eds.), Handbook of Natural Resources and Energy Economics, Vol. I, 395-460.

BOISSON DE CHAZOURNES, L. (1995) The United Nations Framework Convention on Climate Change: On the Road towards Sustainable Development, Graduate Institute of International Studies, University of Geneva Law Faculty.

BOYLE, A. (1994), The Convention on Biological Diversity, in: CAMPIGLIO, L, PINESCHI, L., SINISCALCO, D. & TREVES, T. (eds.), The Environment after Rio. International Law and Economics, 11-127, London: Graham and Trotman.

BRANDER, J. (1995), Strategic Trade Policy, in: GROSSMAN, G. & ROGOFF, K. (eds.), Handbook of International Economics, Vol. III, 1395-1455, Amsterdam: Elsevier Science.

BRANDER, J. & KRUGMAN, P. (1983), A Reciprocal Dumping Model of International Trade: in: Journal of International Economics, Vol. 15, 313-321.

BRANDER, J. & SPENCER, B. (1981), Tariffs and the Extraction of Foreign Monopoly Rents under Potential Entry, in: Canadian Journal of Economics, Vol. 14, 371-389.

BRANDER, J. & SPENCER, B., (1983), International R&D Rivalry and Industrial Strategy, in: Review of Economic Studies, Vol. 50, 707-722.

BRANDER, J. & SPENCER, B. (1984), Tariff Protection and Imperfect Competition, in: KIERZKOWSKI, H. (ed.), Monopolistic Competition and International Trade, 194-206, Oxford: Clarendon Press.

BRANDER, J. & SPENCER, B. (1985), Export Subsidies and International Market Share Rivalry, in: Journal of International Economics, Vol. 18, 83-100.

BRANDER, J. & TAYLOR, S. (1998), Open Access Renewable Resources: Trade and Trade Policy in a Two-country Model, in: Journal of International Economics, Vol. 44, 181-209.

BROWN, K., PEARCE, D., PERRINGS, C. & SWANSEA, T. (1993), Chapter 3 from: The Conservation of Global Biological Diversity, GEF Working Paper 2, Washington D.C..

BULOW, J., GEANAKOPLOS, J. & KLEMPERER, P. (1985), Multimarket Oligopoly: Strategic Substitutes and Complements, in: Journal of Political Economy, Vol. 93, 488-511.

BURGESS, J. (1994), The Environmental Effects of Trade in Endangered Species, in: OECD (ed), The Environmental Effects of Trade, 123-152, Paris.

CAIRNCROSS, F. (1993), International Business Community and Environmental Protection, in: Wirtschaftspolitische Blätter, Vol. 40, 317-326.

CAMERON, J. (1993), Environmental Protection, Sustainable Development and International Trade - Mutually Supportive or Exclusive?, in: Wirtschaftspolitische Blätter, Vol. 40, 385-398.

CARRARO, C. & SINISCALCO, D. (1992), The International Dimension of Environmental Policy, in: European Economic Review, Vol. 36, 379-387.

CHAKARIAN, J. (1994), PPMs and General Policy Issues, in: OECD Trade and Environment: Processes and Production Methods, 113-120, Paris.

CHARNOVITZ, S. (1992), Environmental and Labour Standards in Trade, in: The World Economy, Vol. 13, 335-356.

CHARNOVITZ, S. (1993), Environmentalism Confronts GATT Rules, in: Journal of World Trade, Vol. 27, 37-53.

CHARNOVITZ, S. (1995), Improving Environmental and Trade Governance, in: International Environmental Affairs, Vol. 7, 59-91.

CHOI, E. K. & JOHNSON, S. R. (1992), Regulation of Externalities in an Open Economy, in: Ecological Economics, Vol. 5, 251-265.

CLINE, W. (1991), Scientific Basis for the Greenhouse Effect, in: Economic Journal, vol. 101, 904-909.

COASE, R. (1960), The Problem of Social Cost, in: Journal of Law and Economics, Vol. 1, 1-44.

COMMISSION OF THE EUROPEAN COMMUNITIES (1991), A Community Strategy to Limit Carbon Dioxide Emissions and to Improve Energy Efficiency, Communication from the Commission to the Council, SEC (91), 1744, Brussels.

COMMISSION OF THE EUROPEAN COMMUNITIES (1995), Communication from the Commission to the Council on Trade and Environment, SEC (95), Brussels.

CONRAD, K. (1993), Taxes and Subsidies for Pollution-Intensive Industries as Trade Policy, in: Journal of Environmental Economics and Management, Vol. 35, 121-135.

CONRAD, K. (1996), Optimal Environmental Policy for Oligopolistic Industry under Intra-industry Trade, in: CARRARO, C. ET AL. (eds.), Environmental Policy and Market Structure, 65-83, Dordrecht: Kluwer Academic Publishers.

COPELAND, B. (1993), Process Standards, Pollution Content Taxes, and the Control of Cross-Border Pollution, Discussion Paper No. 93-42, University of British Columbia, Vancouver.

COPELAND, B. (1994), International Trade and the Environment: Policy Reform in a Polluted Small Open Economy, in: Journal of Environmental Economics and Management, Vol. 26, 44-65.

CORNES, R. & SANDLER, T. (1986), The Theory of Externalities, Public Goods, and Club Goods, Cambridge: Cambridge University Press.

CROPPER, M. & OATES, W. (1992), Environmental Economics: A Survey, in: Journal of Economic Literature, Vol. 30, 675-740.

DEBREU, G. (1983), Mathematical Economics - Twenty Papers of Gerard Debreu, Cambridge: Cambridge University Press.

DEATON, A. & MUELLBAUER, J. (1980), Economics and Consumer Behaviour, Cambridge: Cambridge University Press.

DIXIT, A. (1984), International Trade Policy for Oligopolistic Industries, in: Economic Journal, Vol. 94 suppl., 1-16.

DIXIT, A. (1985), Tax Policy in Open Economics, in: AUERBACH, A. & FELDSTEIN, M. (eds.), Handbook of Public Economics, Vol. 1, 313-374, Amsterdam: North-Holland.

DIXIT, A. (1988), Anti-dumping and Countervailing Duties under Oligopoly, in: European Economic Review, Vol. 32, 55-68.

DÜERKOP, M. (1994), Trade and Environment: International Trade Law Aspects of the Proposed EC Directive Introducing a Tax on Carbon Dioxide Emissions and Energy, in: Common Market Law Review, Vol. 31, 807-844.

ECKAUS, R. (1993), Laissez Faire, Collective Control or Nationalization of the Global Commons, Nota di Lavoro 31.93, Milan: Fondazione Eni Enrico Mattei.

EGLIN, R. (1993), International Economics, International Trade, International Environmental Protection, in: Wirtschaftsppolitische Blätter, Vol. 40, 304-317.

EGLIN, R. (1995), Trade and Environment in the World Trade Organisation, in: World Economy, Vol. 18, 769-779.

EKINS, P. & SPECK, S. (1998), The Impacts of Environmental Policy on Competitiveness: Theory and Evidence, in: BARKER, T. & KÖHLER, J. (eds), International Competitiveness and Environmental Policies, International Studies in Environmental Policy Making, 33 - 70, Cheltenham: Edward Elgar Publishing Ltd..

ENDERS, A. & PORGES, A. (1992), Successful Conventions and Conventional Success: Saving the Ozone Layer, in: ANDERSON, K. & BLACKHURST, R. (eds.), The Greening of World Trade Issues, 130 - 144, New York: Harvester Wheatsheaf.

ESTY, D. (1994), Greening the GATT - Trade, Environment and the Future, Washington, D.C.: Institute for International Economics.

FEESS, E. (1998), Umweltökonomie und Umweltpolitik, 2nd edition, München: Verlag Vahlen.

FEKETEKUTY, G. (1993), The Link between Trade and Environmental Policy, in: Minnesota Journal of Global Trade, Vol. 2, 171-205.

FREDERIKSSON, P. (1995), Capital Mobility, Pollution Taxes, and Environmental Federalism, Seminar Paper 95-14, Department of Econonomics, University of Adelaide.

FRENCH, H. (1993a), Costly Tradeoffs: Reconciling Trade and the Environment, World Watch Paper 113.

FRENCH, H. (1993b), The GATT: Menace or Ally ?, in: World Watch, Sept./Oct., 12-19.

FUDENBERG, D. & TIROLE, J. (1991), Game Theory, Cambridge: MIT Press.

GANDOLFO, G. (1994), International Economics I -The Pure Theory of International Trade, 2nd ed., Berlin: Springer.

GARDNER, B. (1994) Environmental Regulation and the Competitiveness of US Agriculture, paper prepared for presentation at the International Agricultural Trade Research Consortium Symposium on Agricultural Trade and the Environment: Understanding and Measuring the Critical Linkages, Toronto.

GATT (1970), Border Tax Adjustment - Report of the Working Party, adopted Dec. 2 1970, BISD 18S/97, Geneva.

GATT (1991), Dispute Settlement Panel Report on United States Restrictions on Imports of Tuna, Doc DS21/R, Geneva.

GATT (1992), Trade and the Environment, Geneva.

GATT (1994), Results of the Uruguay Round of Multilateral Trade Negotiations - Legal Texts, Geneva: GATT Secretariat.

GORNIG, G. & SILAGI, M. (1992), Vom Ökodumping zum Ökoprotektionismus, in: Europäische Zeitung für Wirtschaftsrecht, Heft 24, 753-759.

GRAY, W. & SHADBEGIAN, R. (1993), Environmental Regulation and Manufacturing Productivity at the Plant Level, NBER Working Paper 4634, Cambridge.

GROSSMAN, G. & KRUEGER, A. (1994), Economic Growth and the Environment, NBER Working Paper 4634, Cambridge.

HANSSON, G. (1990), Harmonisation and International Trade, London: Routledge.

HARDIN, G. (1968), The Tragedy of the Commons, in: Science, Vol. 162, 1243-1248.

HARTMANN, M. (1993), The Effects of EC Environmental Policies on Agricultural Trade and Economic Welfare, in: Journal of Economic Integration, Vol. 8, 219-244.

HARTMANN, M. (1994), National and International Effects of a Pesticide Ban - Simulations with the Trade Model TEPSIM, in: MICHALEK, J. & HANF, C. (eds.), The Economic Consequences of a Drastic Reduction in Pesticide Use in the EU, 64-80, Kiel.

HAUSER, H. & SCHANZ, K.-U. (1995), Das neue GATT - die Welthandelsordnung nach Abschluß der Uruguay Runde, München: Oldenbourg Verlag.

HAUT, B. (1997), Neuere Außenwirtschaftstheorie, Sockelübungsskript, Hannover.

HAZARI, B. (1978), The Pure Theory of International Trade and Distortions, London: Croom Helm.

HELM, C. (1995) Sind Freihandel und Umweltschutz vereinbar? Ökologischer Reformbedarf des GATT/WTO Regimes, Berlin: Ed. Sigma.

HELM, C. (1996), Umwelt- und Handelspolitik in einer globalisierten Wirtschaft, in: SIMONIS, U. (ed.), Weltumweltpolitik - Grundriß und Bausteine eines neuen Politikfeldes, 219-242, Berlin: Ed. Sigma.

HERBERG, H. & KEMP, M. (1971), Factor Market Distortions, the Shape of the Locus of Competitive Outputs, and the Relation between Product Prices and Equilibrium Outputs, in: BHAGWATI, J., JONES, J., MUNDELL, R. & VANEK, J. (eds.), Trade, Balance of Payments and Growth. Papers in International Economics in Honour of C. P. Kindleberger, Amsterdam: North Holland.

HILLMAN, A. (1989), The Political Economy of Protectionism, Chur: Harwood Academic Publishers.

HILLMAN, A. & URSPRUNG, H. (1992), The Influence of Environmental Concerns in the Political Determination of Trade Policy, in: ANDERSON, K. & BLACKHURST, R. (eds), The Greening of World Trade Issues, 195-220, New York: Harvester Wheatsheaf.

HILLMAN, A. & URSPRUNG, H. (1993), Greens, Supergreens and International Trade Politics: Environmental Concerns and Protectionism, Nota di Lavoro 21.93, Miland: Fondazione Eni Enrico Mattei.

HOEKMAN, B. & LEIDY, M. (1992), Environmental Policy Formation in a Trading Economy: A Public Choice Perspective, in: ANDERSON, K. & BLACKHURST, R. (eds), The Greening of World Trade Issues, 221-246, New York: Harvester Wheatsheaf.

HOEKMAN, B. & LEIDY, M. (1994), 'Cleaning Up' While Cleaning Up? Pollution Abatement, Interest Groups and Contingent Trade Policies, in: Public Choice, Vol. 78, 241-258.

HOEL, M. (1993), Should a Carbon Tax Be Differentiated Across Sectors?, Memorandum from Department of Economics No. 9, University of Oslo.

HOEL, M. (1989), Global Environmental Problems: The Effects of Unilateral Action Taken by One Country, Memorandum from Department of Economics No. 11, University of Oslo.

HOUGHTON, J., JENKINS, G. & EPHRAUMS, J. (1990), Climate Change: IPCC Scientific Asessment, Cambridge: Cambridge University Press.

IMF SURVEY (1997), WTO Ministerial Conference Seeks to Strengthen the Multilateral Trading System, in: IMF Survey, January 13, 1997, 5-7.

JAFFE A., PETERSON, P, PORTNEY, P. & STAVINS, R. (1995), Environmental Regulation and the Competitiveness of US Manufacturing: What does the Evidence Tell Us?, Journal of Economic Literature, Vol. 33, 132-163.

JOHNSON, H. (1950), Optimum Welfare and Maximum Revenue Tariffs, in: Review of Economic Studies, Vol. XIX, 28-35.

JOHNSON, H. (1953/4), Optimum Tariffs and Retaliation, in: Johnson, H. (1958), International Trade and Economic Growth Studies in Pure Theory, (reprinted from Review of Economic Studies, Vol. XXI, 142-153), 31-55, London: George Allen & Unwin.

JOHNSON, H. (1971), The Implications of Free or Freer Trade for Harmonisation of other Policies, London: George Allen & Unwin.

JOHNSON, H. (1987), Optimal Trade Intervention in the Presence of Domestic Distortions, in: BHAGWATI, J. (ed.), International Trade: Selected Readings, 235-263, Cambridge: MIT Press.

JONES, R. (1971), Distortions in Factor Markets and the General Equilibrium Model of Production, in: Journal of Political Economy, Vol. 79, 437-459.

KARL, H. & RANNE, O. (1997), Öko-Dumping: Ein stichhaltiges Argument für ökologische Ausgleichszölle?, in: WiSt, No. 6, 284-289.

KENNEDY, P. (1994), Equilibrium Pollution Taxes in Open Economies with Imperfect Competition, in: Journal of Environmental Economics and Management, Vol. 27, 49-63.

KIRCHGÄSSNER, G. & MOHR, E. (1995), Trade Restrictions as Viable Means of Enforcing Compliance with International Environmental Law: An Economic Assessment, Discussion Paper No. 9509, Department of Economics, University of St. Gallen.

KLEPPER, G. (1992), The Political Economy of Trade and the Environment in Western Europe, in: LOW, P. (ed), International Trade and the Environment, World Bank Discussion Papers 159, 247-259, Washington: World Bank.

KLEPPER, G. (1994), Trade Implications of Environmental Taxes, Kiel Working Paper No. 628.

KLEVORICK, A. (1996), Reflections on the Race to the Bottom, in: BHAGWATI, J. & HUDEC, R. (eds.), Fair Trade and Harmonization, Vol 1: Economic Analysis, 459-467, Cambridge: MIT Press.

KOOPMANN, G. (1995), Die Welthandelsordnung nach der Uruguay Runde - Von der Liberalisierung zur Harmonisierung, HWWA Discussion Paper 21, Hamburg.

KRAUSS, M & JOHNSON, H. (1974), General Equilibrium Analysis, London: George Allen & Unwin.

KRUEGER, A. (1987), The Political Economy of the Rent-Seeking Society, in: BHAGWATI, J. (ed), International Trade: Selected Readings, 291-309, Cambridge: MIT Press.

KRUGMAN, P. (1984), Import Protection as Export Promotion: International Competition in the Presence of Oligopoly and Economics of Scale, in: KIERZKOWSKI, H. (ed.), Monopolistic Competition and International Trade, 180-193, Oxford: Clarendon Press.

KRUGMAN, P. & OBSTFELD, M. (1997), International Economics - Theory and Policy, 4th ed., Reading: Addison-Wesley.

KRUMM, R. (1996), Internationale Umweltpolitik. Eine Analyse aus umweltökonomischer Sicht, Berlin: Springer.

KRUTILLA, K. (1991), Environmental Regulation in an Open Economy, in: Journal of Environmental Economics and Management, Vol. 20, 127-142.

KUHN, M. & TIVIG, T. (1996), Ecological Dumping and Environmental Capital Flight - The Economics Behind the Propaganda, Diskussionsbeiträge SFB 178 Internationalisierung der Wirtschaft, Uni Konstanz.

KULESSA, M. (1995), Umweltpolitik in einer offenen Volkswirtschaft, Baden-Baden: Nomos Verlagsgesellschaft.

LALLAS, P., ESTY, D., & HOOGSTRATEN, D. (1992), The Environmental Protection and International Trade: Towards Mutually Supportive Rules and Policies, in: Harvard Environmental Law Review, Vol. 16, 271-342.

LANG, W. (1993), International Environmental Agreements & the GATT: The Case of the Montreal Protocol, in: Wirtschaftspolitische Blätter, Vol. 40, 364-372.

LEE, J. (1994), Process and Product - Making the Link Between Trade and the Environment , in: International Environmental Affairs, Vol. 6, 320-347.

LEONARD, H. (1988), Pollution and the Struggle for the World Product, Cambridge: Cambridge University Press.

LEVIN, G. (1992), The Environment and Trade - A Multilateral Imperative, in: Minnesota Journal of Global Trade, Vol. 1, 231-267.

LEVINSON, A. (1996), Environmental Regulations and Industry Location: International and Domestic Evidence, in: BHAGWATI, J. & HUDEC, R. (eds.), Fair Trade and Harmonization, Vol. 1: Economic Analysis, 429-457, Cambridge: MIT Press.

LLOYD, P. (1992), The Problem of Optimal Environmental Policy Choice, in: ANDERSON, K. & BLACKHURST, R. (eds.), The Greening of World Trade Issues, 49-71, New York: Harvester Wheatsheaf.

LOCKWOOD, B. (1987), Pareto Efficiency, in: EATWELL, J. ET AL. (eds), The New Palgrave, 811-813, London: Macmillan.

LONG, N. VAN & SIEBERT, H. (1989), Institutional Competition Versus Ex-Ante Harmonisation: The Case of Environmental Policy, Kiel Working Papers No. 396.

LOW, P. (1992), International Trade and the Environmental: An Overview, in: LOW, P. (ed.) International Trade and the Environment, World Bank Discussion Paper No. 159, 1-14, World Bank, Washington.

LOW, P. & YEATS, A. (1992), Do 'Dirty' Industries Migrate?, in: LOW, P. (ed.) International Trade and the Environment, World Bank Discussion Paper No. 159, 89-103, World Bank, Washington.

LUDEMA, R.D. & WOOTON, I. (1994), Cross-Border Externalities and Trade Liberalisation: The Strategic Control of Pollution, in: Canadian Journal of Economics, Vol. XXVII, 950-966.

LUDEMA, R.D. & WOOTON, I. (1997), International Trade Rules and Environmental Cooperation under Asymmetric Information , in Economic Review, Vol. 38, 605-625.

MÆSTAD, O. (1998), On the Efficiency of Green Trade Policy, in: Environmental and Reseource Ecnomics, Vol. 11, 1-18.

MAGEE, S. (1971), Factor Market Distortions, Production, Distribution, and the Pure Theory of International Trade, in: Quaterly Journal of Economics, Vol. 85, 623-643.

MAGEE, S. (1973), Factor Market Distortions, Production and Trade: A Survey, in: Oxford Economic Papers, Vol. 3, 1-43.

MAGEE, S. (1976), International Trade and Distortions in Factor Markets, New York: Marcel Dekker.

MAGEE, S., BROCK, W. & YOUNG, L. (1989), Black Hole Tariffs and Endogenous Policy Formation, Cambridge: Cambridge University Press.

MARKANDYA, A. (1991), Economis and the Ozone Layer, in: PEARCE, D. (ed.), Blueprint 2: Greening the World Economy, 63-74, London: Earthscan.

MARKUSEN, J. (1975), International Externalities and Optimal Tax Structures, in: Journal of International Economics, Vol 5, 15-29.

MARKUSEN, R., MELVIN, J., KAEMPFER, W. & MASKUS, K. (1995), International Trade Theory and Evidence, 2nd ed., New York: McGraw-Hill International Editions.

MARKUSEN, J., MOREY, E. & OLEWILER, N. (1992), Noncooperative Equilibria in Regional Environmental Policies when Plant Locations are Endogenous, NBER Working Paper No. 4051.

MAS-COLELL, A., WHINSTON, M. & GREEN, J. (1995), Microeconomic Theory, New York: Oxford University Press.

MATTOO, A. & MAVROIDIS, P. (1996), Trade, Environment and the WTO: How Real is the Conflict?, in: STUDENTENINITIATIVE WIRTSCHAFT UND UMWELT E.V. (ed.), Welthandel und Umweltschutz: Wie Handeln wir Ökologisch?, 61-83, Münster.

MCGUIRE, M. (1982), Regulation, Factor Rewards, and International Trade, in: Journal of Public Economics, Vol. 17, 335-354.

MEINHEIT, E. (1996), Handelspolitik als Umweltpolitik im Agrarbereich?, Kiel: Wissenschaftsverlag Vank.

MERRIFIELD, J. (1988), The Impact of Selected Abatement Strategies on Transnational Pollution, the Terms of Trade, and Factor Rewards: A General Equilibrium Approach, in: Journal of Environmental Economics and Management, Vol. 15, 259-284.

METZLER, L. (1949), Tariffs, the Terms of Trade, and the Distribution of National Income, in: Journal of Political Economy, Vol. LVII, 1-29.

MIKESELL, R. (1993), GATT Trade Rules and the Environment, in: Contemporary Policy Issues, Vol. 11, 14-18.

MOLINA, M. & ROWLAND, F. (1974), Stratospheric Sink for Chlorofluorocarbons: Chlorine Atom-catalysed Destruction of Ozone, in: Nature, Vol. 249, 810-812.

MOTTA, M. & THISSE, J. (1994), Does Environmental Dumping Lead to Delocation?, in: European Economic Review, Vol. 38, 563-576.

NASH, J. (1950), Equilibrium Points in n-Person Games, in: Proceedings of the National Academy of Sciences, USA, Vol. 36, 48-49.

NASH, J. (1951), Non-Cooperative Games, in: Annals of Mathematics, Vol. 54, 286-295.

NICOLETTI, G. & OLIVEIRA-MARTINS, J. (1993), Global Effects of the European Carbon Tax, in: CARRARO, C. & SINISCALCO, D. (eds.), The European Carbon Tax: An Economic Assessment, 15-48, Dordrecht: Kluwer Academic Publishers.

OATES, W. & SCHWAB, R. (1988), Economic Competition Among Jurisdictions: Efficiency Enhancing or Distortion Inducing?, in: Journal of Public Economics, Vol. 35, 333-354.

OBERTHÜR, S. (1992a), Die Zerstörung der Stratosphärischen Ozonschicht als Internationales Problem, in: Zeitschrift für Umweltpolitik und Umweltrecht, Vol. 15, 155-185.

OBERTHÜR, S. (1992b), Die internationale Zusammenharbeit zum Schutze des Weltklimas, in: Aus Politik und Zeitgeschichte, Beiträge zur Wochenzeitung das Parlament, Vol. 42, 9-19.

O'CONNOR, D. (1994), The Use of Economic Instruments in Environmental Management: The East-Asian Experience, in: OECD (ed.), Applying Economic Instruments to Environmental Policies in OECD and Dynamic Non-member Countries, 33-58, Paris.

OECD (1993), Summary Report of the Workshop on Environmental Policies and Industrial Competitiveness, Paris.

OECD (1994), The Use of Economic Instruments in OECD Member Countries, in: OECD (ed.), Applying Economic Instruments to Environmental Policies in OECD and Dynamic Non-member Countries, 15-31.

OECD (1995a), Environmental Taxes in OECD Countries, Paris.

OECD (1995b), Report on Trade and Environment to the OECD Council at Ministerial Level, OECD Working Papers No. 47, Paris.

OECD (1996), Implementation Strategies for Environmental Taxes, Paris.

OZONE SECRETARIAT (1993), Handbook for the Montreal Protocol on Substances that Deplete the Ozone Layer, 3rd ed., Nairobi.

PALMETER, D. (1993), Environment and Trade: Much Ado about Little?, in: Journal of World Trade, Vol. 27, 55-70.

PANAGARIYA, A., PALMER, K., OATES, W. & KRUPNICK, A. (1993), Toward an Integrated Theory of Open Economy Environmental and Trade Policy, Working Paper No. 938, Department of Economics, University of Maryland.

PARETO, V. (1909), Cours d'Économie Politique, Paris: M. Giard.

PEARCE, D. (1993), Should the GATT be Reformed for Environmental Reasons?, Centre for Social and Eonomic Research on the Global Environment, London.

PEARSON, C. (1987), Environmental Standards, Industrial Relocation, and Pollution Havens, in: PEARSON, C. (ed.), Multinational Corporations, Environment, and the Third World, Durham: Duke University Press.

PEARSON, C. (1993), The Trade and Environment Nexus: What is New since '72?, in: ZAELKE, D., ORBUCH, P. & HOUSMAN, R. (eds.), Trade and the Environment: Law, Economics, and Policy, 23-32, Washington D.C.: Island Press.

PEARSON, M. & SMITH, S. (1991), The European Carbon Tax: An Assessment on the European Commission's Proposal, London: Institute of Fiscal Studies.

PETERSMANN, E.-U. (1993a), International Trade Law and International Environmental Law Prevention and Settlement of International Environmental Disputes in GATT, in: Jounal of World Trade, Vol. 27, 43-81.

PETERSMANN, E.-U. (1993b), The Settlement of International Environmental Disputes in GATT and the EEC, in: Wirtschaftspolitische Blätter, 372-383.

PETERSMANN, E.-U. (1995), International and European Trade and Environmental Law after the Uruguay Round, London: Kluwer Academic Publishers.

PETHIG, R. (1976), Pollution, Welfare, and Environmental Policy in the Theory of Comparative Advantage, in: Journal of Environmental Economics and Management, Vol. 2, 160-169.

PETHIG, R. (1983), Reciprocal Transfrontier Pollution, in: SIEBERT, H. (ed.), Global Environmental Resources - Staatliche Allokationspolitik im Marktwirtschaftlichen System 2, 57-93, Frankfurt: Verlag Peter Lang.

PIGOU, A. (1932), The Economics of Welfare, London: Macmillan.

PULVENIS, J. (1994), The Framework Convention on Climate Change, in: CAMPIGLIO, L., PINESCHI, L., SINISCALCO, D. & TREVES, T. (eds), The Environment after Rio: International Law and Economics, 71-110, London: Graham & Trotman/Martinius Nijhoff.

RANNE, O. (1996), Ökonomische Überlegungen zum Begriff des Öko-Dumping, Diskussionspapier 96-04, Agrar- und Ressourcenökonomik Universität Bonn.

RASMUSEN, E. (1989), Games and Information - An Introduction to Game Theory, Oxford: Basil Blackwell Ltd..

RAUSCHER, M.(1991a), National Environmental Policies and the Effects of Economic Integration, in: European Journal of Political Economy, Vol. 7, 313-329.

RAUSCHER, M. (1991b), Foreign Trade and the Environment, in: SIEBERT, H. (ed.), Environmental Scarcity - The International Dimension, 17-31, Tübingen: J.C.B. Mohr.

RAUSCHER, M. (1992a), Economic Integration and the Environment: The Effects on Members and Non-Members, in: Environmental and Resource Economics, Vol 2, 221-236.

RAUSCHER, M. (1992b), Umweltpolitik und wirtschaftliche Integration, in: Homo Oekonomicus, Vol IX, 81-102.

RAUSCHER, M. (1992c), International Economic Integration and the Environment: The Case of Europe, in: ANDERSON, K. & BLACKHURST, R. (eds.), The Greening of World Trade Issues, 173-191, New York: Harvester Wheatsheaf.

RAUSCHER, M. (1992d) Environmental Policy and International Capital Movements, Manuscript.

RAUSCHER, M. (1993a), Foreign Trade and Renewable Resources, Nota di Lavoro 25.93, Milan: Fondazione Enrico Eni Mattei.

RAUSCHER, M. (1993b), Provision of Public Inputs and the Effects of Successful Lobbying in Open Economies, Discussion Paper No. 807, London: Centre for Economic Policy Research.

RAUSCHER, M. (1994), On Ecological Dumping, in: Oxford Economic Papers, Vol. 46, 822-840.

RAUSCHER, M. (1995a), Environmental Regulation and the Location of Polluting Industries, in: International Tax and Public Finance, Vol 2, 229-244.

RAUSCHER, M. (1995b), Protectionists, Environmentalists and the Formation of Environmental Policy in an Open Economy, SFB 178 Internationalisierung der Wirtschaft, Diskussionsbeiträge Serie II No. 256, Universität Konstanz.

RAUSCHER, M. (1995c), Strategic Environmental Policy in Oligopolistic Markets, Nota di Lavoro 65.95, Milan: Fondazione Enrico Eni Mattei.

RAUSCHER, M. (1995d), Environmental Legislation as a Tool of Trade Policy, in: BOERO, G. & SILBERSTON, Z. (eds.), Proceeding of a Conference held by the Confederation of European Economic Associations at Oxford, 1993 CEEA Conference, 73-90, Basingstoke: Macmillan.

RAUSCHER, M. (1997), International Trade, Factor Movements and the Environment, Oxford: Oxford University Press.

REPETTO, R. (1993), Trade and Environment Policies: Achieving Complementarities and Avoiding Conflicts, Washington D.C.: World Research Institute.

REVESZ, R. (1994), Rehabilitating Interstate Competition: Rethinking the 'Race-To-The-Bottom' Rationale for Federal Environmental Regulation, in: Land Use and Environmental Law Review, 373-417.

ROBERTSON, D. (1992), Trade and the Environment: Harmonisation and Technical Standards, in: LOW, P. (ed), International Trade and the Environment, World Bank Discussion Paper, No. 159, 309-324, Washington, D.C..

ROBERTSON, D. (1994), Environment, Trade and Development, Economics Division, Research School of Pacific and Asian Studies, The Australian University.

ROBISON, H. (1988), Industrial Pollution Abatement: The Impact of the Balance of Trade, Canadian Journal of Economics, 187-199, Vol. 21.

RODRIK, D. (1995), Politican Economy of Trade Policy, in: GROSSMAN, G. & ROGOFF, K. (eds.), Handbook of International Economics, Vol. III, 1457-1494, Amsterdam: Elsevier Science.

ROTH, E. (1983), Sämtliche Menschen, München: Karl Hauser Verlag.

RÜBESAMEN, D. (1998), Technischer Fortschritt, Wirtschaftsstruktur und Leistungsbilanzentwicklung, Frankfurt: Verlag Peter Lang.

SANDLER, T. (1992), After the Cold War, Secure the Global Commons, in: Challenge, Vol. 35, 16-23.

SANDS, P., TAROFSKY, R. & WEISS, M. (1994), Documents in International Environmental Law, Principles of Environmental Law IIA, Manchester: Manchester University Press.

SCHNEIDER, K. & WELLISCH, D. (1995), Eco-Dumping, Capital Mobility, and International Trade, Dresdner Beiträge zur Volkswirtschaftslehre.

SCHULZ, J. (1994), Environmental Reform of the GATT-WTO International Trading System, in: World Competition, Vol. 18, 77-113.

SHRYBMAN, S. (1990), International Trade and the Environment: An Environmental Assessment of the General Agreement on Tariffs and Trade, in: The Ecologist, Vol. 20, 30-34.

SHRYBMAN, S. (1992), Trading Away the Environment, in: World Policy Journal, Vol. 9, 93-110.

SIEBERT, H. (1977), Environmental Quality and the Gains from Trade, in: Kyklos, Vol. 30, 657-673.

SIEBERT, H. (1979), Environmental Policy in the Two Country Case, in: Zeitschrift für Nationalökonomie, Vol. 39, 259-274.

SIEBERT, H. (1990a), Natürliche Ressourcen und Weltwirtschaft, in: Weltwirtschaftliches Archiv, Vol. 126, 1-24.

SIEBERT, H. (1990b), The Harmonisation Issue in Europe: Prior Agreement or Competitive Process?, in: SIEBERT, H. (ed), The Completion of the Internal Market - Symposium 1989, 53-90, Tübingen: J.C.B. Mohr.

SIEBERT, H. (1994), Außenwirtschaft, 6th ed., Stuttgart: Gustav Fischer Verlag.

SIEBERT, H. (1995a), Economics of the Environment, 4th ed., Theory and Policy, Berlin: Springer.

SIEBERT, H. (1995b), Ein Regelwerk für eine Zusammenwachsende Welt, Kieler Diskussionsbeiträge 251.

SIEBERT, H. (1996), Trade Policy and Environmental Protection, Kiel Working Paper No. 730.

SIMONIS, U. & WEIZSÄCKER, E.-U. VON (1990), Global Environmental Problems, in: Economics, Vol. 42, 39-53.

SLOOTEN, R. VAN (1994), The Case of the Montreal Protocol, in: OECD (ed.), Trade and Environment Processes and Production Methods, Paris.

SNAPE, R. (1992), The Environment, International Trade and Competitiveness, in: ANDERSON, K. & BLACKHURST, R. (eds.), The Greening of World Trade Issues, 73-92, New York: Harvester Wheatsheaf.

SOHMEN, E. (1976), Allokationstheorie und Wirtschaftspolitik, Tübingen: J.C.B. Mohr.

SOLOW, R. (1991), Is there a Global Warming Problem?, in: DORNBUSCH, R. & POTERBA, J. (eds.), Global Warming: Economic Policy Responses, Cambridge: MIT Press.

SORSA, P. (1992a), GATT and Environment, in: The World Economy, Vol. 15, 115-133.

SORSA, P. (1994), Competitiveness and Environmental Standards: Some Exploratory Results, World Bank Policy Reseach Working Paper 1249, Geneva.

SORSA, P. (1995), Environmental Protectionism, North-South Trade, and the Uruguay Round, International Monetary Fund Working Paper, Geneva.

SRINIVASAN, T. (1993), The Environment, Economic Development, and International Trade: Some Issues, Occasional Paper No. 13, Bureau of Economic Studies, Macalester College, St. Paul.

STACKELBERG, H. VON (1934), Marktform und Gleichgewicht, Berlin: Springer.

STEVENS, C. (1994), Synthesis Report Trade and Environment: PPM Issues, in: OECD (ed.), Trade and Environment Processes and Production Methods, 7-22, Paris.

STEVENS, C. (1995), Eco-Dumping: More Myth than Reality, in: Internationale Politik und Gesellschaft, Vol. 2, 174-180.
STEWARDSON, R. (1994), The Case of Carbon Taxes, in: OECD (ed.), Trade and Environment Processes and Production Method, 93-108.
SUBRAMANIAN, A. (1992), Trade Measures: A Nearly Empty Box, in: The World Economy, Vol. 15, 135-152.
THOMAS, C. & TEREPOSKY, G. (1993a), The NAFTA and the Side Agreement on Environmental Cooperation, in: Journal of World Trade, Vol. 27, 5-34.
THOMAS, C. & TEREPOSKY, G. (1993b), The Evolving Relationship Between Trade and Environmental Regulation, in: Journal of World Trade, Vol. 27, 23-45.
TIROLE, J. (1988), The Theory of Industrial Organization, Cambridge: MIT Press.
TREBILCOCK, M. & HOWSE, R. (1995), The Regulation of International Trade, London: Routledge.
TSCHOFEN, F. (1992), Legal Content of the Notion 'Global Commons', World Development Report 1992, Background Paper No. 16, Washington D.C.: World Bank.
TUDINI, A. (1993), Trade and Environment: The Issue of Process and Production Methods, Nota di Lavoro 7.93, Milan: Fondazione Enrico Eni Mattei.
TWUM-BARIMA, R. & CAMPBELL, L. (1994), Protecting the Ozone Layer Through Trade Measures: Reconciling the Trade Provisions of the Montreal Protocol and the Rules of GATT, Environment and Trade 6, United Nations Environmental Programme, Geneva.
ULPH, A. (1992), The choice of Environmental Policy Instruments and Strategic International Trade, in: PETHIG, R. (ed.), Conflicts and Cooperation in Managing Environmental Resources, 111-129, Berlin: Springer Verlag.
UNEP (1989), Economic Panel Report: Montreal Protocol on Substances that Deplete the Ozone Layer - Final Report of the Economic Assessment Panel, Nairobi.
UNFCCC (1997), Kyoto Protocol to the UN Framework Convention of Climate Change, FCCC/CP/1997/L.7/Add. 1, New York.
URSPRUNG, H. (1992), The Political Economy of Environmental Decision Making, SFB 178 Internationalisierung der Wirtschaft, Diskussionsbeitrag No 176.
VANGRASSTEK, C. (1992) The Political Economy of Trade and the Environment in the United States, in: LOW, P. (ed.), International Trade and the Environment, World Bank Discussion Paper 159, 227-246, Washington, D.C..
VAUGHAN, S. (1994), PPMs and International Environmental Agreements, in: OECD (ed.), Processes and Production Methods, 127-136, Paris.
VERDIER, T. (1993), Strategic Trade and the Regulation of Pollution by Performance or Design Standards, Nota di Lavoro 58.93, Milan: Fondazione Eni Enrico Mattei.
VOGLER, J. (1995), The Global Commons: A Regime Analysis, Chichester: John Wiley & Sons.
VOUSDEN, N. (1990), The Economics of Trade Protection, Cambridge: Cambridge University Press.
WALTER, I. (1975), International Economics of Pollution, London: Mcmillan Press.
WALZ, U. & WELLISCH, D. (1997), Is Free Trade in the Interest of Exporting Countries When There Is Ecological Dumping?, in: Journal of Public Economics, Vol. 66, 275-291.
WEIZSÄCKER, C.-C. VON & WELSCH, H. (1991), Institutional Arrangements for Transfrontier Air Pollution, in: SIEBERT, H. (ed.), Environmental Scarcity: The International Dimension, 117-134, Tübingen: J.C.B. Mohr.
WHALLEY, J. (1991), The Interface Between Environmental and Trade Policies, in: The Economic Journal, Vol. 101, 180-189.
WHALLEY, J. (1996), Trade and Environment Beyond Singapore, NBER Working Paper 5768.

WILSON, J. (1996), Capital Mobility and Environmental Standards: Is There a Theoretical Basis for a Race to the Bottom?, in: BHAGWATI, J. & HUDEC, R. (eds.), Fair Trade and Harmonization, Vol. I, Economic Analysis, 393-427.

WORLD BANK (1992), Development and the Environment, World Development Report 1992, Oxford: OUP:

WTO (1995), WTO Trade and Environment Bulletin No. 2, Geneva.

WTO (1996a), Report of the WTO Committee on Traden and Environment, Press/TE 014, Geneva.

WTO (1996b), WTO Committee on Trade and Environment Discusses Proposals on MEAs, Ecolabelling, Transparency, Market Access, and Domestically Prohibited Goods, Press/TE/011, Geneva.

WTO (1997), WTO Committee on Trade and Environment Discusses Environmental Reviews, BTA, Ecolabelling and Packaging, a WTO Environmental Database, and Market Access, Press/TE/018, Geneva.

ZIMMERMANN, H. (1992), Ökonomische Aspekte Globaler Umweltprobleme, in: Zeitschrift für Angewandte Umweltforschung, Vol. 5, 310-321.

Appendix: GATT/WTO Texts

This Appendix contains GATT/WTO texts which provide background information relevant to part III of our study. These texts are extracted from

1. The General Agreement on Tariffs and Trade (GATT 1947),
2. the Preamble to the Marrakesh Agreement Establishing the World Trade Organization (1994),
3. the Trade Ministers' Marrakesh Decision on Trade and Environment (1994).

1. EXTRACTS FROM THE GENERAL AGREEMENT ON TARIFFS AND TRADE (GATT 1947)

Article I

General Most-Favoured-Nation Treatment

1.With respect to customs duties and charges of any kind imposed on or in connection with importation or exportation or imposed on the international transfer of payments for imports or exports, and with respect to the method of levying such duties and charges, and with respect to all rules and formalities in connection with importation and exportation,.......any advantage or favour, privilege or immunity granted by any contracting party to any product originating in or destined for any other country shall be accorded immediately and unconditionally to the like product originating in or destined for the territories of all other contracting parties.

Article III

National Treatment and Internal Taxation and Regulation

1.The contracting parties recognize that internal taxes and other internal charges, and laws, regulations and requirements affecting the internal sale, offering for sale, purchase, transportation, distribution or use of products, and internal quantitative regulations requirement the mixture, processing or use of products in specified amount or proportions, should not be applied to imported or domestic products so as to afford protection to domestic products.

2.The products of the territory of any contracting party imported into the territory of any other contracting party shall not be subject, directly or indirectly, to internal taxes or other internal charges of any kind in excess of those applied, directly or indirectly, to like domestic products....

Article VI

Anti-Dumping and Countervailing Duties

1.The contracting parties recognise that dumping, by which products of one country are introduced into the commerce of another country at less than the normal value of the products, is to be condemned if it causes or threatens material injury to an established industry in the territory of a contracting party or materially retards the establishment of a domestic industry.....

3.No countervailing duty shall be levied on any product of the territory of any contracting party imported into the territory of another contracting party in excess of an amount equal to the estimated bounty or subsidy determined to have been granted, directly or indirectly, on the manufacture, production or export of such product in the country of origin or exportation, ... The term 'countervailing duty' shall be understood to mean a special duty levied for the purpose of offsetting any bounty or subsidy bestowed, directly or indirectly, upon the manufacture, production or export of any merchandise......

Article XX

General Exemptions

Subject to the requirement that such measures are not applied in a manner which would constitute a means of arbitrary of unjustifiable discrimination between countries where the same conditions prevail, or a disguised restriction on international trade, nothing in this Agreement shall be construed to prevent the adoption or enforcement by any contracting party of measures:.....

(b) necessary to protect human, animal or plant life and health;......

(e) relating to the products of prison labour;......

(g) relating to the conservation of exhaustible natural resources if such measures are made effective in conjunction with restrictions on domestic production and consumption;

(h) undertaken in pursuance of obligations under any intergovernmental commodity agreement which conforms to criteria submitted to the CONTRACTING PARTIES and not disapproved by them or which is itself so submitted and not so disapproved;....

Article XXV

Joint Action by the Contracting Parties

5.In exceptional circumstances not elsewhere provided for in this Agreement, the CONTRACTING PARTIES may waive an obligation imposed upon a contracting party by this agreement; Provided that any such decision shall be approved by a two thirds majority of the votes cast and that such majority shall comprise more than half of the contracting parties.....

2. EXTRACT FROM THE PREAMBLE OF THE MARRAKESH AGREEMENT ESTABLISHING THE WORLD TRADE ORGANIZATION

The *Parties* to this Agreement,

Recognizing that their relations in the field of trade and economic endeavour should be conducted with a view to raising standards of living, ensuring full employment and a large and steadily growing volume of real income and effective demand, and expanding the production of and trade in goods and services, while allowing for the optimal use of the world's resources in accordance with the objective of sustainable development, seeking both to protect and preserve the environment and to enhance the means for doing so in a manner consistent with their respective needs and concerns at different levels of economic development, ...

3. EXTRACTS FROM THE DECISION ON TRADE AND ENVIRONMENT

Ministers,......

Considering that there should not be, nor need be, any policy contradiction between upholding and safeguarding an open, non-discriminatory and equitable multilateral trading system on the one hand, and acting for the protection of the environment, and the promotion of sustainable on the other,

Desiring to coordinate the policies in the field of trade and environment, and this without exceeding the competence of the multilateral trading system, which is limited to trade policies and those trade-related aspects of environmental policies which may result in significant trade effects for its members,

Decide:

- ...to establish a Committee on Trade and Environment ......
- that..........
  a) to identify the relationship between trade measures and environmental measures, in order to promote sustainable development;
  b) to make appropriate recommendations on whether any modifications of the provisions of the multilateral trading system are required, ..., as regards, in particular:
- the need for rules to enhance positive interaction between trade and environmental measures, for the promotion of sustainable development, with special consideration to the needs of developing countries.....
- the avoidance of protectionist trade measures, and the adherence to effective multilateral disciplines to ensure responsiveness of the multilateral trading system to environmental objectives
- surveillance of trade measures used for environmental purposes, of trade-related aspects of environmental measures which have significant trade affects, and of effective implementation of the multilateral disciplines governing those measures,

constitutes ..... the terms of reference of the Committee on Trade and Environment,

- that, within these terms of reference, and the aim of making international trade and environmental policies mutually supportive, the Committee will initially address the following matters, in relation to which any relevant issue may be raised:
  - the relationship between the provisions of the multilateral trading system and trade measures for environmental purposes, including those pursuant to multilateral environmental agreements;
  - the relationship between environmental policies relevant to trade and environmental measures with significant trade effects and the provisions of the multilateral trading system;
  - the relationship between the provisions of the multilateral trading system and:
    a) charges and taxes for environmental purposes;

   b) requirements for environmental purposes relating to products, including standards and technical regulations, packaging, labelling and recycling;
- the provisions of multilateral trading system with respect to the transparency of trade measures used for environmental purposes and environmental measures and requirements which have significant trade effects;
- the relationship between the dispute settlement mechanisms in the multilateral trading system and those found in multilateral environmental agreements;
- the effect of environmental measures on market access, especially in relation to developing countries, in particular the least developed among them, and environmental benefits of removing trade restrictions and distortions;
- the issue of exports of domestically prohibited goods,......

- that the Committee on Trade and Environment will consider the work programme envisaged in the Decision on trade in Services and the Environmental and the relevant provisions of the Agreement of Trade-Related Aspects of Intellectual Property Rights an integral part of its work, with the above terms of reference;.....

Economy & Environment

1. F. Archibugi and P. Nijkamp (eds.): *Economy and Ecology: Towards Sustainable Development.* 1989 ISBN 0-7923-0477-2
2. J. Bojö, K.-G. Mäler and L. Unemo: *Environment and Development: An Economic Approach.* 1990 ISBN 0-7923-0802-6
3. J. B. Opschoor and D. W. Pearce (eds.): *Persistent Pollutants: Economics and Policy.* 1991 ISBN 0-7923-1168-X
4. D.J. Kraan and R. J. in 't Veld (eds.): *Environmental Protection: Public or Private Choice.* 1991 ISBN 0-7923-1333-X
5. J.J. Krabbe and W.J.M. Heijman (eds.): *National Income and Nature: Externalities, Growth and Steady State.* 1992 ISBN 0-7923-1529-4
6. J. Bojö, K.-G. Mäler and L. Unemo: *Environment and Development: An Economic Approach* (revised edition). 1992 ISBN 0-7923-1878-1
7. T. Sterner (ed.): *Economic Policies for Sustainable Development.* 1994 ISBN 0-7923-2680-6
8. L. Bergman and D.M. Pugh (eds.): *Environmental Toxicology, Economics and Institutions.* The Atrazine Case Study. 1994 ISBN 0-7923-2986-4
9. G. Klaassen and F.R. Førsund (eds.): *Economic Instruments for Air Pollution Control.* 1994 ISBN 0-7923-3151-6
10. K. Uno: *Environmental Options: Accounting for Sustainability.* 1995 ISBN 0-7923-3513-9
11. K. Uno and P. Bartelmus (eds.): *Environmental Accounting in Theory and Practice.* 1997 ISBN 0-7923-4559-2
12. J.C.J.M. van den Bergh, K.J. Button, P. Nijkamp and G.C. Pepping: *Meta-Analysis in Environmental Economics.* 1997 ISBN 0-7923-4592-4
13. S. Faucheux, M. O'Connor and J. v.d. Straaten: *Sustainable Development: Concepts, Rationalities and Strategies.* 1998 ISBN 0-7923-4884-2
14. P. Kågeson: *Growth versus the Environment: Is there a Trade-off?.* 1998 ISBN 0-7923-4926-1
15. J.C.J.M. van den Bergh and M.W. Hofkes (eds.): *Theory and Implementation of Economic Models for Sustainable Development.* 1998 ISBN 0-7923-4998-9
16. J.N. Lekakis (ed.): *Freer Trade, Sustainability, and the Primary Production Sector in the Southern EU: Unraveling the Evidence from Greece.* 1998 ISBN 0-7923-5151-7
17. M. Boman, R. Brännlund and B. Kriström (eds.): *Topics in Environmental Economics.* 1999 ISBN 0-7923-5897-x
18. S.M. de Bruyn: *Economic Growth and the Environment.* An Empirical Analysis. 2000 ISBN 0-7923-6153-9
19. C. Kraus: *Import Tariffs as Environmental Policy Instruments.* 2000 ISBN 0-7923-6318-3

KLUWER ACADEMIC PUBLISHERS – DORDRECHT / BOSTON / LONDON

MIX
Papier aus verantwortungsvollen Quellen
Paper from responsible sources
FSC® C105338

If you have any concerns about our products,
you can contact us on
ProductSafety@springernature.com

In case Publisher is established outside the EU,
the EU authorized representative is:
Springer Nature Customer Service Center GmbH
Europaplatz 3, 69115 Heidelberg, Germany

Printed by Libri Plureos GmbH
in Hamburg, Germany